IBM PRESS NEWSLETTER

Sign up for the monthly IBM PRESS NEWSLETTER at
ibmpressbooks.com/newsletters

LEARN

- **NEW PODCASTS**
  from your favorite authors

  - **ARTICLES & INTERVIEWS**
    with authors

- **SPECIAL OFFERS**
  from IBM Press and partners

  - **NOTICES & REMINDERS**
    about author appearances and conferences

WIN

Sign up for the IBM PRESS NEWSLETTER and
you will be automatically entered into a
QUARTERLY GIVE-AWAY
for 3 months access to Safari Books Online –
online access to more than 5000 books
A $150 VALUE!

Safari
Books Online

Sign up at **ibmpressbooks.com/newsletter**

REGISTER YOUR BOOK

ibmpressbooks.com/ibmregister

REGISTRATION ENTITLES YOU TO:

- Supplemental materials that may be available
- Advance notice of forthcoming editions
- A coupon that can be used on your next purchase from ibmpressbooks.com

IBM
Press

Visit ibmpressbooks.com
for all product information

Related Books of Interest

Service-Oriented Architecture (SOA) Compass
Business Value, Planning, and Enterprise Roadmap

by Norbert Bieberstein, Sanjay Bose,
Marc Fiammante, Keith Jones, and Rawn Shah
ISBN: 0-13-187002-5

In this book, IBM® Enterprise Integration Team experts present a start-to-finish guide to planning, implementing, and managing Service-Oriented Architecture. Drawing on their extensive experience helping enterprise customers migrate to SOA, the authors share hard-earned lessons and best practices for architects, project managers, and software development leaders alike.

Well-written and practical, *Service-Oriented Architecture Compass* offers the perfect blend of principles and "how-to" guidance for transitioning your infrastructure to SOA. The authors clearly explain what SOA is, the opportunities it offers, and how it differs from earlier approaches. Using detailed examples from IBM consulting engagements, they show how to deploy SOA solutions that tightly integrate with your processes and operations, delivering maximum flexibility and value. With detailed coverage of topics ranging from policy-based management to workflow implementation, no other SOA book offers comparable value to workingIT professionals.

WebSphere Business Integration Primer
Process Server, BPEL, SCA, and SOA

by Ashok Iyengar, Vinod Jessani,
and Michele Chilanti
ISBN: 0-13-224831-X

Using WebSphere® Business Integration (WBI) technology, you can build an enterprise-wide Business Integration (BI) infrastructure that makes it easier to connect any business resources and functions, so you can adapt more quickly to the demands of customers and partners. Now there's an introductory guide to creating standards-based process and data integration solutions with WBI.

WebSphere Business Integration Primer thoroughly explains Service Component Architecture (SCA), basic business processes, and complex long-running business flows, and guides you to choose the right process integration architecture for your requirements. Next, it introduces the key components of a WBI solution and shows how to make them work together rapidly and efficiently. This book will help developers, technical professionals, or managers understand today's key BI issues and technologies, and streamline business processes by combining BI with Service Oriented Architecture (SOA).

Related Books of Interest

The New Language of Business
SOA & Web 2.0

By Sandy Carter
ISBN: 0-13-195654-X

In *The New Language of Business*, senior IBM executive Sandy Carter demonstrates how to leverage SOA, Web 2.0, and related technologies to drive new levels of operational excellence and business innovation.

Writing for executives and business leaders inside and outside IT, Carter explains why flexibility and responsiveness are now even more crucial to success — and why services-based strategies offer the greatest promise for achieving them.

You'll learn how to organize your business into reusable process components — and support them with cost-effective IT services that adapt quickly and easily to change. Then, using extensive examples — including a detailed case study describing IBM's own experience — Carter identifies best practices, pitfalls, and practical starting points for success.

 Listen to the author's podcast at:
ibmpressbooks.com/podcasts

IBM WebSphere
Deployment and Advanced Configuration

by Roland Barcia, Bill Hines, Tom Alcott, and Keys Botzum
ISBN: 0-13-146862-6

If you're a WebSphere Application Server administrator or developer, this is your advanced guide for delivering applications rapidly, running them smoothly, and administering them efficiently. Four leading IBM consultants draw on their years of experience to illuminate the key steps involved in taking WebSphere Application Server applications from development to production. They focus on the areas most crucial to success, including application assembly and build, application and infrastructure configuration and administration, and application testing and verification. Along the way, they show how to implement automated deployment processes that can be executed frequently, reliably, and quickly — so you can get your applications to market fast. The focus is on WebSphere Application Server Version 5.1, but much of the information applies to other versions.

Related Books of Interest

Enterprise Java Programming with IBM WebSphere
Second Edition

by Kyle Brown, Dr. Gary Craig, Greg Hester,
David Pitt, Russell Stinehour, Mark Weitzel,
Jim Amsden, Peter M. Jakab, and Daniel Berg

ISBN: 0-321-18579-X

*Enterprise Java™ Programming with IBM
WebSphere, Second Edition* is the definitive guide
to building mission-critical enterprise systems
with J2EE™, WebSphere, and WebSphere
Studio Application Developer. Fully updated for
Versions 5.x of WebSphere Application Server
and WebSphere Studio Application Developer,
it combines expert architectural best practices
with a case study that walks you through
constructing an entire system.

The authors are an extraordinary team of
WebSphere insiders: developers, consultants,
instructors, and IBM WebSphere development
team members. Together, they offer unprec-
edented insight into the use and behavior of
WebSphere's APIs in real-world environments
— and systematic guidance for delivering
systems of exceptional performance,
robustness, and business value.

IBM WebSphere and Lotus

Lamb, Laskey, Indurkhya
ISBN: 0-13-144330-5

Enterprise Messaging Using JMS and IBM WebSphere

Yusuf
ISBN: 0-13-146863-4

IBM WebSphere System Administration

Williamson, Chan, Cundiff,
Lauzon, Mitchell
ISBN: 0-13-144604-5

Outside-in Software Development

Kessler, Sweitzer
ISBN: 0-13-157551-1

Enterprise Master Data Management

Dreibelbis, Hechler, Milman,
Oberhofer, van Run, Wolfson
ISBN: 0-13-236625-8

Executing SOA

IBM Press

The developerWorks® Series

The IBM Press developerWorks Series represents a unique undertaking in which print books and the Web are mutually supportive. The publications in this series are complemented by their association with resources available at the developerWorks Web site on ibm.com. These resources include articles, tutorials, forums, software, and much more.

Through the use of icons, readers will be able to immediately identify a resource on developerWorks which relates to that point of the text. A summary of links appears at the end of each chapter. Additionally, you will be able to access an electronic guide of the developerWorks links and resources through ibm.com/developerworks/dwbooks that reference developerWorks Series publications, deepening the reader's experiences.

A developerWorks book offers readers the ability to quickly extend their information base beyond the book by using the deep resources of developerWorks and at the same time enables developerWorks readers to deepen their technical knowledge and skills.

For a full listing of developerWorks Series publications, please visit: **ibmpressbooks.com/dwseries**.

IBM
PRESS

Executing SOA
A Practical Guide for the
Service-Oriented Architect

developerWorks® Series

Norbert Bieberstein
Robert G. Laird
Dr. Keith Jones
Tilak Mitra

IBM Press
Pearson plc
Upper Saddle River, NJ • Boston • Indianapolis • San Francisco
New York • Toronto • Montreal • London • Munich • Paris • Madrid
Capetown • Sydney • Tokyo • Singapore • Mexico City
ibmpressbooks.com

IBM Press Program Managers: Tara Woodman, Ellice Uffer

Cover design: IBM Corporation

Associate Publisher: Greg Wiegand

Marketing Manager: Kourtnaye Sturgeon

Publicist: Heather Fox

Acquisitions Editor: Katherine Bull

Development Editor: Ginny Bess Munroe

Managing Editor: Kristy Hart

Designer: Alan Clements

Project Editor: Chelsey Marti

Copy Editor: Keith Cline

Indexer: Brad Herriman

Senior Compositor: Gloria Schurick

Proofreader: Water Crest Publishing

Manufacturing Buyer: Dan Uhrig

Published by Pearson plc

Publishing as IBM Press

IBM Press offers excellent discounts on this book when ordered in quantity for bulk purchases or special sales, which may include electronic versions and/or custom covers and content particular to your business, training goals, marketing focus, and branding interests. For more information, please contact:

U.S. Corporate and Government Sales
1-800-382-3419
corpsales@pearsontechgroup.com

For sales outside the U.S., please contact:

International Sales
international@pearsoned.com.

The following terms are trademarks or registered trademarks of International Business Machines Corporation in the United States, other countries, or both: IBM, the IBM logo, IBM Press, CICS, Component Business Model, DataPower, developerWorks, IMS, Lotus, MVS, OMEGAMON, Rational, Rational Unified Process, Redbooks, RequisitePro, RUP, Tivoli, Tivoli Enterprise Console, WebSphere and z/OS. Java and all Java-based trademarks are trademarks of Sun Microsystems, Inc. in the United States, other countries, or both. Microsoft, Windows, Windows NT, and the Windows logo are trademarks of Microsoft Corporation in the United States, other countries, or both. Linux is a registered trademark of Linus Torvalds in the United States, other countries, or both. Other company, product, or service names may be trademarks or service marks of others.

This Book Is Safari Enabled

The Safari® Enabled icon on the cover of your favorite technology book means the book is available through Safari Bookshelf. When you buy this book, you get free access to the online edition for 45 days. Safari Bookshelf is an electronic reference library that lets you easily search thousands of technical books, find code samples, download chapters, and access technical information whenever and wherever you need it.

To gain 45-day Safari Enabled access to this book:

- Go to http://www.awprofessional.com/safarienabled.
- Complete the brief registration form.
- Enter the coupon code HXLI-NDXM-4LDM-7UMT-LQP8.

If you have difficulty registering on Safari Bookshelf or accessing the online edition, please e-mail customer-service@safaribooksonline.com.

Library of Congress Cataloging-in-Publication Data

Executing SOA : a practical guide for the service-oriented architect / Norbert Bieberstein ... [et al.]. — 1st ed.

    p. cm.

Includes index.

ISBN 0-13-235374-1

1. Web services. 2. Computer network architectures. 3. Business enterprises—Computer networks. 4. Computer architecture. I. Bieberstein, Norbert.

TK5105.88813.E96 2008

004.6′5—dc22

2008006598

ISBN-13: 978-0-13-235374-8
ISBN-10: 0-13-235374-1

Text printed in the United States on recycled paper at R.R. Donnelley in Crawfordsville, Indiana.
First printing May 2008

*To my family, my mother, my wife, Joanna,
and my daughters, Katherina, Caroline, and Julia.*
—Norbert Bieberstein

*I'd like to dedicate this book to Amy Laird, my wife,
who was very insightful in providing the first level of review and
was supportive throughout.*
*To my sons, Thomas and Jack, who didn't get to
play with their dad quite so much while he was writing.*
—Robert G. Laird

*To my wife, Gillian, and my sons,
Simon and Philip.*
—Dr. Keith Jones

*To my very special wife, Tania,
my father, Dibakar, and my mom, Manjusree,
without whose continuous support this would not have been possible.*
*I dedicate this book to my great grandfather,
the late Narendranath Mitra,
a renowned Bengali novelist par excellence,
who has been my inspiration to take up the pen.*
—Tilak Mitra

Contents

Foreword

Service-oriented architecture (SOA) is no longer new. Indeed, it suffers from some retrenchment and backlash as the "hype curve" settles, with many pointing to examples of failed attempts. Why is that? If this direction was so compelling, why are some turning to a degree of skepticism and outright cynicism? The major reason lies in our collective failure to understand that this kind of transition is difficult and requires discipline, in-depth understanding, and active involvement from the business as well as the IT infrastructure. Discipline is needed in collaborative alignment and cross-group processes that we tend to associate with broader organizational thinking—not individual, localized "quick fixes" or silos. As a result, many initial attempts fail for a variety of good reasons:

- A failure to establish effective governance or even realize that governance must change to establish enduring benefits in delivering shared, useful, and effective services.
- An attempt to introduce a services discipline into organizational silos without drastically altering the culture of collaboration and information-process sharing. This oversight absolutely results in failure.
- A failure to understand how to integrate new thinking around services into preexisting technology assets and directions.
- Believing that a single technology or tool will deliver the desired results.
- Believing that speed comes from agility, where *agility* equates to a simplistic view of "delivering quickly" on isolated, individual projects without regard to organizational life cycle. This is otherwise known as unstructured chaos.

In my view, the fundamental motivation or reason to pursue an SOA is more prevalent today than ever before. The pressure to compete with greater speed and innovation as a business model remains. The pressure on enterprises, ecosystems, and supply chains to globalize is accelerating. The dependency on IT systems to scale businesses constantly grows, and technology continues to pervade all facets of commerce and of everyday life.

Many of the scale issues in any shift in business models comes from the growing reach and choice afforded by the ever more ubiquitous Internet. The Internet is changing and evolving. Bandwidth continues to increase, and the resulting network effects are providing opportunity for new businesses and business models while also wreaking havoc on the existing ones. All we have to do is look to everyday examples in the music industry (indeed, in entertainment as a whole). Telecom service providers (TSPs) are classic examples where vertical integration of industry and the billing models have been torn asunder by the introduction of pervasive IP-based services and devices. The interaction of the two (entertainment and TSPs) is even more dramatic and has downstream effects on consumer electronics, automotive, and so on. The growing choices and resulting shifts in global supply chains and sourcing affect everything from manufactured goods to intellectual property and talent. There is no place to hide.

IT systems are forced to enable or to lead this trend; if not, the associated businesses will fail to compete and fade into irrelevance. Key to enabling flexibility and scale are the tenets of service-oriented architectures. As has been said before, there is no magic in SOA. In many ways, it is the evolution of the ever-present and old concept of "modularity" and structural decomposition applied to better alignment of IT and business at a global, open scale. However the raw scale issues of modularity and sharing in successful services-based architectures to be deployed on the Internet in support of truly globalized business has never before been attempted.

I experienced this scale issue in transforming Rational® in IBM®. I embarked on trying to use SOA to effect both a cultural and a technical evolution in Rational's business and Rational's technology. The Jazz direction and architecture are prime examples of a shift in strategy that stems not just from an Internet-based architecture but from a rethinking of both the business and the technology underlying development tools and platforms. It puts us in a position to generate new products, evolve from existing ones, and take advantage of emerging business models (pricing and packaging) in delivering value to our customers. In line with the book, it required a shift in culture, a shift in governance models—organization, technology assumptions, information architectures, and collaboration services. It required rethinking the business of software development and modeling it as a series of business processes that need to establish and report through dynamic monitoring of metrics with services that can be delivered on internets in a globally distributed model. The jury is out yet on whether we have turned vision into execution, but I am convinced now, more than ever, that it was the right thing to do.

In that spirit, I encourage you to view this book as an update that imparts the benefit of extensive experience in SOA-based engagements with ourselves and our customers over the past four years. The first edition set the stage and brought out many of the key issues and thinking. This version delves deeply into key issues such as governance, management of services, and especially the challenges of life cycle. It addresses many of the failure issues I highlighted in the beginning of the Foreword. The team that put it together is experienced and has boiled down best practices and delivered a practical and thoughtful roadmap to implementing successful SOA transformations. Enjoy the ride. After all, if it were easy, anyone could do it!

Daniel Sabbah
GM, Rational Software
IBM Software Group

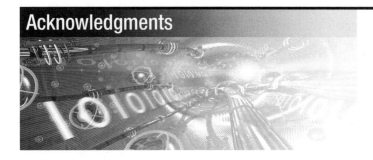

Acknowledgments

We thank the IBM management team for allowing us the time necessary to write this book. All books written at IBM get support from management. We acknowledge this support and the ability to access the necessary resources to write the book. Thank you to our executive sponsors at IBM Software Group and IBM Global Services, especially Robert LeBlanc, GM, IBM Global Consulting Services, and SOA.

We thank the people at IBM Press and Pearson Education, the publishers and staff who have helped market and complete the production work that goes into publishing a book like this. At IBM Press, we thank Tara Woodman and her team. At Pearson Education, we want to thank Greg Wiegand, who helped us during the proposal phase, and Katherine Bull, who acted in the role of senior editor to get our work in line and meet the standards. We thank development editor Ginny Bess Munroe and copy editor Keith Cline for their eye on comprehensiveness and for helping us express ourselves better, and we thank Sue Outterson for her technical review and for finding inconsistencies. We also thank the production and marketing teams at Pearson who helped make the book real.

We also want to thank all the amazingly talented people who make the effort and take the time to write the myriad articles published in the public domain on IBM developerWorks (www.ibm.com/developerworks) and IBM Redbooks® (www.ibm.com/redbooks). In the case of Chapter 5, "Leveraging Reusable Assets," this includes Alan Brown, Mikko Kontio, Dr. Tracy Gardner, Larry Yusuf, John Lord, Eoin Lane, Clive Gee, John Medicke, Feng-Wei Chen, Margie Mago, Scott Linehan, Kevin Williams, John Ganci, Amit Acharya, Jonathan Adams, Paula Diaz de Eusebio, Gurdeep Rahi, Diane Strachan, Kanako Utsumi, Noritoshi Washio, and Grant Larsen.

Finally, we want to thank the many individuals who contributed to chapters in the book. Clive Gee, from IBM UK, has been working with customers for years regarding governance. His keen insight into what works and makes sense contributed to our work on SOA governance and organizing for SOA. Randy Langel, from IBM U.S., taught us about the business aspects of SOA governance and the subset of SOA governance. Bruce Hawken, from IBM Australia, showed his insightfulness and dedication to making SOA governance real and inspiring. We thank all three for their contribution to our work on SOA governance. We also thank Dr. Ali Arsanjani, IBM Distinguished Engineer, for the numerous discussions we had about SOMA over the past couple of years and for what we learned from him on this subject. We also thank Patrick Haren, IBM Executive Architect, whose critical reviews and suggestions helped us "run the last mile" when writing Chapter 4, "A Methodology for Service Modeling and Design." We thank Marc Fiammante, IBM Distinguished Engineer, who, no matter how busy, somehow made time for those of us who needed his insight and leadership. We thank Rosalind Radcliffe, STSM from IBM Tivoli®, for providing key insights into some of the SOA infrastructure products, and we thank Sankar Singha, IBM Senior Architect, who helped bring all the pieces together when we were writing Chapter 6, "Realization of Services." Last but not least, we are very thankful to Thomas Schaeck, IBM Distinguished Engineer, Lotus® Quickr, and WebSphere® Portal Web 2.0 Development. He gave us a great insight to the collaborative solutions that help to take broad advantage from SOA-based IT in the enterprise.

About the Authors

Norbert Bieberstein works for IBM's SOA Advanced Technologies organization supporting worldwide publication and communication of SOA-related topics. He gained firsthand experiences from customer projects in various industries striving to migrate to SOA-based solutions. Norbert published several articles on SOA-related topics, coordinated the IBM Systems Journal issue 44-4 on SOA, and was the lead author of *Service-Oriented Architecture Compass* (IBM Press, 2005). In 2007, the book *SOA for Profit* was published, for which Norbert acted as one of the three lead authors. He also co-authored two IBM Redbooks: *Introduction to Grid Computing with Globus* and *Enabling Applications for Grid Computing with Globus*. In 1993, he published his first book, *CASE-Tools*. Norbert joined IBM software development labs as a software engineering consultant in 1989. In total, he has more than 27 years of experience in information technology and computer sciences. In his career, he worked as an application developer at a smaller software vendor and as a scientific programmer at Aachen University of Technology (RWTH), where he received his Master's degree in Mathematics and Geography. In 2006, he graduated from a corporate MBA program at Henley Management College in Henley, United Kingdom.

Robert G. Laird is an IT Architect with IBM in the SOA Advanced Technologies group, performing worldwide consulting for IBM customers in the area of SOA governance and SOA architecture since May 2006. He is a member of the industry TOGAF (The Open Group Architecture Framework) SOA Governance working group.

Robert has more than 20 years experience in the telecom industry at MCI and Verizon Business. He was the MCI chief architect, leading the enterprise architecture group and working across the entire order-to-cash suite of applications. He led the development of the SOA-based single-stack strategy to simplify the multiple network and applications silos. Bob has driven the strategy, planning, and execution of MCI's product development in the area of contact centers, IP/VPN, VoIP, IMS™, and managed services. For OSS, he has led successful implementations to automate network provisioning, network restoration, and network management.

Before joining MCI, Robert worked as a consultant for American Management Systems (AMS) and Ideation, Inc. He has a Master's degree and a Bachelor degree in Computer Science from Purdue University and has been granted two patents in the area of telephony. He has spoken at various industry forums, written for the *SOA Magazine,* and been quoted in *CIO Insight, Telecommunications, InfoWorld,* and *Computerworld.*

Dr. Keith Jones is currently an executive IT architect with IBM in the SOA Advanced Technologies team where he focuses on the definition and implementation of service-oriented architectures with leading-edge customers. He has 30 years experience in the IT industry as a systems engineer, software architect, strategist, and author of many middleware publications. Keith's professional interests center on building transactional, message-oriented and service-oriented middleware infrastructures in support of business processes in a wide range of enterprise environments. Most recently, these have included infrastructures at major financial services, retail services, automotive manufacturing, online media, and auction enterprises. Keith has a PhD in Chemistry and lives with his family in Boulder, Colorado, United States.

Tilak Mitra is a Certified Executive IT Architect with IBM Global Business Services, performing global consulting for IBM in the areas of enterprise architecture, helping clients realize their adoption of SOA from its vision through its design and implementation.

Tilak has more than 10 years of industry experience in retail, banking, media and entertainment, health-care, and transportation industries, wherein he has worked in various leadership capacities, ranging from business to IT transformations, leading into solution implementation and delivery. Tilak works closely with the IBM SOA Center of Excellence, in which capacity he contributes to the development of various IBM SOA offerings and authors white papers and technique papers on IBM SOA assets. His current focus is on building assets and techniques that foster a radical simplification of the development of SOA-based composite applications that are executable on various vendor platforms (for example, IBM WebSphere and SAP NetWeaver).

Tilak has a Master of Engineering degree in Electrical Engineering from Indian Institute of Science (IISc), India, and a Bachelor of Science degree in Physics from Presidency College, India. He is a contributing editor of the *Java Developers Journal (JDJ)* and is a frequent author in IBM developerWorks and in *JDJ* and *WebSphere Developer's Journal* (both from SYS-CON Publications). He also speaks at various U.S. universities on topics that cover the gamut of SOA.

SOA is the architectural style of choice. However, the implementation of an SOA has an avalanche of consequences, some of which are not yet discovered. There is not just one methodology that leads to an SOA. We have to learn from doing and build on experiences and best practices. This book provides valuable insights into the consequences of applying SOA. It offers approaches, principles, and guidelines for the full service life cycle based on experiences. The book is a must read for every enterprise architect.

Martin van den Berg
Lead Enterprise Architect
Sogeti Netherlands

Many current publications on service-oriented architecture (SOA) focus on technology and tools only. *Executing SOA: A Practical Guide for the Service-Oriented Architect* takes a broader view. One whole chapter each is dedicated to the business implications of SOA, the governance of SOA, and a methodology for the SOA architect.

Some of the key statements:

1. SOA primarily focuses on business agility and not on IT.

2. SOA is an architectural style and is not to be equated with technologies such as WebServices.

3. The principles of SOA are not new and were not invented in the moment the acronym came up.

We need more publications that are headed in this direction!

Prof. Dr. Bernhard Humm

A thorough and practical book I found valuable for its in-depth descriptions of SOA governance and the complete view of services, from the architectural view through to actual realization. This book is useful to any enterprise architect looking to address the hard parts in SOA. The chapters on how to approach asset reuse, the human aspects of SOA, and the descriptions of where tooling fits in make it a book well worth reading and using. Through the extensive references to other materials available, it can also serve as a guide to further reading online

Erik van Ommeren
Director of Innovation
Sogeti USA LLC / VINT
Washington D.C., USA

Chapter 1

Introducing SOA

"Yet another book on service-oriented architecture (SOA)," you might think. Hundreds of titles are already for sale at bookstores. After four good years in use, the acronym SOA has developed such a strong market value that you can buy almost anything as "SOA-something." Marketers quickly detected the strong drive and so renamed or described products as SOA compliant, made with SOA, built for SOA, and SOA whatever. And even with the vast number of books that cover SOA, a number of issues have yet to be covered. So, in this book, we discuss the "missing items."

The principles of SOA are not new and were not invented concurrently with the acronym, and many vendors "feel justified" claiming an SOA basis for their products. Sure, when you examine IT solutions, you can find SOA principles that were implemented decades ago. For example, some homegrown mainframe-based solutions running at IT shops of financial service companies have been wisely built with the purpose of future reuse and change requests, in a loose coupling approach. In some cases, an architectural structure that we now call an enterprise service bus (ESB) is used; those units are not being identified as such, but they do operate according to SOA requirements. Architecture principles were not invented recently, and you can consider them the foundation of SOA.

Before we delve into the details, let's take a close look at the history of SOA. Where did SOA come from? The answer to this question quickly shows the key elements for successfully executing SOA. However, history isn't enough; service-oriented architects who lead the transformation toward SOA must also address a number of new issues.

1.1 SOA in Retrospect

The strong adoption of SOA probably stems from its link between IT and business. It promises to bridge the chasm that divides the two camps. The involved parties at an enterprise want to break down the wall over which the requirements have been thrown and behind which an IT organization tries to figure out what the business people want.

When IT was new in the 1950s and 1960s, it was peopled by specialists who spoke a secret language and knew how to operate magical business machines. Those machines (with their first applications) enabled the quicker calculation of interest/tax and automated certain business processes. A team of highly paid experts could easily understand simple business requirements and then realize them as software programs on those machines. With the dawn of the personal computer, the knowledge about how to program, and not just how to enter data in given fields on green screens, created a more computer-savvy community of users who understood how to articulate more sophisticated demands on IT shops. In the 1970s, more and more software vendors appeared on the market offering operation automation for many industries.

The market enabled enterprises to compare and evaluate alternative software solutions, often against their own in-house IT shop. Subsequently, companies began looking at outsourcing IT, as it became too complicated, and as in-house teams failed to master the backlog of requirements that required urgent implementation to beat the competition. Strategic outsourcing became a significant market in the IT industry; often, in fact, the whole IT organization was acquired by an IT service company that offered fixed levels of service and promised to take away all IT "worries" from the company. Concentration on the core business soon became the motto of the day.

Instead of gaining speed and flexibility via this takeover of IT by "experts" who ensured service levels, escalation processes, terms and conditions, and so on, these outsourced services ultimately drifted further away from the daily business of the enterprise than when IT had been in-house. The service providers had been asked by their customers and forced by competition to offer the lowest possible cost for the sake of long-term contracts that meant secured income streams. As one way to achieve this, providers standardized and reused existing IT infrastructure and solutions.

Mergers and acquisitions occurred in increasingly larger dimensions in the 1990s, so that several incompatible enterprise IT solutions needed to be integrated. For example, these enlarged companies had to align various assets and demands; operations became a problem. Standardized software packages represented one solution to this issue; however, existing enterprise resource planning (ERP) systems had been heavily customized, and in some cases ERP solution providers had taken over their competitors and needed to integrate their packages themselves. In some cases, software vendors released several streams of software solutions that targeted specific needs of individual operational units in certain industries, not caring for integration in the first place. The lack of industry business models as accepted standards for those systems added its share to the dilemma.

These so-called *silo* solutions each focused on a specific business subject and data set (and accordingly, functions operating on this data). Driven by the separation of business concerns in the various enterprise units, these silos exemplified the mentality of optimized operation within each unit. The overall view got lost as optimizing the business most efficiently meant concentrating on the inner operations of the business units.

As mentioned previously, one driver for integration between the units was mergers and acquisitions, with the resulting entity needing to achieve the envisioned savings from reusing units such as HR, invoicing, procurement, and sales administration. The first attempt was to create integration automation between dedicated applications, so that a user could enter the same data just one time to be applied in various systems; alternatively, a batch process transferred information from one system to another. Enterprise application integration (EIA) systems appeared that offered sophisticated support to establish point-to-point integration of dedicated applications.

To automate the integration, various mediation languages and adapters were developed; often, standard software providers offered sets of application programming interfaces (APIs) to better integrate their solutions with others built for different purposes. These first attempts to map horizontal information flows and business processes across the enterprise generated an integration software and service market, but still the languages and transformation rules had individual definitions, and they had been tailored to a specific use in a given business process.

The need for the quicker integration of IT systems in an enterprise, the increasingly specific business unit requirements not yet addressed by standard software packages, and the necessity of cooperation among Internet-based new businesses (often interoperating across borders) drove the need for IT industry standards. Under the name of *web services*,[1] the large software vendors and the ever-growing crowd of small IT providers around the world defined and supported a set of standards.

A.1.1

With these definitions, the first interoperability terms were set. It was well accepted that any service offered via the World Wide Web could be described (how it could be found, how it could be invoked, what the standard formats were, and so on). However, this did not yet mean an IT architecture definition, except for the fundamental concept of a provider-consumer registry that was defined to standardize how web services could be publicly found, propagated, and accessed by consuming units.

The hub-and-spoke architecture predominant in most EAI systems inspired another step toward an SOA. These systems provided a central controlling unit that ensured the invocation of the proper function of a registered application, dealing in addition to issues such as access rights, format conversion, assured delivery, and so on. Abstracting this idea and generalizing it for enterprise-wide utilization, the concept of an ESB was born. The IBM® reference architecture for SOA was created to illustrate this approach. In Bieberstein et al. (2006), you can find an in-depth discussion about ESB and how it supports IBM's SOA reference architecture.

Those services, requiring human interaction, can be configured so that the whole system operates according to immediate customer needs. The SOA reference architecture thus becomes a clear framework for any enterprise operation. This framework can finally provide a basis for end-user-built front ends and applications built according to web 2.0 service definitions, such as mashups, and the quick deployment of user-oriented applications written in AJAX or similar on-the-glass development tools.

SOA was seen as the way out of the backlog at IT shops, as it was architecture that could serve various needs of business and of IT. In the first book of this series, *Service-Oriented Architecture (SOA) Compass*, by Bieberstein et al. (2006), we looked at various definitions of SOA as it was used in those early days just after the turn of the millennium. Finally, a definition was provided that turned out to best fit the understanding and use of SOA then and today. The definition reads as follows:

> **A service-oriented architecture is a framework for integrating business processes and supporting IT infrastructure as secure, standardized components—services—that can be reused and combined to address changing business priorities.**

Several authors have adopted this definition, and the definition has determined the SOA marketing direction, which is toward an approach that combines business and IT demands to gain a market advantage via more-agile business operations. Flexibility became the driving force it is today. Enterprises recognized that speed to market and offering the best solutions to their customers meant winning in the global market.

One way to gain speed with supporting IT solutions (and with business processes operating within them) was to reuse assets. This reuse implies a common set of standards (industry-wide or just within the globally operating corporation) both for IT items and for business subjects. Finally, it means gaining an operational set of components aligned and realigned just in time according to actual demand.

1.2 New Items to Consider

The initial focus of SOA was on architecture and how to design IT for the enterprise in such a way that it becomes flexible. The pressure to become flexible came from growing backlogs and business demands for agility because businesses faced an increasingly dynamic market and global competition. The immediacy of the Internet and modern communication let innovation conquer a worldwide market quicker than ever before.

For architects, this interconnectedness meant no longer solving an isolated problem for a concrete business issue. Instead, architects were forced to integrate any new solution into an existing and increasingly interwoven IT system within the company and beyond it. The IT architect became a city planner rather than a person asked to build a single house. Myriad publications have described the roles of IT architects, SOA architects, and enterprise architects, with the emphasis always on the mediator role between IT and business.

The changes underlying an SOA-based IT landscape impact the organization and the people inside and external to the enterprise. The technical aspects provided by web 2.0 and in general collaborative tools used within the enterprise and beyond bring new opportunities and risks for an enterprise operating in a globalizing market.

Ever since humankind started trading, standards have been established: measures for the goods, a monetary system that enables comparison of the values, and technical norms that enable the construction of complex machines and technical equipment with parts from various providers. More and more, the metric system is the global standard in technology and science. Based on convenience, however, some exceptions apply (for example, standard shipping containers, which are based on feet).

Being first with a new idea and achieving market success with it means setting the standards for the market. In every industry (including IT, especially software), there has been a run for the first spot, to establish one's own standards as the norm for the industry. In the IT industry, this race started with binary coding and the ASCII standard; it continues today. With regard to SOA, the standards summarized under the term *web services* have become the widely accepted norm within the software technological base.

For many business purposes, however, these standards do not yet suffice because they define only how to package, describe, access, and find services within the network. The standards lack the context/semantics relevant for many business users. To aid users, for example, business terms need to be standardized to facilitate access and operability. Situation-specific innovation will lead to the most suitable approach.

A.1.2

Foremost, however, developers must identify essential elements and understand how to control them (so that things don't execute blindly according to hard-and-fast, inflexible rules). Reuse—building for it and actually doing it most efficiently—is a question of survival, of how effectively and quickly a solution can be built. The time to market—from recognition of a business opportunity to getting a system and the organization ready to deal with it—decides market survivability much more than ever before.

Efficiency no longer comes just from using an optimized system that has been developed based on diligent research, but on how quickly you can extend a running system by having people on board who know how to solve issues using services provided by the system.

Tools are being developed to manage both the technical issues and the business aspects. Business process management becomes more than just a pencil-and-paper approach. The well-defined processes can be orchestrated from services and changed more quickly. Employees within the enterprise, customers, and business partners from outside become part of the process. They can build ad hoc processes that relevantly react to changing situations based on well-defined and reliable sets of services and so on.

In this book, we deal with technical aspects and their impact, but we do not cover business transformation and change management necessary to reach the most suitable organization for SOA-based enterprises. After all, several articles, blogs, and other forums (including, surely, more business books) provide guidance on that. Nevertheless, we offer the solutions and ideas described herein in a practical way so that you can apply them to your individual situation.

A.1.3

1.3 What Makes This Book Different?

You might ask why you should read a book that promises to describe how to execute SOA when we just said that SOA has been used in many places already (and was so even before the acronym came into use).

We and an increasing number of our colleagues and partners around the world have been involved in various projects in which customers of many industries have engaged in projects with the goal to realize solutions based on SOA principles. Various issues, not just related to IT installations and enterprise guidelines, influenced certain elements or rules. Some situations triggered the development of innovative software features and products that make it easier to succeed, and which are applicable in many other situations, too.

A.1.4

New standards emerged that can enable businesses to put elements of independent origin together to create a solution. The new products have to meet the expectations of the customers and their IT organizations; and because IT and lines of business are purportedly getting closer to each other, the end user comes into the picture more than ever before.

In this book, we highlight those approaches that are supported by appropriate tools and those that consist of organizational and behavioral changes among the employees and the management in the enterprises and beyond. We base the essentials for successful SOA discussed herein on our experience with thousands of projects and customers who come from many industries all over the world, who often operate across borders in a "flat world" and share production and development work between continents on a 24-hour basis.

1.4 Who Is This Book For?

This book is not a beginner's guide to SOA. Several books already provide the fundamentals to build a service-oriented economy and discuss how to start the business transformation associated with the journey toward it.

The readers for whom we wrote this book are foremost practitioners working in an enterprise, business consultants and enterprise architects charged with driving business transformation toward SOA. We do not offer silver bullets or 100 percent-proven solutions; instead, we rely on our and our colleagues' experience in real-life projects. Situations used in the book are abstracted to be easily applied by the advanced professional.

A.1.5

As with our earlier book, *SOA Compass*, which gained acceptance at hundreds of libraries at universities and research institutions, we attempt to address an academic audience and give input to research projects.

A.1.6

We expect that most of our readers will have an IT and business background. Normally, this so-called T-shape role requires a broad range of business and technical knowledge and a detailed understanding of and experience with specific subjects. For this type of person, this book will prove helpful and strengthen the individual T-shape.

1.5 What Is Covered in This Book?

When postulating a closer interlock between IT and lines of business in the enterprise, it is important for any IT architect to consider business arguments. Chapter 2, "Unveiling the Benefits," provides insight into the minds of executives based on data from various surveys. We relate that insight to the architectural foundation for service orientation and develop matching patterns in both worlds. At a certain level of abstraction, you can find parallels between the business organization and IT structures that are the core of SOA. IT architecture, business architecture, and enterprise architecture show a number of commonalities, and the players in each area can benefit from cross-pollination. In the end, this leads to the expected and required link between IT and business. Several supporting indicators are recognizable today.

From the many projects that have been realized, one aspect has become crucial: namely *how to approach SOA governance to organize the project and the enterprise for SOA.* Certain elements and organizational structures have proven favorable to success with the transition toward an SOA-based enterprise. Chapter 3, "SOA Governance," explains their importance.

A.1.7

Having set the fundamentals for success by establishing and incorporating SOA governance, the next important step is the *methodological approach to services.* Chapter 4, "A Methodology for Service Modeling and Design," provides practical guidelines to run a project successfully based on a theory that has been derived from various SOA projects around the world.

As we have already hinted, it is important to manage the services within the enterprise, and even more important to gain advantage by *leveraging reusable assets.* Therefore, we dedicated Chapter 5, "Leveraging Reusable Assets," to the issues that arise from introducing a repository; semantic issues; and how, when, and why to use a repository to achieve the most efficient solutions.

Based on the leveraging of reusable assets, a set of tools enables the *realization of services.* These tools build an integrated platform and enable team members in different roles to cooperate most effectively. Chapter 6, "Realization of Services," examines topics such as which tool to select, when to use it, and how to set up a development environment for SOA.

Data is essential to any business. Data becomes information (knowledge) and is accessed by various people for different purposes. *Information services* in an SOA provide and transform necessary and relevant data for users. Chapter 7, "Information Services," discusses innovative technologies based on recent research that may help to get all essentials to the right person in the enterprise.

Employees, as well at customers and business partners of companies, work together to utilize service-oriented concepts. Chapter 8, "Collaboration Under SOA: The Human Aspects," considers SOA in combination with the means that come under the term *web 2.0* and other innovative products and solutions. Human interaction with modern tools is also discussed, with examples based on experience.

Finally, Chapter 9, "The Future of SOA," offers our perspectives about recent developments and emerging trends (visible on the horizon or just in the "talking" phase right now but promising enough to merit consideration).

1.6 Links to developerWorks Articles

There are no specific papers at IBM developerWorks® (dW) to point to from this chapter, but we recommend the following sites for additional reference. These sites lead to the forums and landing pages about SOA:

A1.1 dW web services standards site.
www.ibm.com/developerworks/webservices/standards/

A1.2 "SOA" search on IBM redbooks.
www.redbooks.ibm.com/cgi-bin/searchsite.cgi?Query=%20SOA&SearchMax=250&SearchOrder=1

A1.3 Web services and SOA forum landing page.
www.ibm.com/developerworks/forums/dw_wsforums.jspa

A1.4 dW webcasts by IBMers and IBM business partners.
www.ibm.com/developerworks/views/global/webcasts.jsp[2]

A1.5 The dW subscription newsletter.
www-128.ibm.com/developerworks/newsletter/

A 1.6 SOA Compass at developerWorks.
http://www.128.ibm.com/developerworks/dwbooks/soacompass.html

A1.7 The IBM SOA newsletter (Besides the dW website, you might want to bookmark this subscription newsletter.)
www.ibm.com/soa/newsletter

1.7 References

Bieberstein et al. *Service-Oriented Architecture (SOA) Compass: Business Value, Planning, and Enterprise Roadmap,* IBM Press, Pearson Education, 2006.

OASIS SOA standard definitions. www.oasis-open.org/committees/tc_cat.php?cat=soa.

W3C web services standard definitions. www.w3.org/2002/ws/.

Endnotes

1. The "References" section lists two standards organizations relevant to SOA and web services.

2. Note: Enter the keyword "SOA" for related topics; this URL just lands at the site with the most recent webcast on top.

Chapter 2

Unveiling the Benefits

One of the images I have in mind when I contemplate the universe, is that it is constructed upon a simple pattern of order that may be seen in any and all phenomena, no matter how complex.

—Jonas Edward Salk, 1914–1995, *The Anatomy of Reality*

When a business executive is asked whether he has an SOA, he is more than likely to answer "an SO what?." The truth is that many business executives around the world have heard about SOA, but many think it is something that their IT departments might be implementing. Although this situation is evolving, we believe that until the management recognizes a strategic objective to become "service oriented," the full benefit of an SOA will not be realized.

2.1 Why the Business Should Care About SOA

The term *SOA*, and specifically, the *A* part of the acronym (architecture) is often a significant barrier for a meaningful conversation with business managers and professionals. It is almost always easier to secure executive sponsorship by avoiding the technical buzzwords and instead highlighting the IT department's ability to make business processes, transactions, and information flows faster and more agile. We don't need more technology; SOA is more about business-oriented solutions that the business will understand and readily endorse.

Businesses have long "tolerated" Information Technology as a black box into which much corporate treasure was poured. Initially, the returns on investment were positive. There was obvious value in automating the clearly automatable processes such as billing, accounts payable and receivable, ordering, and sales.

However, business changed. In one situation, a company might have acquired several businesses that were accretive to earnings and pruned several others that were not growing. All of a sudden, several differentiated IT system "silos" were hard to manage separately. There were different IT departments, and they didn't like each other much. One might have used all IBM technology, and the other might have used all Microsoft technology, and a third had a mixture of everything. So, the company poured more and more capital and expense dollars into the IT box, and never seemed to get anything back that was of real benefit to the business. The separate groups or silos said they were working with each other, and everyone did seem to be trying, but all turned into a technical mumbo jumbo, that in the end had zero impact on the business. So, when the question is asked at the end of the year, "What did we gain from IT?," there were shrugs and rolling of the eyes.

It is vital to talk a common language between business and IT organizations. The concept of a "service" is a natural way to think about the business of an enterprise. What does a business consist of? Business is a set of *business services* arranged in a *workflow* to create a *business process* that accomplishes what the business needs to accomplish. This is what SOA is about! It's not the technology, it's the business!

In addition, businesses change, and that change is accelerating. IT must be able to support and quickly enable that change. "The best companies are the best collaborators. In the flat world, more and more business will be done through collaborations within and between companies, for a very simple reason: The next layers of value creation... are becoming so complex that no single firm or department is going to be able to master them alone."[1]

2.1.1 Industry Trends Drive the Need for a Business-Oriented Approach

A.2.1

Let's take a step back and look at the big picture. The leadership of an organization should be thinking about certain industry trends and planning for now. Dave Newbold, an IBM Distinguished Engineer and Chair of the IBM CIO Technology team, authored the 2010 CIO Outlook report. Six trends with the most business impact in 2010 include (note that we emphasize the SOA implications in italic) the following:

- **Global integration**—Businesses need to respond rapidly to global opportunities. This means enterprise employees need to leverage the best global intellectual capital both in and outside the enterprise and discover previously unknown capabilities. Such ability will be a key differentiator. This includes *creating, discovering, and reusing business service* capabilities that enable fast time to market ahead of the competition.
- **Participatory Internet**—The idea here is to capture and reuse customer interactions on the Internet and understand the wisdom of users and apply it to products and future interactions. For example, this powers Google's page ranking, eBay's seller ratings, and Amazon's product reviews. This technique provides a powerful information source that accumulates value quickly and builds high loyalty. This will require you to have a *single view of your customers and the ability to combine and analyze interactions with them across your enterprise.*

- **Workforce demographics**—In the developed world, corporations are now starting to experience the first of what will be a massive wave of retirements, thereby losing subject matter expertise. Their replacements assume transparent and accessible data and fluid connections with colleagues. *Making sure that enterprise data is available via robust service interfaces is vital to this process.*
- **Software as a service**—Software as a service (SaaS) is transforming the packaged software business. These hosted applications and data are less expensive, easier to maintain and improve, very easy to integrate and support, and available anywhere. *Your current applications are probably not easy to maintain and improve or easy to integrate. The vendor packages you are using are expensive to run and maintain and difficult to integrate with the rest of your enterprise, putting your corporation at a competitive disadvantage to those using SaaS/services.*
- **Virtualized data and devices**—Applications and data will be moved to network delivery and storage, enabling any platform with a web browser to access data that you choose to make available. *Your ability to provide data that matters to your stakeholders, anywhere they might be, will differentiate your company.*
- **Simplicity from design**—As the world gets more complex, the race will go to those who can *provide simple methods of interaction.* This "simplicity" requires design and discipline, but has growing market value as businesses and consumers seek simplicity and confidence in the services they use.

There are two consistent themes in the 2010 CIO Outlook:

- Business services that are easy to interact with
- Easily accessible and correct data about the business

What are the skills that your workforce needs in this rapidly changing world? How well is your organization positioned to support these changes? For most organizations, unfortunately, the answer is "We're not." So what are you doing about it? What's your plan to fix this situation? Your target year is just two years away. That's a long time (except it's not!) for you to take charge and make business services and business data and workforce enhancement a reality instead of a wish.

2.1.2 Accessible Business Services

Which business services make your business operate successfully? This is not a difficult question. It's natural for the business to think about services. For example, customers buy products that consist of one or more services that add value for them. The products are created via a production process that consists of business services such as "Develop delivery schedule," "Monitor production runs," "Collect in-process samples," and "Produce finished products." The product is ordered and shipped to the customer via services such as "Create Order," "Perform Order Management," and "Pick, Pack, and Ship Order."

The business and IT organizations must think about and analyze these business processes, break them down into business services and their subcomponents, figure out how to optimize a new and better business process, and then create reusable business services. This is part of creating your business architecture, which is discussed later in this chapter. The rest of the book is about the SOA methods and techniques that make your business architecture a reality. The point is, SOA is about the business and the manner in which you make your business agile and responsive to the needs of the business stakeholders.

2.1.3 Easily Accessible and Correct Data

If your organization is like most organizations, the data that you need to run your business in the most optimal fashion is parsed out among a set of separate line-of-business databases that contain differing and overlapping information. Your customers know this, because they have to tell your customer service representatives about the transaction with the small business group that the consumer group knows nothing about. Or the information for one network is not integrated with the information for another network, and your costs are higher as a result. Examples abound, and we are sure that you can come up with your own that are much worse. The negative implications in revenue lost, increased costs, and opportunities missed should make even the most myopic business person distraught.

Why does this enterprise accept this as "the way it is and always will be"? It shouldn't! There should be a single view of the customer, a provisioning process, a sales pipeline, financial records, and any other set of information important to the business. Let's start treating your data, which is the lifeblood of the organization, with respect. It deserves to be cleansed. It deserves to be federated. In some cases, it might even have to undergo the painful process of integration. The bottom line is that the business has every right, indeed, the duty to demand that IT produce easily accessible and correct data.

Chapter 7, "Information Services," delves into the SOA methodology that can make this happen.

2.1.4 The Skills Needed in the Rapidly Changing Workforce

In his seminal book *The World Is Flat,* Thomas Friedman states, "Y2K became a huge flattener because it demonstrated to so many different businesses that the combination of the PC, the Internet, and fiber-optic cable had created the possibility of a whole new form of collaboration and horizontal value creation: outsourcing. Any service, call center, business support operation or knowledge work that could be digitized could be sourced globally to the cheapest, smartest, or most efficient provider." (Friedman, 2005, 108–109).[2]

What does this mean for the way we work and are organized? Today, enterprises tend to be organized around products, geography, or functions. Such organizations tend to be vertical in nature and optimize what needs to be done within that vertical group. Although this made sense in the twentieth century, the advent of the global flattening that Friedman so eloquently discusses has made such organizations obsolete. A horizontal organization focused on a process from beginning to end enables outsourcing of portions of the process that are commoditized and where no business advantage is to be obtained while at the same time promoting in-sourcing of core portions of the process chain that confer competitive advantage.

This is what makes business process management (BPM) so important. BPM adopts a more formal management of the organization's business processes. A BPM-driven organization is able to manage the process from an enterprise perspective rather than from a functional or domain perspective, and this creates synergies and optimization that are impossible in a vertical organization. Governance and structured methods, policies, metrics, practices, and tools are implemented that continually optimize business processes in a holistic manner.

Certain functions in IT have become or are becoming commodities. This doesn't mean that those functions will go away, but just that the best companies understand what skills they need to grow and keep in-house and what skills they can collaborate on and outsource. For example, in a horizontally organized, services-focused organization, there is less "coding" and more "assembling" of existing and reusable capabilities. Those capabilities might have been created internally or obtained from the set of global services or SaaS services that are increasingly available in the market today.

The rise of BPM means that certain business-oriented skills are increasingly necessary. For example, a "Business Process Designer" must be able to work with both the business and IT and be able to understand an existing end-to-end business process, optimize this process for the benefit of the enterprise, and design the set of business services that must be created or assembled to realize the goal of creating the flexibility needed. The Business Process Designer must be fluent with business goals and able to interface well with technology and IT. Many companies are taking people with business skills and rotating them through various business units and IT jobs. They can be business people with a bent for technology or IT professionals who are capable of learning the commercial big picture. How many people in the world have these skills today? Not many. What is your organization doing to build this skill set? Now let's explore this topic further.

2.2 Architecture

Many business executives and professionals, although highly focused on defining their strategy, managing their operations, and conducting their businesses, do not focus on "architecture." Whether service oriented or not, architecture is something that IT professionals are concerned with but business professionals are not (according to popular myth).

This situation is also changing. There is gathering momentum behind the idea that many of the same principles that are applied by IT architects to information systems[3] can, and should, also be applied by "business architects" to business systems.

How might this momentum help unveil the benefits of an SOA? Here we open up the discussion to expose some fruitful avenues to business value by applying architectural principles.

2.3 Focus on Business Architecture

Not that long ago, information systems were seen as support for business organizations and goals only. Computer systems were introduced to perform manual tasks quickly and more accurately. Today, that situation has evolved to the point where information systems not only improve business efficiency, but they often play a critical role in the corporate strategy for achieving competitive advantage in complex marketplaces. It is almost impossible to be in business today without explicitly deciding the role that information systems must play as a weapon in the corporate armory.

The initial focus of any business architecture is to identify a set of common business concepts and relationships that will ultimately unify deployed business systems and related information systems. These common business concepts are used to organize business knowledge about any given commercial enterprise. Requirements for both business systems and information systems arising from that knowledge are expressed in a common language and satisfied by SOA custom development or by matching existing assets such as SaaS systems.

Architecture has been defined in many ways, but if we accept the IEEE 1471-2000 standard definition,[4] business architecture should be "the fundamental organization of a [business] system, embodied in its components, their relationships to each other and the environment, and the principles governing its design and evolution." Defining such an architecture is not intended to guide others to build business systems, but to help others understand the nature of the business systems.

By applying the same systems engineering discipline to business systems and to information systems using a common set of underlying concepts and their relationships, a giant step is taken forward. However, this step is not easy. First, no business executive finds it easy to set aside the time and resources required to establish the common business concepts and the use of a common business language within an organization. To achieve this, an organic process must be allowed to evolve within a framework of strong discipline and governance over a significant period of time. When different departments refer to "customers," they must all refer to the same concept whether ultimately implemented uniformly or not.

Second, the conceptual model defined must enable clear articulation of requirements for origination or change and clear guidance as to how to organize work in an organization. Such an approach has already been described[5] and successfully deployed. Many projects in several countries have focused on building enterprise ontologies to provide a robust foundation for future business and information system architectures.

After the conceptual model is defined, it becomes obvious that business architectures are concerned with domains of *accountability* within which work is organized to achieve a set of well-defined outcomes. This way of looking at business systems focuses on getting results, and often, this is expressed as a chain of value-adding delivery mechanisms. Of course, adopting this approach depends on a clear definition of the business model and the business strategy that underlies accountability for results.

2.4 Business Process

Within each accountability domain, work is organized, resources are provisioned, and appropriate monitoring is defined. In recent years, the design of workflows to achieve specific results has received a great deal of attention. No matter how appealing, the notion that work may be organized systematically and explicitly managed in the form of *business processes* is not yet uniformly accepted by enterprises around the world. In fact, many businesses have not yet responded to the challenge of becoming "process-oriented" in their thinking and planning for the future.

The next major step toward unveiling the full potential benefit of SOA is often taken by enterprises as they focus on the modeling, specification, deployment, and monitoring of processes for achieving specific business results. Many factors promote the focus on process, once disguised under the labels of "organization and method" and later "workflow." Collaboration among many enterprises has recently resulted in a proposed industry standard notation for describing business processes.

This standard Business Process Modeling Notation[6] (BPMN) provides businesses with the capability of understanding their internal business procedures in a graphical notation and gives organizations the capability to communicate these procedures in a standard manner. This modeling ensures that businesses will understand themselves and that participants in them will enable organizations to quickly adjust to new internal circumstances and business circumstances.

This standard notation has become the basis for many computer-based tools that may be used to model, simulate, and monitor business processes. The availability of these tools is in part a catalyst for the migration toward process-oriented thinking behind business and information systems. An additional factor is the development of computer-based tools for describing the execution of business processes in a standardized fashion. The Business Process Execution Language[7] (BPEL) was developed by a consortium of software vendors and is now supported by many IT platforms. At a high level, BPEL enables business professionals to describe their business processes and then have them translated, semi-automatically, into live running information systems that support those business processes.

Each business process is composed of sequences of business tasks or activities that must be performed, whether by human hand or by machine, to achieve defined business results. Some processes are simple, involving relatively few tasks. Others may be complicated, involving hundreds of tasks punctuated by decisions that must be made to ensure the correct outcome. Best practices for building efficient business processes have emerged from skilled practitioners and patterns of activity captured as models for future users. All of these factors contribute to the growing movement toward "process-oriented" business thinking.

It would be inefficient to assume that all the business processes needed to deliver the results for a particular domain of accountability must be wholly contained within the boundaries of that domain. This "stovepipe" inefficiency is dramatically reduced when different accountability domains collaborate by sharing key "subprocesses." This sharing becomes possible as each business process is broken down into constituent subprocesses and business tasks. Because each task is assumed to require human skills, capital expenditure, operational costs, raw materials, supplied goods, and many other "resources," this leap of faith implies shared responsibility for the shared key subprocess. This shared responsibility, when managed well, achieves reduced operating costs by encapsulating the need for resources and optimizing their use in a well-defined manner.

2.5 Business Components

The sum total of business processes and subprocesses implemented or included by collaboration with partners within a particular domain of accountability might be categorized into activities that relate to specific business functions. These groups of subprocesses are often called business components because they comprise atomic functional elements that may be the focus of executive reasoning for the future.

Figure 2-1 illustrates a methodology developed by IBM[8] for identifying and reasoning about business components. Each vertical column is composed of components related to a particular functional business capability. The horizontal rows organize those components according to their impact on the business at Executive (Direct), Management (Control), or Operational (Execute) levels. For example, Sales is a component in the Servicing and Sales capability domain at the operational level.

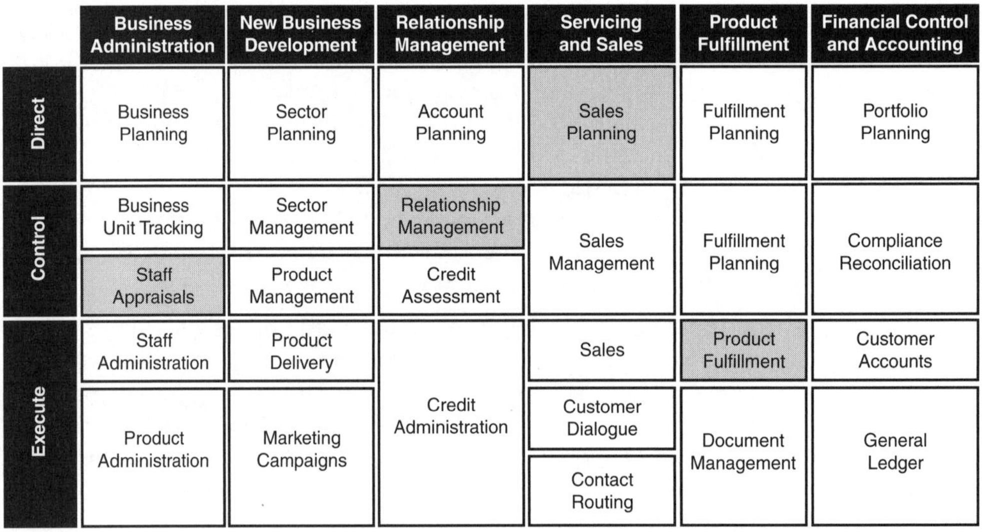

	Business Administration	New Business Development	Relationship Management	Servicing and Sales	Product Fulfillment	Financial Control and Accounting
Direct	Business Planning	Sector Planning	Account Planning	Sales Planning	Fulfillment Planning	Portfolio Planning
Control	Business Unit Tracking	Sector Management	Relationship Management	Sales Management	Fulfillment Planning	Compliance Reconciliation
	Staff Appraisals	Product Management	Credit Assessment			
Execute	Staff Administration	Product Delivery	Credit Administration	Sales	Product Fulfillment	Customer Accounts
	Product Administration	Marketing Campaigns		Customer Dialogue	Document Management	General Ledger
				Contact Routing		

Figure 2-1   The Component Business Model

After an analysis of business activities has identified a map of business components, it becomes possible to identify those core to a business and those that might be outsourced, those specific to an enterprise, and those that are generic capabilities within an industry. Business goals within a strategy may then be mapped to those components that require enhancement in some way to achieve desired results and those where cost savings may be achieved.

The combination of analyses that focus on business components and on business processes can be powerful indeed. Whereas business components group related business activities, their resources, and their methods into the "building blocks" for an enterprise, the business process analysis yields an understanding of the threads of activity that interrelate those components to achieve business goals. Some business processes may be wholly contained within a particular component, whereas others might involve the capabilities of several components. This level of understanding of a business architecture and its component parts brings us yet another step closer to unveiling the benefits of SOA. But how could that be? If SOA is not about technology but about a framework for building on-demand business enterprises, the big picture becomes clearer.

2.6 Lifting the Veil

When business processes and subprocesses are identified and assigned to specific business components, each with its strategic value and impact to the enterprise identified, it becomes possible to narrow focus to particular functions and their sequence of activities for enhancement. Getting to this point is no mean feat. However, when this point has been reached, it is possible to identify certain sequences of business tasks, whether implemented using human skills or machine-automated capabilities, as *critical to the business*. These sequences are called *business services* by IT architects and should also be called *business services* by business architects. Ah-ha! There is a eureka moment when business and IT worlds intersect. Both communities should be working to identify an optimum set of business services that not only serve to deliver the goals of the business, but also are the highest impact aspects of supporting information systems.

By identifying services that are critical to the business, it becomes possible to reason about those that exist but need enhancement or replacement and those that don't yet exist but must be introduced to achieve strategic goals. Recent developments in IT have made it possible to mirror this thinking in the business community. Business services can be "encapsulated" into units of capability that can not only be bought and sold, acquired, and outsourced but also combined by business architects in creative ways to assemble new capabilities that might make the difference between competitive advantage and disadvantage in a chosen marketplace. This is the true value of SOA unveiled: the synergy between business creativity and powerful information systems capabilities.

In Chapter 1, "Introducing SOA," we opened up the discussion with a realization that SOA is an emerging but nevertheless real influence in business systems around the world. The marketing hype may be waning, but leading adopters of SOA are pronouncing the value that SOA has brought them in ways that range from modest gains in time to market to impressive game-changing advances in positioning their business in a highly competitive marketplace.

In this chapter, we discussed, in outline only, the real meaning of SOA to business executives, managers, and professionals and the recent advances in business architecture, BPM, business components, and how these advances together create a context in which the full potential for SOA may be realized. Unveiling the benefits requires vision, strong direction, discipline, and knowledge—knowledge of the business and knowledge of the IT capabilities that can be applied.

2.7 Link to developerWorks Article

A2.1 Laningham, developerWorks Interviews: Dave Newbold on the IBM CIO 2010 Outlook. www.ibm.com/developerworks/podcast/dwi/cm-int061907txt.html.

2.8 References

Amenta, Peter S. *Histology,* 4th ed., 1993, 138. Medical Outline Series. Norwalk, CT: Appleton & Lange.

Baker, James A. "The Stakes for Them—and Us," *Newsweek,* April 6, 1993, 24–26.

"Descriptive Geometry," *Encyclopedia Britannica* (1986), 7, 292.

Friedman, Thomas. *The World is Flat,* Farrar, Straus, and Giroux, 2005, 352–353.

Ibid 108–109.

Endnotes

1 Friedman, Thomas. *The World is Flat,* Farrar, Straus, and Giroux, 2005, 352–353.

2 Friedman, Thomas. *The World is Flat,* Farrar, Straus, and Giroux, 2005, 108–109.

3 Note that the phrase *information systems* is used here to denote the focus on information flow within an enterprise. Information technology is applied to implement those information systems. The phrase *IT systems* does not correctly describe the purpose of those systems.

4 IEEE Std 1471-2000 Systems and Software Engineering—Recommended Practice for Architectural Description of Software-intensive Systems [2007-07-15].

5 McDavid, D. W. "A Standard for Business Architecture Description," *IBM System Journal,* 38: 1, 1998.

6 See "Object Management Group / Business Process Management Initiative" at www.bpmn.org.

7 See "Business Process Execution Language for Web Services" at www.ibm.com/developer-works/library/specification/ws-bpel/.

8 See "A Component-Based Approach to Strategic Change" at www-935.ibm.com/services/us/igs/cbm/html/bizmodel.html.

Chapter 3

SOA Governance

Governance is the intentional usage of policies, plans, procedures, and organizational structures to make decisions and control an entity to achieve the objectives of the business. SOA governance focuses on the services that need to be or are created in the realization of an SOA.

A major reason to have an SOA is to create business and IT agility. SOA is a reusable services approach to implementing the corporate business strategy using the enterprise architecture. Creating an environment in which reusable services flourish and the benefits are fully realized requires a well thought-out, explicit, implemented, and maintained governance plan. The real benefit of an SOA is the creation of a service-oriented enterprise (SOE). An SOE is about connecting business processes in a much more horizontal fashion.

A.3.1

A.3.2

We have witnessed two extremes in the governance models used at global corporations and public entities. In the generation after World War II, a military manner of governance predominated, guided by those in the workforce who had received their leadership training in the armed forces. Projects tended to be lengthy with strict bureaucratic controls and a huge paper exercise, resulting in a big bang result or a project cancellation. This form of governance still exists at many government organizations.

In reaction to this and seeing the need for speed, the next generation of governance tended to err in the opposite direction. Business units controlled their own IT development or IT development groups were focused on their vertical areas with locally optimized decision making and a focus on delivering projects on time with minimal regard or understanding about the impacts to the enterprise as a whole. This, combined with the effects of merger and acquisitions, resulted in redundant systems with several different applications for every business problem.

An SOE chooses the middle road. Some controls are necessary, but the right ones—that is, those that add value to the creation of "good" services and agility without being heavy-handed. The needs of the business drive IT and not the other way around. The governance model tends to be more federated with multiple organizations focused on individual tasks that are loosely coordinated via common governance policies, plans, procedures, and metrics. In this manner, an SOE can grow both "top down" via an enterprise architecture and resultant business and IT strategy and "bottom up" to enable the organic creation of services to leverage existing set of systems or projects that identify an opportunity to create reusable services.

SOA is a catalyst for IT-enabled change that, when done properly, will align business and IT for competitive advantage. For example, many companies have an infrastructure group of some sort, perhaps responsible for all messaging middleware. It is relatively easy to upgrade an organization and introduce SOA technical architecture capabilities such as the usage of an enterprise service bus (ESB) or eXtended Markup Language (XML) messages to share data across different systems. Although this is valuable and is in many cases the first phase on the road of an SOA journey, upgrading technical architecture alone misses the real benefit. From an infrastructure point of view, concepts such as XML and Web Services Description Language (WSDL) are powerful and useful. Yet, in and of themselves, they are just the latest surge of the technology tide. Indeed, SOA does not require usage of XML and WSDL. Certainly, other techniques beyond XML will manifest themselves in the years ahead that will be even more valuable from a technology perspective.

Because SOA is a distributed approach to architecture that crosses lines of business and IT, there is a greater need for effective governance of what happens between these organizations. Indeed, the introduction of SOA into an organization may often be the tipping point for moving from weak governance to strong governance.

A.3.3

This chapter focuses on the elements that should be considered in your SOA governance with practical techniques to address them. Your enterprise will not necessarily be ready today for all of these elements. This is fine. As long as you are cognizant of them and intentional in your decisions ("I didn't know" is no longer acceptable!), you are well on your way to creating a competent SOA governance function. This chapter explores three main areas of consideration for SOA governance:

- Governance of the SOA strategy
- Organizing for SOA
- SOA governance considerations

We intentionally take a top-down approach when considering SOA governance. That is, we start with a strategic and business focus and work our way down to a more day-to-day SOA governance design and implementation set of patterns. Many organizations starting on an SOA journey will find that they are not ready initially for a strategic leap using SOA and need to first build more technical expertise. This is another way of saying that SOA will frequently start in an IT organization, where expertise must be created and nurtured, before being ready to move up the value chain and consider a full-on, business-focused, and SOA-based transformation. In these cases, the SOA governance practitioner should take note of

the governance of the SOA strategy, but should start with implementation of relevant portions of the "Organizing for SOA" section and the "SOA Governance Considerations" section in this chapter. In fact, a phased approach is usually taken for SOA governance with
focus initially on the service development life cycle, then SOA project management (using
the processes described in the "SOA Governance Considerations" section), and finally the
transition to an agile enterprise (see Figure 3-1).

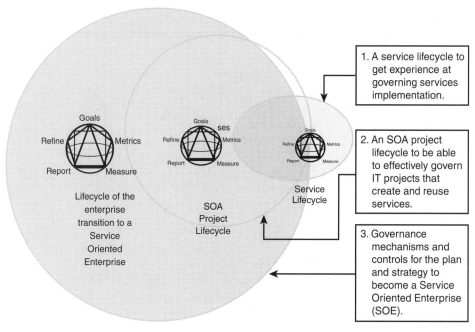

Figure 3-1   Typical SOA governance phasing

Where appropriate, a fictional organization known as Ideation Communications is used as
an example.

3.1 Governance of the SOA Strategy

A maximally effective SOA governance must be able to control and help advance the enterprise strategy for creating an SOE. This requires that IT (the information technology group)
be aligned with and work with the business. In addition, many IT groups are used to working comfortably in their silos and have neither the skills nor interest in considering the
entire order to cash cycle, let alone what the business wants beyond the immediate project
requirements. SOA governance, which is responsible for governing the business agility
effort, needs to change that (see Figure 3-2). This change requires working closely with the
enterprise architecture group and business groups and putting the necessary controls in

place to drive the agility strategy forward. Without an intentional plan, the enterprise will never be able to make the leap to become an SOE.

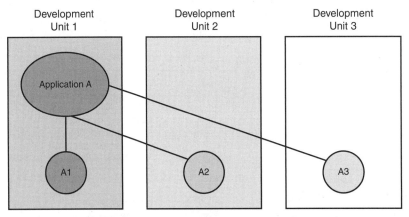

Figure 3-2   For this example, Development Unit 1's process is two thirds dependent on the integrity, performance, reliability, and currency of services managed by other development units. Without governance, Unit 1 will go its own way instead of using reusable services.

3.1.1 IT Governance Considerations

A.3.4

Ideally, a well thought-out IT governance capability already exists that can be leveraged for SOA governance. Certainly, it would be inadvisable for SOA governance to be separate from and in competition with IT governance. IT governance itself fits within the context of corporate governance, as, for example, articulated in the OECD Rules of Corporate Governance. Ideally, SOA governance should be focused on the "service" enhancements necessary to IT governance as it fits within the overall context of corporate governance.

SOA is often a paradigm shift for both the business and IT groups in how they work together and need to be governed. Frequently, aspects of a best practice IT governance are unknown or have been neglected in favor of each vice-president doing things his own way. It behooves the SOA governance practitioner to assess the current state and maturity of IT governance and be prepared to include corrective action in a governance transition plan. Building SOA governance on top of nonexistent or weak IT governance is like building a house on quicksand (see Figure 3-3). Fortunately, existing entities have thought quite extensively about IT governance.

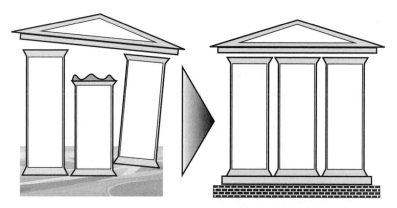

Figure 3-3   Should you build your SOA governance on quicksand or a solid foundation?

Control Objectives for Information and related Technology (COBIT) was created by the Information Systems Audit and Control Association (ISACA) and the IT Governance Institute (ITGI). COBIT provides a set of generally accepted measures, processes, and best practices for maximizing the benefits of information technology and developing IT governance. You can find additional information on COBIT at www.isaca.org/cobit.

The SOA governance practitioner should assess the current state of IT governance using COBIT or an equivalent set of IT governance best practices. Some of the IT governance deficits can be addressed using industry best practices such as the Information Technology Infrastructure Library (ITIL). ITIL provides operational guidance in the areas of service management, infrastructure management, security management, and applications management. For more information on ITIL, refer to www.itil.org.

While patterns for creating strategic business agility do exist, there is no equivalent in this area to the set of detailed best practices that were created for IT operations by ITIL. As a major objective of SOA is to create fundamental understanding of business process and models that inform the creation of business services and corresponding IT design, the SOA Governance of this area is almost always going to be above and beyond what the current IT Governance is managing.

The remainder of this section addresses SOA governance in the areas of alignment and agility.

3.1.2 Business and IT Alignment

Business and IT speak different languages. Business uses terms such as *sales pipeline, market segmentation,* and *monetize.* IT uses terms such as *J2EE, XML,* and *form factors.* Whereas an enterprise architect will be comfortable in both worlds, most people are not. However, SOA expects the two groups to work intelligently and cooperatively with each other. To do this, there needs to be governance consideration given to the process of Business and IT alignment.

The purpose of this section of SOA governance is to discuss governing the identification and alignment of the business goals and the IT goals. The goals are used to guide the SOA strategy and portfolio management for the enterprise.

The business goals may be articulated in a nice, neat document, and the only thing the practitioner must do is to politely ask to obtain a copy. Clarification of the document via interviews with the appropriate business stakeholders will probably still be necessary. For the un-rare occasion where such a document does not exist, governance needs to ensure that the business stakeholders are interviewed and business goals are then articulated. This may include talking to the CEO, COO, or business unit managers. The business users are used to dealing with IT as a technical resource, usually in terms of "their" IT applications and things such as PCs and e-mail support. SOA governance must ensure that the right stakeholders for business and IT are brought to the table, and that this discussion is a business discussion. The business leaders at Ideation Communications have the following business goals:

- Bring new products to market in 2 months or less.
- Cut operational costs by 5 percent per year during the next 2 years.
- Achieve 2.5 percent uplift in our average revenue per user (ARPU) within 12 months.

In the absence of IT goal creation from the business goals, the IT goals tend to be technical in nature. The business needs will be the right ones to drive the IT portfolio and used to guide the SOA journey. From the business goals listed for Ideation Communications, the following IT goals were created:

- A single product catalog must be created that is integrated for order entry, fulfillment, and billing, allowing new products to be introduced without coding changes.
- Separate product operation support systems (OSS) must be federated with a single user interface allowing operational excellence and cost reduction.
- Customer information must be mapped to a canonical data model. A federated customer information model will be created that enables a single customer view.

Left to its own devices, would IT have created these strategic goals without the corresponding business goals? While these are high-level examples, the basic idea should be employed by the SOA governance practitioner. That is, governing the process of using business goals to inform and create IT goals.

3.1.3 Business Agility

Business agility is the ability to change or create a new business process in a readily adaptable manner. How did the current business processes come to exist as they are today? Did a strategic planning process result in a completely rational and seamless set of business processes? Is everything automated that can be automated? Is the corporation addressing all the functional areas that it should be addressing or are there gaps? Are multiple groups performing the same business function; for example, are there any significant overlaps resulting in redundant or nonoptimized business operations?

Business agility is one of the main drivers for SOA adoption. Questions like the preceding ones need to be analyzed to create the SOA strategy that will provide agility. It is the job of SOA governance to make sure that the right team exists and addresses these questions and others like them that are important for the business and that such business decisions are then governed and used throughout the organization. Ideally, this process uses a combination of enterprise architecture, business users with a broad understanding of how things currently work, several business visionaries, and possibly outside consultants. Failure to understand and address business needs and priorities will leave the enterprise SOA journey to be a Sisyphean task, rolling the business value rock up the hill, but always having it escape to roll down the hill again when IT project crunch time comes. The needs of the business must be paramount and the driver for SOA. Any SOA task (or for that matter, any IT project) that cannot be mapped back to a business driver should probably be eliminated or, at least, noted for what it is: an IT maintenance project with no direct business value. In doing so, it will often be the case that the reduction of capital investment in projects with no business driver frees up the funding necessary to create services and a truly agile enterprise.

SOA governance must ensure that the right resources are engaged in this task. A good way to attack this opportunity is to make sure that enterprise architecture uses a standard industry functional map that can be used to map the enterprise's current business processes. Next, identify the current business groups and their business responsibilities. Interviews with these groups will achieve an understanding of the business functions supported and the different market segments within those functions. Pain points within each business function can be elicited and understood. A gap or overlap analysis should then be employed to identify areas of strength, as well as areas of opportunity for business agility.

For example, for the telecommunications industry, the TeleManagement Forum (TM Forum) has created the industry standard TM Forum Business Process Framework also known as enhanced Telecommunications Operations Map (eTOM) (http://www.tmforum.org/browse. aspx?catID=1648). Figure 3-4 shows the Operations subset of the TM Forum Business Process Framework.

For our fictional company, Ideation Communications, SOA governance, working with the enterprise architecture group, used eTOM in interviews with the business units and identified that four separate business groups performed the eTOM function of "2.5 Instance & Service-Specific Rating." In some cases, different pricing was available on the same service from a different sales group within the company. Consequently, it became a business goal to create a single rating function for all Ideation Communication products, and an SOA business service was created with the name Create Rating. This service then consisted of a set of subservices—Mediate Usage Records, Rate Usage Records, and Analyze Usage Records—as per the eTOM Level 3 business functional map. In this manner, an industry business process map drives both a business discussion that results in measurable benefit to the business, but also the planning of the SOA business services creation strategy! In addition, the business agility discussion is a good time to establish key performance indicators (KPI). In the example on rating, an obvious KPI created might be "single source of pricing for all products by the end of the year." A more business-focused KPI in this case might be "DSL product margin increased 2 percent due to elimination of pricing mistakes."

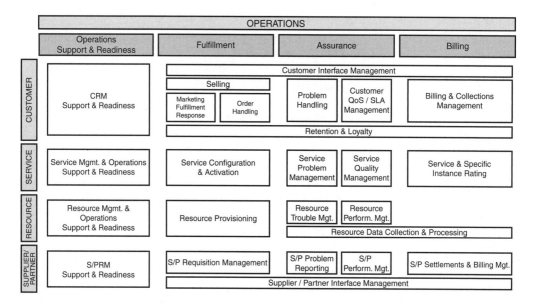

Figure 3-4   Use an Industry Functional Component Model to guide the business agility discussion and analysis, such as the TM Forum Business Process Framework (aka eTOM) Level 2 shown.

Ideation Communications also used the eTOM in identifying the impact of the high-value business priority of having a 360-degree view of the customer. Enterprise architecture identified significantly different customer views in Fulfillment (Selling and Order Handling), Assurance (Problem Handling and Customer QoS & SLA Management), and Billing (Billing & Collections Management). Each of these areas was managed by a separate general manager (GM), one for the business and one for IT. The business and IT GM in Fulfillment agreed with each other that their view of the customer was the right one. Unfortunately, their counterparts in Assurance and in Billing had similar opinions as to the primacy of their own customer views. We discuss this in more detail in the "Information Agility" section; the point here is that the Industry Functional Component Model is a good place to start in any business agility analysis to identify the pain points that will drive governance of the SOA strategy.

3.1.4 Technical Agility

Technical agility is the ability to take up new technologies while eliminating old ones as the needs of the business dictate in a readily adaptable manner. Many organizations are not ready for business agility and should start their SOA journey focused on technical agility. This is especially true when IT is leading the SOA initiative and is finding it difficult to gain the attention of the business. Gaining experience with services and creating technical agility is a valid first step in the SOA journey and sets the foundation of SOA capabilities that will be leveragable later for business services. Governance control of the service development life cycle is key here and is discussed in more detail later in this chapter.

Many enterprises, unfortunately, allow each development group to have complete control over the selection of particular technical services and functions for their projects. In addition, as a result of mergers and acquisitions (M&A), an enterprise may consist of myriad technical capabilities that were separately selected. As a result, the integration problem to be addressed is more difficult than it would be otherwise. Further, the enterprise fails to gain the synergies of economies of scale in its purchasing and maintenance contracts with software vendors that a more focused procurement approach would engender. It is much easier to negotiate a significant discount with a single vendor that has $20 million per year in spend than 20 vendors that each has $1 million per year in spend.

A technology life cycle should be implemented to manage the evaluation, adoption, and later retirement of services technologies to be used at the enterprise. This should be an enhancement to the IT governance technology life cycle. If such a function doesn't exist yet in IT governance, it will be necessary for SOA governance to initiate this cycle, as shown in Figure 3-5.

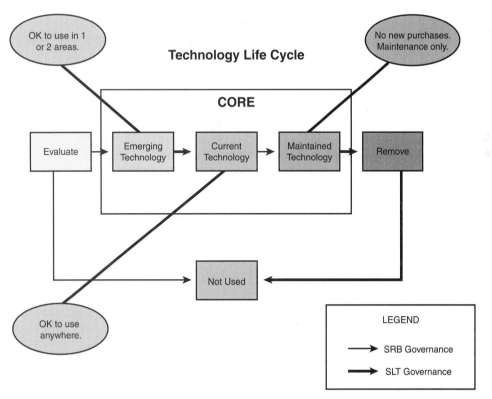

Figure 3-5   SOA governance will maintain technology vitality by setting controls in place for a services technology management lifecycle.

Governance needs to help drive the enterprise to make decisions on the two or three vendors (at most) for each area that you will continue to drive future purchase funding to.
Other vendors should be sunsetted over a period of time. Procurement is a key organization
in this endeavor. All purchase orders (PO) must be negotiated and approved through procurement, which will enact a quality gate of consulting their enterprise technical reference
model with approved vendors. Development groups attempting to buy outside the
approved vendor list will have their PO rejected and must either change to an approved vendor package or receive an exception from the appropriate SOA governance control point.

3.1.5 Information Agility

Information agility is the ability to understand, control, and leverage the information assets
of the corporation in a useable and readily adaptable manner. Information agility tends to
be the "redheaded stepchild" of the SOA strategy. This is unfortunate and needs to be corrected by the SOA governance group, because there is tremendous business leverage in a well
thought-out and implemented information strategy as part of the enterprise SOA strategy.

It is well known within the IT function at today's enterprises that application integration is
a nontrivial problem to solve. Applications have usually been developed without benefit of
an enforced enterprise data model. COTS (commercial off the shelf) software comes with its
own data schema and an implied business process, which the IT group must either adapt to
or engage in an expensive process of adapting to the current enterprise business model. Of
course, this is a process that keeps on giving pain. Further adaptation is necessary whenever
either a new release of the already purchased COTS must be implemented or changes to the
business cause enhancements to the message structure.

The usual solution for application integration has been point-to-point interface solutions,
as depicted in Figure 3-6. Such solutions, while operationally efficient, result in an ossifica-
tion of the enterprise business model. It is expensive and risky to change out one application for another or even make changes to an existing application because of the complex
nature of the information and functional model. Changes to one system's interface can
result in multiple changes and testing of all the myriad systems that must adapt to this
change. It's not unusual for such projects to consume 1 to 2 years in analysis, design, and
testing before being ready for production. In the meantime, the business has moved on, and
IT is judged to be inflexible.

More generically, the following are regarded as typical problems that most IT departments
must deal with:

- A multitude of technologies and platforms support the business systems.
- Business process models include a mixture of people practices, application code,
  and interactions between people and systems or systems and systems.
- Changes to one system tend to imply ripples of changes at many levels and to
  many other systems.
- No single, fully functional solution will "talk to" or work with all other functional
  solutions.

- Deployment of any single, proprietary integration solution across the enterprise is complex, costly, and time-consuming.
- No single data, business, or process model spans, much less extends beyond, the enterprise.

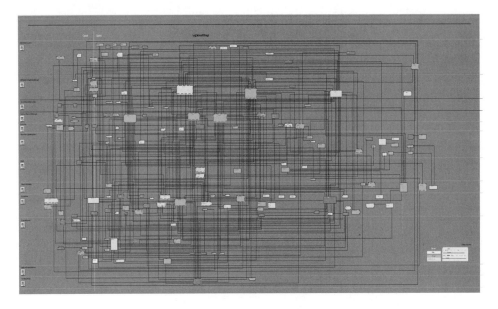

Figure 3-6   Agility is impossible when point-to-point solutions are the norm.

SOA is ultimately about providing IT systems that allow the business to be flexible and change at the pace that the business needs to change. SOA stresses interoperability as one of its key principles. Interoperability refers to the ability of services deployed using different technologies and platforms to communicate with each other. Chapter 7, "Information Services," discusses the usage of information patterns and information services in more detail.

SOA governance can help drive integration agility by demanding and directing this as part of the SOA journey. An enterprise data group is responsible for creating information standards, and the SOA development life cycle governance verifies those standards are followed.

Data ownership is another key concern for SOA governance. Many different business and IT groups will claim to be the primary user and therefore owner of a particular set of data. SOA governance should seek to identify the business owner of each major information area. This will become important in the future as hard business decisions need to be made to rationalize this information and enable information agility.

3.1.6 Portfolio Management

A.3.5

Portfolio management is responsible for analyzing and selecting the programs and projects to be performed at the enterprise and to manage and control those programs. A portfolio is one of a number of mechanisms, constructed to actualize significant elements in the enterprise business strategy. It contains a selected, approved, and continuously evolving collection of initiatives that are aligned with the organizing element of the portfolio, and that contribute to the achievement of goals or goal components identified in the enterprise business strategy.

SOA governance for portfolio management involves many aspects, including the business, technical, and information agility previously mentioned. The portfolio structure should provide oversight of all the enterprise's programs. The associated business case should be reviewed and validated. It is necessary to develop and approve plans, continuously adjust direction, and exercise control through periodic assessment and review of conformance to expectations.

Most large organizations conduct a yearly budgeting exercise. This is an area where SOA governance must be fully engaged. Proposed projects must now be assessed in a manner that gives priority to those that improve the agility of the organization. The return on investment (ROI) or similar calculation that is used to decide which projects are above the line must be adjusted to take creation of agility into account. In this manner, the portfolio will be adjusted over time to support a larger percentage of agility-creation projects.

3.2 Organizing for SOA

Although it is true that SOA may grow "organically" for a time, such an approach will inevitably sputter out without a group dedicated to its vision and vitality.

3.2.1 Organization

If a group already exists within the enterprise that is responsible for strategic and tactical vision, has good interface and alignment between the business and IT, performs business case and financial analysis, and has a portfolio oversight role, this group should also take on the responsibility of governing the SOA. If such a group does not exist, a new governance organization should be created (see Figure 3-7). Surveying the names used for this group has turned up SOA Center of Excellence (CoE), Integration Competency Center (ICC), Integration Center of Excellence (ICE), and Program Management Authority (PMA). It doesn't matter what you call it; it does matter that you have an organization that is responsible for SOA governance. We use Center of Excellence (CoE) for the remainder of this chapter.

This group would have the following tasks:

- Govern and work with all IT and business groups on SOA.
- Perform SOA governance tasks and not SOA implementation tasks.

> **NOTE**
>
> It might be the case that in the beginning of the SOA journey certain service capabilities do not yet exist in IT (for example, services designer skills, service implementation skills, SOA technology skills, and even enterprise architecture skills). In such a situation, expertise should be instantiated here and loaned to IT projects implementing SOA services.

- Lead in governing the creation and implementation of SOA governance principles, policies, and procedures that guide the SOA journey.
- Govern SOA strategic, tactical, and operational processes.
- Govern the SOA service life cycle.
- Monitor the vitality of the SOA program and lead in making adjustments, including improving skills, identifying new and changing roles, taking corrective actions, and identifying and leading necessary change that improves the maturity of the SOA program and the ability of the enterprise to be agile.

The CoE should have a CoE steering committee responsible for providing the immediate oversight of the CoE. It should include stakeholders from the various developer areas, enterprise architecture, the program management office (PMO), and the business. Projects that are nonconformant to SOA governance policies may appeal to this group for an exception if not granted by the CoE.

The SOA executive steering committee is the group that provides oversight and direction of the SOA initiative. The steering committee has an executive sponsor who is the leader of the SOA effort at the enterprise and works with the CIO, the board of directors, and other leaders within the corporation. This person is sometimes referred to as the chief transformation officer or SOA champion and should be someone with experience, vision, passion, and who commands respect in both the business and IT.

The architecture review board is responsible for reviewing all projects during the SOA development cycle and validating that all mandated SOA policies are being followed and that proper reuse of existing services and creation of new services for each project is taking place.

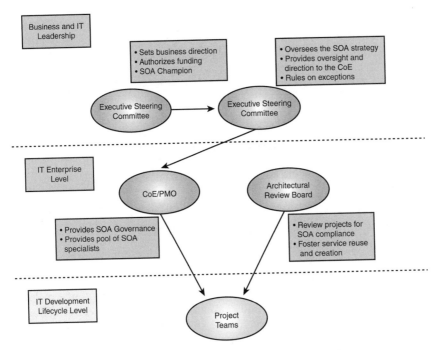

Figure 3-7 How the SOA organizations function with each other

3.2.2 Roles and Responsibilities

Certain roles and responsibilities should be considered for the SOA implementation at the enterprise. Not all of these will be germane to your enterprise, but they should be considered and either accepted, rejected, or adapted as appropriate. Depending on the size of the SOA effort and resource constraints, several different roles can be assigned to the same staff person. Most of these positions will be in the line organizations, but some of them may be housed in the SOA CoE, especially during the first year of SOA implementation or for roles that would benefit from a more enterprise level of control. The following SOA roles and responsibilities have been found to be a worthwhile starting point for consideration:

- The CoE leader is the leader of the SOA governance function within the enterprise. The CoE leader is responsible for making sure that the SOA activities occur, but does not usually perform them. They are responsible for governing the SOA for the enterprise. This means leading in the creation of the principles, policies, and procedures for the services-oriented approach and ensuring that those are followed.
- Service architects are services technology experts. They are responsible for working across the enterprise, providing expertise in service technology and guiding and adapting projects to governance and technology standards for SOA as agreed to at the enterprise.

- Service designers are solution architects responsible for creating a consistent and complete service design that meets all the technical and business requirements and standards. This role may initially be part of the CoE to provide consistency and expertise, but should eventually migrate to the line organizations.
- The service developer is a software engineer who builds services based on a service specification as given by the service designer.
- The service tester is a testing engineer who builds services test plans and validates that the service works correctly, including for nonfunctional requirements. They understand how the service fits in the service hierarchy and validate that service changes do not adversely impact other services roles.
- The service registrar is the keeper of the organization's service assets. They work with the architecture and development groups to enforce the services agility strategy and make sure that services are in their proper service state.
- An SOA governance specialist has primary day-to-day responsibility for overseeing the SOA governance tasks, including validation of governance policies and procedures, as well as monitoring the overall vitality of the SOA effort. Without this capability, the groups being governed will soon lose the vitality necessary to continue progress on the SOA journey. Although automated tools will help with governance, the human element is necessary.
- A business services leader is responsible for vitality and analysis and creation of the business services strategy. Usually, this is a businessperson with excellent IT understanding or an IT staff person with business subject matter expertise.
- A business process analyst models and optimizes complete business processes and individual tasks within the process to reengineer existing business processes or define new business processes. Because of the depth of business knowledge needed, business analysts are typically specialists in a few specific areas of business activity.
- Business process developers create executable processes based on a modeled business process, which then executes in a suitable environment role, usually with an ESB.

3.3 SOA Governance Considerations

As SOA governance practitioners, we must take a more structured approach to the art of governing, and turn it, as much as possible, into a science. To do so, we have to consider and define a paradigm for governance to be used in the remainder of this chapter. After the governance paradigm is defined, a number of governance components, including the service development life cycle, are explained in more detail. You may well have additional governance components beyond the ones described in this chapter, and the governance paradigm described here is meant to be a reusable governance framework, equally applicable to those components. It will help you derive the policies, standards, responsible parties, procedures, mechanisms, and metrics that you will need to govern additional governance components not described in this chapter.

But first, a few definitions of governance terms are needed to get us started:

- **Governed component**—Identifies the specific capability requiring governance.
- **Policy**—A definite course or method of action selected from among alternatives and in light of given conditions to guide and determine present and future decisions.[1] A policy applies to the governed component.
- **Standard**—Something established by authority, custom, or general consent as a model or example.[2] The governed component must adhere to the agreed standards.
- **Responsible party**—A person or group of people responsible for managing the governed component. It must be clear for each component who this responsible party is.
- **Procedure**—A particular method for performing a task. The procedure identifies how a component will be governed.
- **Mechanism**—A particular method for performing a task. This is where an asset, methodology, or best practice is applied to assist in the governance of this component.
- **Metric**—A standard of measurement.[3] It is important to put in place the measurements for the success of this governance component.

3.3.1 SOA Governance Paradigm

It is necessary for the governance practitioner to have a paradigm that is consistently applied to the entities to be governed. The governance entity-relationship diagram in Figure 3-8 uses the definitions we just discussed and has been successfully used in various governance consulting assignments. It seems to be a reasonable one to follow based on empirical evidence. You might decide to use a variation, but this is a commonsense place to start.

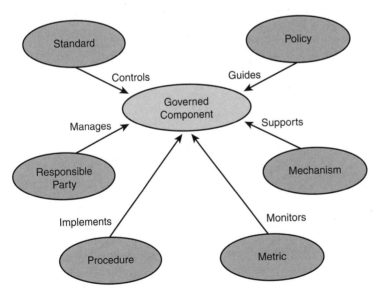

Figure 3-8 Governance paradigm

3.3.2 SOA Governance Checklist

Now that we have our governance definitions and governance paradigm, we're ready to consider each of the various governance components for SOA governance. We use the SOA governance paradigm to give a standard framework to the discussion of each component. To provide meaningful context, we use Ideation Communications as the enterprise being governed. Yours will undoubtedly be different, but these examples are meant to be practical and useful.

3.3.2.1 Services Development Life Cycle (SvDLC)

This area is concerned with reviewing and enforcing the rigor of the agreed-to enterprise policies and procedures upon system development, which may or may not involve services for a particular system or project. Unfortunately, it is quite common for projects and their corresponding development teams to take shortcuts to meet project deadlines. Although these shortcuts provide a short-term benefit, they have a long-term price and compromise the ability to achieve the lasting benefits of an SOE approach. Identifying these issues as soon as possible in the SvDLC is paramount to achieving delivering on time and budget. Of particular importance are the following for an *SvDLC Controls Handbook,* performed in this order:

1. **Solution review**—The solution architect will have created a solution architecture document that has identified the solution approach and high-level design to be taken, including identifying the services to be created or reused on this project. This is a vital time to optimize the services plan and the project development plan, as follows:

   a. If there is any opportunity to reuse existing services that has not been used, the architecture document should be updated. If the architects anticipate any messaging interface changes to the existing service, they must note any backward compatibility and service versioning requirements here.

   b. If there is any opportunity to create additional services, that should be addressed here.

   c. Particular attention should attend that the interface documents are following all information and technical standards.

   d. The project risk profile should be assessed and options to decrease risk identified and chosen.

   e. Validate that the business requirements are being met. The test team responsible for integration testing should review the Solution Architecture Document and request clarification and change as needed.

   f. The Service Registrar should be alerted to new services or changes.

2. **Service design review**—The service design document must be validated before commitment of development resources is allowed:

   a. The service specification must adhere to all policies and standards in effect.

   b. The service design document must be validated as adhering to the solution architecture document, including any business, information, or technical agility requirements, as well as security and compatibility requirements.

   c. All service producer and consumer concerns must be addressed, including nonfunctional requirements (NFR).

     d. Requirements traceability should be validated. The test team responsible for integration testing should review and validate that they understand the service design and are able to perform the necessary testing of the service. Runtime policy must be reviewed. For example, specific WS-Policy should be verified as adequate.

     e. The security design should be assessed as to whether it follows the minimum security baseline standards.

3. **Development to test review**—Handoff from development to integration test occurs:

     a. The developers will review the scope of the development, including interfaces and messaging, and present the service and component unit testing performed.

     b. The test team responsible for integration testing will review their service's integration test plan and ask for feedback. Verify that the service has a test plan that sufficiently tests the service's design, interfaces, and integration with other services and applications. If an existing service has changed, it must be verified that sufficient regression testing is taking place.

     c. Requirements traceability will be reviewed.

4. **Test to acceptance review**—Handoff from integration testing to user acceptance testing occurs:

     a. The testers review the results of their testing with the users, including solution, integration, and performance testing.

     b. The users will review their user acceptance test plan and ask for feedback

     c. Requirements traceability will be reviewed.

5. **Certification signoff**—Users have validated that requirements have been met:

     a. The registrar is notified and updates the service registry.

     b. The registrar ensures that backward compatibility and versioning for existing service consumers is properly employed.

     c. The registrar verifies that metadata for the runtime policy is correctly reflected in the service registry.

> **NOTE**
>
> IBM's WebSphere Service Registry and Repository performs all the registry functions mentioned in this chapter and is a key tool for SOA governance.

Ideation Communications used the following SvDLC (see Figure 3-9).

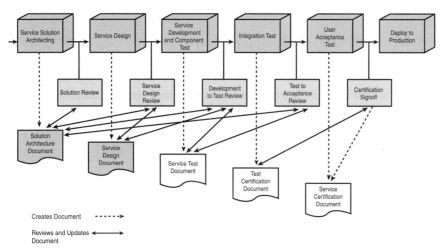

Figure 3-9 Modified SvDLC for Ideation Communications

Now, let's put the SvDLC and controls that we've adopted into our SOA governance paradigm framework that was shown in Figure 3-8 and discussed previously in this chapter. Table 3.1 shows the results.

Table 3-1 SvDLC Governance Component Table

Responsible Party	Architecture review board (ARB).
Policy	All projects must undergo an SvDLC controls review checking to consider reusing existing services and determine whether they should be creating new services. Projects must undergo the SvDLC review and meet all the currently accepted criteria. All exceptions must be approved by the ARB. Test plans and results must be reviewed and validated before the service may be deployed in production.
Standard	SvDLC Controls Handbook, business agility service plan, technical agility service plan, information agility plan, IT SOA design standards, IT information design standard, IT test plan design standard.

continues

Table 3-1 continued

Procedure	The SvDLC Controls Handbook is used. The reviews are scheduled and lead by the program management office (PMO), with the program PM creating an artifact to document the results. This artifact is then placed in the SOA governance library for future reference.
Mechanism	The reviews are scheduled and lead by the PMO, with the PM creating an artifact to document the results. This artifact is then placed in the SOA governance library for future reference with the ARB responsible for oversight and the exceptions process.
Metric	Number of services reused and created in analysis, number of changes made during design per project, number of test cases changed per project, number and severity of defects in integration test, number and severity of defects in the user acceptance test.

3.3.2.2 Service Life Cycle

The concept of a service life cycle is a bit different from the standard development approach that the enterprise is used to and therefore requires a separate discussion. See Figure 3-10 for a sample of the service states life cycle that is used in this section.

Reusable services are at the core of the actual creation of an SOA. As discussed in the "Governance of the SOA Strategy" section, the identification of services should grow from both a business strategy viewpoint and organically from project need. All services that have been identified as a result of the business agility, technical agility, or information agility planning, should be entered into the services registry with a "planned" status. Because the services registry will be used, among other functions, as a single source of the identified and planned services for the enterprise, project planners will be able to consult the registry and find planned services that their project is in a position to fund and create. In a similar manner, the solution architect will find the status of services that they contemplate reusing in the services registry and the status of such services. This capability will enable them to then assess the applicability of the service to their project.

After a solution has been architected that includes the services, the service will enter the "solution architected" state. In a similar manner, the status of the service in the service registry will advance via the service registrar as each quality gate in the SvDLC is passed.

The service reflects the business, so as the business changes the service needs to change accordingly. With existing users of the service, however, changes need to be made judiciously so as not to disrupt their successful operation. Therefore, the needs of existing users for stability are in conflict with the needs of users desiring additional functionality.

Service versioning supports these contradictory goals. It enables users satisfied with an existing service to continue using it unchanged, yet allows the service to evolve to meet the needs of users with new requirements. The current service interface and behavior is preserved as one version, while the newer service is introduced as another version. Version compatibility can enable a consumer expecting one version to invoke a different but compatible version.

To have "backward compatibility," it must be verified that existing message interface schema, transport bindings, or operations are not changed. Adding new XML schema types, transport bindings, or operations to a WSDL document should allow for backward compatibility. If backward compatibility cannot be maintained in a new version of a service (this should be the exception, not the rule), governance in the person of the service registrar must take special care to review and address all current consumers of the service. In any case, once a new version is created, the old version enters a state of "deprecated."

SOA governance should make sure that a policy is in place regarding the number of versions of a service that will be maintained. A maximum of two is best, but three is acceptable, too. When a version of a service is finally retired, its service state becomes "sunsetted."

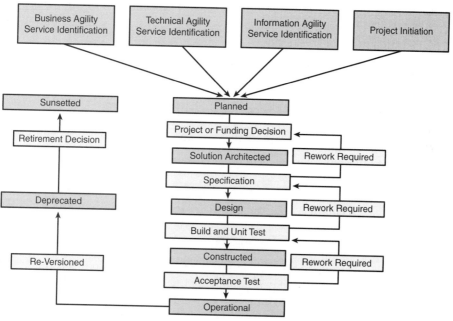

Figure 3-10   Service lifecycle used for Ideation Communications

Now, let's put the service life cycle into our SOA governance paradigm framework that was shown in Figure 3-8 and discussed previously in this chapter. Table 3-2 shows the results.

Table 3.2 Service Life Cycle Table

Responsible Party	Service registrar.
Policy	Service status is updated upon successful completion of an SvDLC control gate. Service versioning must be intelligently controlled and backward compatibility ensured with exceptions being as few as possible. Any service change that is not backward compatible is a "major" version change, for example, from Version 1.2 to 2.0. If the service change is backward compatible, this is a "minor" version change, for example from 1.2 to 1.3.
Standard	The SvDLC Controls Handbook, business agility service plan, technical agility service plan, information agility plan, service life cycle.
Procedure	An SvDLC approach is integrated with service life cycle status.
Mechanism	Service registry with management capabilities from the service registry.
Metric	Number of services in each state, number of services with two, three, or more than three versions.

3.3.2.3 Business Agility

SOA governance must make sure that there is vitality in the creation of business agility.

Ideation Communications implemented the items in Table 3-3 for its SOA governance model of business agility.

Table 3-3 Business Agility Table

Responsible Party	SOA executive steering committee with the CoE.
Policy	Portfolio management priority will be given to projects that advance the stated business agility strategy. The business agility strategy will be reconsidered and updated at least once a year.
Standard	TMF eTOM and Telco Applications Map (TAM) is the industry standard business operations map and application map used by Ideation Communications for business agility analysis, and all agility proposals must map to these standards. The approved business agility plan is the standard to be used for giving priority to IT portfolio priority.

Procedure	The business agility task force will meet quarterly and include global and visionary members of both the business and IT at Ideation Communications. The task force will report back to the SOA executive steering committee, who will review and accept, reject, or modify each task force recommendation. The PMO will use the business agility plan to give priority to projects at Ideation Communications.
Mechanism	Industry modeling software that has implemented the TMF eTOM and TAM.
Metric	Number of planned business services created, number of business services instantiated in the past year.

3.3.2.4 Technical Agility

SOA governance must make sure that there is vitality in the creation process of technical agility and that it is properly implemented. In particular, SOA governance must validate that the requisite groups within the enterprise are following the technical agility policies and standards and that appropriate enforcement is taking place.

Ideation Communications implemented the items in Table 3-4 for its SOA governance model of technical agility.

Table 3-4 Technical Agility Table

Responsible Party	Enterprise architecture with the CoE. CoE steering committee.
Policy	Infrastructure projects that advance the technical agility strategy will be given priority. All projects will follow the hardware and software standards with any buying outside these standards being an exception that must be approved by the chief architect.
Standard	Approved technical agility plan.

continues

Table 3-4   continued

Procedure	The technical agility task force will meet quarterly and include global and visionary members throughout IT at Ideation Communications. The task force will report back to the enterprise architecture chief architect, who will review and accept, reject, or modify each task force recommendation.
	All POs will undergo review by procurement as meeting the requirements of the approved technical agility plan. Exceptions must be approved by the CoE steering committee.
	The CoE will periodically review the SOA development cycle to validate that the technical services plan is being advanced appropriately.
Mechanism	Automated procurement review software.
Metric	Number of planned technical services created, number of technical services instantiated in the past year, number of PO changes as a result of procurement review and amount of money saved, number and type of PO exceptions to policy.

3.3.2.5 Information Agility

SOA governance must make sure that there is vitality in the creation process of information agility and that it is properly implemented. In particular, SOA governance must validate that the requisite groups within the enterprise are following the information agility policies and standards and that appropriate enforcement is taking place.

Ideation Communications implemented the items in Table 3-5 for its SOA governance model of information agility.

Table 3-5   Information Agility Table

Responsible Party	Enterprise architecture with the CoE.
Policy	Projects that advance the information agility strategy will be given priority.
Standard	TMF shared information data (SID) will be used as the starting point for the enterprise data model. Additions to the enterprise data model are as approved by the enterprise architecture group.

Procedure	The information agility task force will meet quarterly and include global and visionary members throughout IT and the business at Ideation Communications. The task force will report back to the enterprise architecture chief architect, who will review and accept, reject, or modify each task force recommendation. The CoE will periodically review the SvDLC to validate that the approved information services plan is being advanced appropriately.
Mechanism	Add information agility to the balanced scorecard and review monthly.
Metric	Number of planned information services created, number of information services instantiated in the past year, number of services and applications using the enterprise data model.

3.3.2.6 Portfolio Management

SOA governance must make sure that projects are picked that advance the enterprises strategic intent for agility. This intent is manifested in the business, technical, and information agility plans that have been discussed earlier. In addition, SOA governance must make sure there is a structure to provide global program management, usually instantiated as a program management office (PMO). SOA governance should work closely with the PMO and make sure that they have the tools, processes, and political backing to get their job done right. Ideation Communications implemented the items in Table 3-6 for its SOA governance model of portfolio management.

Table 3-6   Portfolio Management Table

Responsible Party	PMO with the CoE steering committee.
Policy	The overall portfolio of projects must be advancing the enterprise's agility. Any project that involves multiple development VPs will be managed through the PMO.
Standard	Approved business, technical, information agility plan.
Procedure	A PMO will run the quarterly portfolio planning process and work with finance to create an ROI using the enterprise standard ROI approach. This ROI takes the agility plans into account. The PMO will create an enterprise-wide project-reporting mechanism and review status weekly with the CoE steering committee.

continues

Table 3-6   continued

Mechanism	The program management tool software to assist in tracking programs and producing reports.
Metric	Number of programs delivered on time, number of programs delivered on budget, number of business and information services created.

3.3.2.7 Sourcing

Sourcing, in the context of SOA, addresses how a particular service is created, whether it is built in-house, outsourced, or purchased. SOA governance is responsible for making sure that there are policies and procedures for how this decision is made. Left to their own devices, development groups will decide that only they can build the software right. However, this ignores the industry trend that the intellectual capital of the world is helping to create reusable services that are applicable to many enterprises. A good services registry will provide linking to external Universal Description Discovery and Integration (UDDI) libraries that contain technical information about exposed services from other businesses. These services are generally not core businesses of the enterprise (for example, process credit card transaction) that are better to buy, freeing up scarce resources to develop services in areas that provide a competitive advantage.

Ideation Communications implemented the items in Table 3-7 for its SOA governance model of sourcing.

Table 3-7   Sourcing Table

Responsible Party	Solution architect with the CoE.
Policy	Survey the market and determine whether a service or software package exists that meets our needs. Make sure the vendor is financially viable, has good vision in this area, and that the price is reasonable (per procurement). If evaluating existing code as a source for a service, determine whether the business function is relatively modular (good) or is "spaghetti code" (bad). If evaluating an existing application, determine whether the application function is relatively separated from data input/output and other nonapplication entities. If evaluating an existing application, determine whether it is sufficiently interesting from a business point of view and has process logic that can be reused. Determine whether extracting the business logic will cost less than 20 percent of the original investment.

Policy	If the preponderance of three to five of the above is yes, buy. Otherwise, if one to two of the above are true, then build.
Standard	Procurement standards.
Procedure	Development will assess and create their plans for buy versus build using the sourcing policy. As part of the SvDLC for service-usage review, the development group plan may be overridden in the interests of the enterprise SOA strategy. The development group may appeal the sourcing policy decision and request an exception from the CoE steering committee.
Mechanism	UDDI search, which automatically surveys the Internet for service matches.
Metric	Number of services reused, bought, and built.

3.3.2.8 Business Value

Projects are usually accepted based on an ROI of incremental revenue, cost containment, or both. "Business value" is responsible for ascertaining, after the project has gone into production, that the intended value was actually realized. A finance group at the enterprise is usually responsible for this. Because SOA is about providing agility and value to the business, creating business value becomes even more important. Information on business value is used to guide future portfolio management. Governance can help this process by making sure that the right metrics are being measured to identify the business benefits to be accrued. SOA modeling and monitoring tools have a rich set of features to support this capability.

Ideation Communications implemented the items in Table 3-8 for its SOA governance model of business value.

Table 3-8 Business Value Table

Responsible Party	PMO with the CoE.
Policy	Business value parameters from the business case will be modeled and monitored and used in future portfolio management decisions.
Standard	The business case for the project.

continues

Table 3-8 continued

Procedure	For each project that is funded, the PMO will identify the business value parameters that were part of the business case and communicate these to the project team for inclusion in the modeling and monitoring. The PMO will require and check that validation of the inclusion of these parameters will be part of the acceptance test plan and subsequent verification process.
Mechanism	Middleware for modeling and monitoring.
Metric	Business value parameters will be reported on the balanced scorecard.

3.3.2.9 Regulatory Compliance

Many businesses will have at least some degree of industry or government regulation and compliance required. For example, telecommunications has the Federal Communication Commission (FCC) in the United States and the Office of Communications (Ofcom) in the United Kingdom. Sarbanes-Oxley affects all listed companies in the United States, regardless of country of incorporation. Banks are subject to Basel II for international capital framework requirements. Regulations are constantly changing, and being able to easily provide proof of regulatory compliance is a key aspect of an agile business.

SOA governance must ensure that all services fully comply with the relevant laws. Simply, this requires that there be a checklist of what the regulations are, and that this is communicated at the right points in the SvDLC process for the necessary design and implementation.

Ideation Communications implemented the items in Table 3-9 for its SOA governance model of regulatory compliance.

Table 3-9 Regulatory Compliance Table

Responsible Party	Legal group, architecture review board with the CoE.
Policy	Any service must support the rules and regulations that the enterprise is legally subject to.
Standard	Legal provides an approved regulatory checklist for the enterprise.
Procedure	During design review, the approved regulatory checklist must be checked. Each item on the checklist must either be found to be irrelevant to the service undergoing design review or sufficient as to the design.

Mechanism	Summary of the regulatory checklist and service design review results available for auditor review.
Metric	Number of services supporting regulatory requirements.

3.3.2.10 Security

Security is a difficult but necessary proposition for any application. Functionality needs to be limited to authorized users, and data needs to be protected from interception. The SOA governance must ensure that there is a services security standard and that it is properly adhered to. Access to services has to be controlled and limited to authorized consumers. User identity must be propagated into services and used to authorize data access.

What makes this even more important and difficult for SOA is the changing nature of a service transaction versus a typical silo'd application. The latter tended to do all of its work safely inside the firewall. Services, however, have a more distributed architecture, and the overall security architecture cannot make such simplifying assumptions. Usually, a message based security protocol must be chosen as a standard and then enforced via SOA governance. This includes security for authentication, authorization, encryption, and nonrepudiation.

Ideation Communications implemented the items in Table 3-10 for its SOA governance model for security.

Table 3-10   Security Table

Responsible Party	Security Group, enterprise architecture with the CoE. ARB.
Policy	Any service must support the minimum baseline security standards per the security group. There must be regular audits of SOA security. An overall services security plan must be implemented and periodically updated. The security plan must include usage of runtime security control points.
Standard	Security group minimum baseline security standard.
Procedure	During design review, the service will be assessed for following the minimum security baseline. The service must pass this assessment to exit the design review. During the test plan review, the test plan must show that it is testing for the security requirements. The security group will create, implement, and periodically update the security strategy for a distributed services environment. This plan will be reviewed, modified, and approved by the ARB.

continues

Table 3-10 continued

Mechanism	Software for automated security checks to help security testing. Automated security monitoring hardware and software.
Metric	Number of security violations detected or found to be monitored in balanced scorecard.

3.3.2.11 Service Ownership

The word *ownership* means the act of having or controlling a property. The concepts of *service provider* and *service consumer* are basic in an SOA, and are key concept when considering ownership. An IT group is usually not familiar with the concept of using a service that it does not have development control over. This dependency on the part of the service consumer is a source of friction in the SOA process. The service provider (owner) has always had certain support responsibilities to operations for problem resolution and the business users for modification, but now a third party enters into the equation for problem resolution and modification (that is, for the service consumer).

This is why having good governance around the service ownership process is important for an SOA. A service provider has certain obligations to the service consumer. The service is bound with a contract (the service specification) so that the service consumer knows what they are getting and that the service provider is someone they can trust. Service owners assume responsibility for correctness, allowing/denying permission to execute, consume, or access each service or process. It is necessary to establish the process to handle service reusage requests, problem resolution, and service modification.

SOA governance must also ensure that there is a fair process for changing ownership when necessary. If Group A owns a service, but cannot create a new version that Group B needs for several years, how motivated is Group B going to be to use that service? It is possible that when one group requests the reuse of a service it does not own, the level of activity and current business processes may dictate a change in ownership. The current owning group will fight this, so it is beneficial to have governance policies around the ownership change process figured out ahead of time.

Ideation Communications implemented the items in Table 3-11 for its SOA governance model for service ownership.

Table 3-11   Service Ownership Table

Responsible Party	PMO with the CoE.
Policy	The solution architecture will assign ownership of new services. Ownership changes of existing services shall be performed when necessary by the CoE. The service owner is responsible for supporting the owned service to operations and a service consumer. The service owner is responsible for modifications of the owner service.
Standard	None.
Procedure	Ownership of a new service will be decided during project initiation. The PMO office will have the lead and will work with the CoE. If there is a disagreement, the CoE steering committee will hear the appeal and render a final decision. An ownership change in an existing service is triggered if the developer organization cannot perform an update for a new version in a timely manner or is unable to provide support in a timely fashion, as determined by the CoE. The CoE steering committee will be final arbiter on any disagreements.
Mechanism	Service registry management reports
Metric	Number of different development groups that own services reflected in balanced scorecard.

3.3.2.12 Service Funding

Service funding is concerned with how services development will be funded and how to possibly charge back and reward the service producer for the reuse by the service consumer. There are three main types of possible charging: a one-time charge for the service reuse, a per-usage charge, or the developing department receiving funding as needed from the project funds.

Ideation Communications implemented the items in Table 3-12 for its SOA governance model for service funding.

Table 3-12   Service Funding Table

Responsible Party	IT finance group with the CoE.
Policy	The producer organization funds creation of original service from project funds. Modifications are funded from project requiring modification.
Standard	Finance department standards will be used.
Procedure	Department funding will be tracked by finance group.
Mechanism	Finance department reports.
Metric	Number of reused services.

3.3.2.13 Communications

A services approach is usually a major paradigm shift for both the IT and business organization. In particular, it is natural for the IT group to feel threatened at the changes that are going on about them. The executive management must continually be educated about the benefits of the SOA approach. It is important that the CoE group lead the project when creating and implementing a communication plan that educates and leads the organization.

Ideation Communications implemented the items in Table 3-13 for its SOA governance model for communications.

Table 3-13   Communications Table

Responsible Party	The CoE working with corporate communications.
Policy	Robust communications on how the SOA approach is affecting the organization is important.
Standard	Corporate communications standards will be used.
Procedure	Within the IT group, hold periodic (once a month) 1 to 2 hours all-hands meetings to explain a particular aspect of the current services architecture, technology, or process. Check with the IT developers on areas of interest, and then hold lunch meetings to explain and demonstrate this area. Place SOA information on the company intranet website. Meet with the business services team to explain a services approach.

Procedure	Find a business services member who "gets it," and hold more in-depth follow-ups to help him or her become a "champion." Implement a communication plan per up, down, and across the organization. This includes business units and sub-business units. The CoE head will have 1-hour one-to-one meetings monthly with each of the business VPs to discuss aspects of the SOA journey that is of interest to that stakeholder.
Mechanism	Corporate intranet, company newsletter.
Metric	Include communications effectiveness survey questions on balanced scorecard.

3.3.2.14 Education and Mentoring

Typically, the personnel at an enterprise where SOA is new are not proficient in the concepts of services or the industry standards that are important for SOA. It is important to make training and mentoring available to the development group or any others who care to take advantage of it. Several different paths are typically found for SOA education, including business analyst skills, architect skills, application developer skills, integration development skills, solution deployment skills, and solution administration skills.

If the enterprise has a training department, they should be consulted with on additional services-based training that might be offered. This should include services concepts as well as specific technical training (for example, XML, SOAP, WSDL, and WS-I).

The CoE should contain services experts. These resources need to be leveraged and should perform on-the-job (OTJ) training for project staff. One-on-one mentoring for key development personnel or management will accelerate the services plan. Many enterprises have an explicit mentoring program that can be leveraged for this purpose. If not, the CoE should set up a services mentoring program and make that available to the enterprise.

Ideation Communications implemented the items in Table 3-14 for its SOA governance model for education and mentoring.

Table 3-14 Education and Mentoring Table

Responsible Party	Training group with the CoE.
Policy	An SOA training program will be created using a combination of mentoring, in-house classroom training, self-paced online training, and external classroom courses. The manager will create a yearly training program for each employee, making use of these courses depending on the expected employee assignments. This training plan should be periodically reviewed and agreed on between manager and employee.

continues

Table 3-14 continued

Standard	HR training standards, approved courses.
Procedure	Review staff profiles and work with staff managers, identify and fund training courses, and identify staff that will take the training. "Train the trainer"—Take the best staff and train, and then leverage across the organization. Use online training where it makes sense. Mentor—A mentoring program will assess skill levels and have experienced SOA practitioners mentor inexperienced practitioners.
Mechanism	Online training courses, classroom training, and OTJ training.
Metric	The training and mentoring progress will become part of the enterprise's balanced scorecard.

3.3.3 Operations and Monitoring

A services approach has impacts on the operational processes currently in use at the enterprise. SOA governance must consider these impacts and address them with the operations group. The services certification quality gate at the end of the SvDLC is a good opportunity to hand off the operational information and perform training as needed for operational support.

A composite application, one that combines multiple services, is only as reliable as the services it depends on. Because multiple composite applications can share a service, a single service failure can affect many applications. Service level agreements (SLA) must be defined to describe the reliability and performance consumers can depend on. Service providers must be monitored to ensure that they're meeting their defined SLAs.

A related issue is problem determination. When a composite application stops working, it might be difficult to determine why. It's important to monitor not just how each application is running, but also how each service (as a collection of providers) and individual provider is also running. Correlation of events between services in a single business transaction is critical.

Such monitoring can help detect and prevent problems before they occur. It can detect load imbalances and outages, provide warning before they become critical, and can even attempt to correct problems automatically. It can measure usage over time to help predict services that are becoming more popular so that they can run with increased capacity.

3.3.4 SOA Transition Plan

A best practice for any enterprise undergoing an SOA journey is to have a transition plan that has been reviewed and agreed to by the stakeholders. It becomes difficult for the inevitable naysayer in the company to say no when there is a document that the C-level has said yes to. A transition plan helps bring together all the milestones and communicates and inspires confidence in the community at large that the SOA program and the SOA governance group has a well thought-out plan.

The example presented for Ideation Communications is a portion of the transition plan for the CoE. Yours, of course, will be much more complete, but the transition plan in Figure 3-11 should get you started.

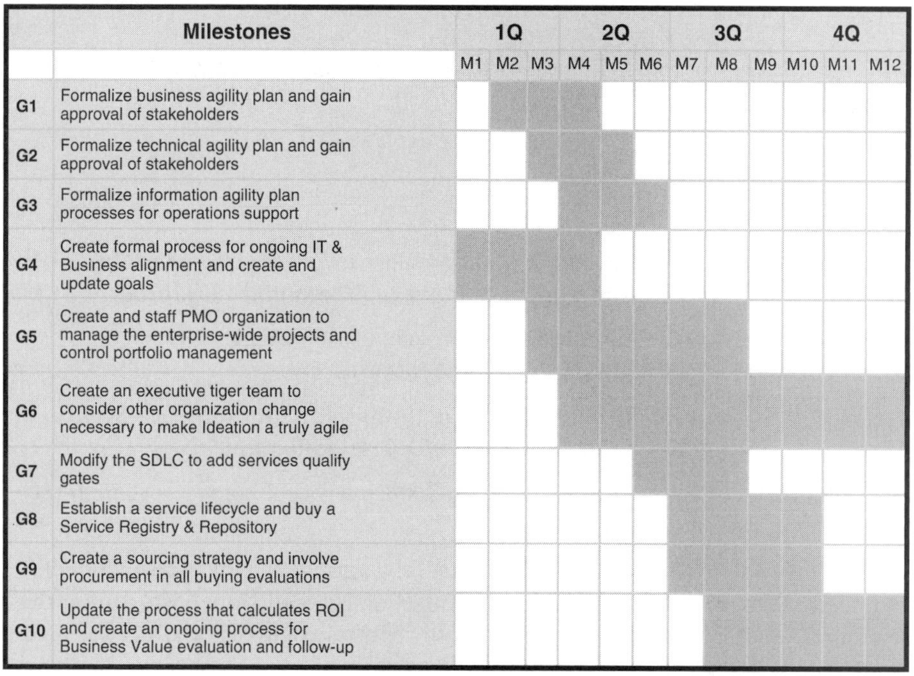

	Milestones	1Q			2Q			3Q			4Q		
		M1	M2	M3	M4	M5	M6	M7	M8	M9	M10	M11	M12
G1	Formalize business agility plan and gain approval of stakeholders		▓	▓									
G2	Formalize technical agility plan and gain approval of stakeholders			▓	▓								
G3	Formalize information agility plan processes for operations support				▓	▓							
G4	Create formal process for ongoing IT & Business alignment and create and update goals	▓			▓	▓							
G5	Create and staff PMO organization to manage the enterprise-wide projects and control portfolio management					▓	▓						
G6	Create an executive tiger team to consider other organization change necessary to make Ideation a truly agile						▓	▓	▓	▓	▓	▓	▓
G7	Modify the SDLC to add services qualify gates						▓	▓					
G8	Establish a service lifecycle and buy a Service Registry & Repository							▓	▓				
G9	Create a sourcing strategy and involve procurement in all buying evaluations								▓	▓			
G10	Update the process that calculates ROI and create an ongoing process for Business Value evaluation and follow-up							▓	▓		▓	▓	

Figure 3-11 SOA governance transition plan

3.4 Conclusion

Getting to a true SOE does not happen by accident. An organization must be intentional and focused. It must have leadership. It must have clear roles and responsibilities. It must have well thought-out and implemented policies and procedures. In other words, it must have SOA governance.

3.5 Links to developerWorks Articles

A3.1 Portfolio Management, an Introduction. www.ibm.com/developerworks/rational/library/oct05/hanford/index.html.

A3.2 A Case for SOA Governance. www.ibm.com/developerworks/webservices/library/ws-soa-govern/.

A3.3 EA & Services Oriented Enterprise (SOE), Services Orientation, Hype of Hope? Structuring the Enterprise around Services. www.enterprise-architecture.info/Images/Services%20Oriented%20Enterprise/EA_ Services-Oriented-Enterprise1.htm.

A3.4 Core Business Architecture for a Service-Oriented Enterprise. www.research.ibm.com/journal/sj/464/nayak.html.

A3.5 OECD Principles of Corporate Governance. www.oecd.org/dataoecd/32/18/31557724.pdf.

3.6 References

Hanford, M. IBM developerWorks, Portfolio Management, an Introduction, October 15, 2005. www.ibm.com/developerworks/rational/library/oct05/hanford/index.html.

Mitra, T. IBM developerWorks, A Case for SOA Governance, August 16, 2005. www.ibm.com/developerworks/webservices/library/ws-soa-govern/.

Nayak, N. et al. *IBM System Journal*, 46:4, 2007, Core Business Architecture for a Service-Oriented Enterprise. www.research.ibm.com/journal/sj/464/nayak.html.

OECD, OECD Principles of Corporate Governance, 2004, www.oecd.org/dataoecd/32/18/31557724.pdf.

Schekkerman, J. Institute for Enterprise Architecture Developments, October 16, 2007, EA & Services Oriented Enterprise (SOE), Services Orientation, Hype of Hope? Structuring the Enterprise around Services. www.enterprise-architecture.info/Images/Services%20Oriented%20Enterprise/EA_Services-Oriented-Enterprise1.htm.

Endnotes

[1] Merriam-Webster Online Dictionary, Policy. www.m-w.com/dictionary/policy.

[2] Merriam-Webster Online Dictionary, Standard. www.m-w.com/dictionary/standard.

[3] Merriam-Webster Online Dictionary, Metric. www.m-w.com/dictionary/metric.

Chapter 4

A Methodology for Service Modeling and Design

When the programming model shifted from the traditional procedural model to that of object-orientation, a major paradigm shift occurred in the world of IT development. The focus was on encapsulating the state and behavior of entities and calling that encapsulation a class. Instances of a class were called objects, which occupied some space in the memory. Object orientation (OO) brought in concepts of inheritance, encapsulation, and polymorphism that could be applied to define relationships between classes. With the prevalence of the use of OO in the programming world, developers and architects started noticing some patterns that can be applied to the usage of OO principles to solve similar types of problems. The patterns depicted the deconstruction of a problem into multiple class entities, together with their interrelationships using the basic concepts of OO, to provide a solution to the problem. The seminal work in this field was done by the Gang of Four authors in the book called *Design Patterns: Elements of Reusable Object-Oriented Software.* (See the "References" section.) Whereas in OO the first-class constructs were objects and classes, the next-generation methodology for building software applications was called component-based development (CBD). In CBD, the first-class constructs were components, where a component was defined by its external specification, which could be used without any knowledge of its internal implementation. As such, the same external specification could be implemented in different programming language (for example, Java, C#). The internal implementation of a component may use multiple classes that collectively provide the implementation of the external specification. The classes could use one or more design patterns, thereby leveraging the advantages of OO principles.

In SOA, the main emphasis is on the identification of the right services followed by their specification and realization. Although some might argue that object-oriented analysis and design (OOAD) techniques can be used as a good starting point for services, its main emphasis is on microlevel abstractions. Services, on the other hand, are business-aligned entities and therefore are at a much higher level of abstraction than are objects and components.

The main first-class constructs in an SOA are *services, service components,* and *process flows.* For the sake of brevity, we refer to process flows as just flows. These are at a level of abstraction that is higher than that of objects, classes, and components. Hence, there needs to be a higher level of modeling and design principles that deal with the first-class constructs of an SOA. Service-oriented modeling and design is a discipline that provides prescriptive guidance about how to effectively design an SOA using services, service components, and flows. Rational Software, now a part of IBM, has provided an extension to Rational Unified Process (RUP) called *RUP-SOMA* (see the "References" section), which is built on a service-oriented analysis and design technique developed by IBM called Service Oriented Modeling and Architecture (SOMA). The rest of this chapter takes you through the SOMA technique and explains how it helps in the identification, specification, and realization of services, service components, and flows.

4.1 An SOA Reference Architecture

A.4.1

When defining a service-oriented solution, it makes sense to keep a reference architecture in context—an architecture that establishes the building blocks of SOA: *services, service components,* and *flows* that collectively support enterprise business processes and the business goals. The reference architecture provides characteristics and definitions for each layer and the relationships between them and assists in the placement of the architectural building blocks onto each layer. This layering facilitates the creation of architectural blueprints in SOA and helps in reusability of solutions and assets within an industry and potentially across industry verticals. Figure 4-1 shows a sample logical SOA reference architecture.

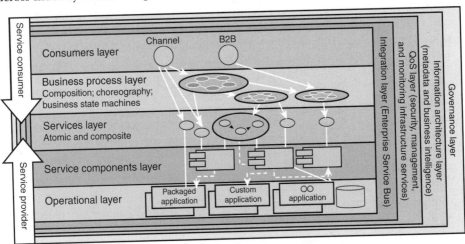

Figure 4-1   Logical view of SOA Reference Architecture

The figure shows a nine-layered architecture with five horizontal layers and four vertical layers. The horizontal layers follow the basic principle of a layered architecture model in which architecture building blocks (ABB) from layers above can access ABBs from layers below, whereas layers below may not access ABBs from layers above. The vertical layers usually contain ABBs that are cross-cutting in nature, which implies that they may be applicable to and used by ABBs in one or more of the horizontal layers. This can also be called a partial layered architecture because any layer above does not need to strictly interact with elements from its immediate lower layer. For example, a specific access channel can directly access a service rather than needing to go through a business process. The access constraints, however, are dictated by the architectural style, guidelines, and principles that apply to a given SOA solution. This view of the SOA reference architecture is independent of any specific technology implementation, and hence is a logical view. Instances of this logical architecture can be developed for a specific platform and technology. Following are definitions of each of the layers:

- **Layer 1: Operational systems**—This layer includes the operational systems that exist in the current IT environment of the enterprise, supporting business activities. Operational systems include all custom applications, packaged applications, legacy systems, transaction-processing systems, and the various databases.
- **Layer 2: Service component layer**—Components in this layer conform to the contracts defined by services in the services layer. A service component may realize one or more services. A service component provides an implementation façade that aggregates functionality from multiple, possible disparate, operational systems while hiding the integration and access complexities from the service that is exposed to the consumer. The consumer thus is oblivious of the service component, which encapsulates the implementation complexities. The advantage of this façade component comes from the flexibility of changing operational systems without affecting the service definition. The service component provides an enforcement point for service realization to ensure quality of service (QoS) and compliance to service level agreements.
- **Layer 3: Services layer**—This layer include all the services defined in the enterprise service portfolio. The definition of each service, which constitutes both its syntactic and semantic information, is defined in this layer. Whereas the syntactic information is essentially around the operations on each service, the input and output messages, and the definition of the service faults, the semantic information is around the service policies, service management decisions, service access requirements, and so on. The services are defined in such a way that they are accessible to and invocable by channels and consumers independent of implementation and the transport protocol. The critical step is the identification of the services using the various techniques that can be employed for the same. The methodology that we focus on in this chapter addresses such identification techniques.
- **Layer 4: Business process layer**—Business processes depict how the business runs. A business process is an IT representation of the various activities coordinated and collaborated in an enterprise to perform a specific high-level business function. This layer represents the processes as an orchestration or a composition of loosely coupled services—leveraging the services represented in the services layer. The layer is also responsible for the entire lifecycle management of the processes along with

their orchestration, and choreography. The data and information flow between steps within each process is also represented in this layer. Processes represented in this layer are the connection medium between business requirements and their manifestation as IT-level solutions using ABBs from other horizontal and vertical layers in the architecture stack. Users, channels, and B2B partner systems in the consumer layer uses the business processes in this layer as one of the ways to invoke application functionality.

- **Layer 5: Consumer layer**—This layer depicts the various channels through which the IT functions are delivered. The channels can be in the form of different user types (for example, external and internal consumers who access application functionality through access mechanisms like B2B systems, portals, rich clients, and other forms). The goal of this layer is to standardize on the access protocol and data format to enable the quick creation of front ends to the business processes and services exposed from the layers below. Some such standards have emerged in the form of portlets, service component architecture (SCA) components, and Web Services for Remote Portlets (WSRP). The adherence to standard mechanisms for developing the presentation layer components for the business processes and services helps in providing template solutions in the form of standard architecture patterns, which helps the developer community to adopt common front-end patterns for service consumption.

- **Layer 6: Integration layer**—This layer provides the capability for service consumers to locate service providers and initiate service invocations. Through the three basic capabilities of mediation, routing, and data and protocol transformation, this layer helps foster a service ecosystem wherein services can communicate with each other while being a part of a business process. The key nonfunctional requirements such as security, latency, and quality of service between adjacent layers in the reference architecture are implemented by the architecture building blocks in this layer. The functions of this layer are typically and increasingly being collectively defined as the enterprise service bus (ESB). An ESB is a collection of architecture patterns that uses open standards and protocols to implement the three basic capabilities of this layer and provide a layer of indirection between the service consumers and the service provider by exposing the services only through the ESB. ESB products usually add some specialized features to provide differentiated capabilities in the marketplace.

The integration capabilities are most commonly used by ABBs residing between Layer 2 through Layer 5. As an example, in Layer 5 there can be many consumers accessing enterprise services through different channel types. Each channel type can use different protocols—HTML, WML (for mobile users), and Voice XML (for IVR users), to name a few. Each of these protocols and message formats may be passed through an Extensible Stylesheet Language Transformations (XSLT) engine before the actual service is invoked. This XSLT transform is usually an ESB-provided feature. The beauty of the ESB-based integration layer is that any feature or function that can be exposed in a manner that follows open standards and protocols for access can be plugged into the ESB so that it is enabled to take part in a service-based ecosystem. Figure 4-2 depicts a logical view of the ESB.

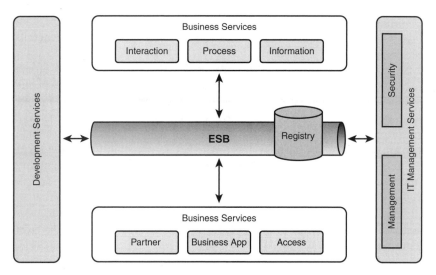

Figure 4-2 Logical view of an ESB in the integration layer

As Figure 4-2 suggests, the ESB provides capabilities for service consumers and providers to connect to each other, for services to be discovered using the registry, for services to be managed and for secure invocations, and provides application programming interfaces (API) to facilitate the development of service connectivity.

- **Layer 7: QoS layer**—This layer focuses on implementing and managing the non-functional requirements (NFR) that the services need to implement. Although SOA brings some real value proposition through the new architectural style, the programming model that supports the building of the first-class SOA constructs adds some inherent challenges that are nontrivial to address. The challenges arise while trying to comply with the essential tenets of SOA: abstraction, open standards and protocols, distributed computing, heterogeneous computing infrastructures, federated service ecosystem, and so on. Adherence to these compliance requirements often makes the implementation of the NFRs that much more complicated. This layer provides the infrastructure capabilities to realize the NFRs. It captures the data elements that provide the information around noncompliance to NFRs at each of the horizontal layers. Standard NFRs that it monitors for noncompliance is security, availability, scalability, and reliability.

- **Layer 8: Information architecture layer**—This layer ensures a proper representation of the data and information that is required in an SOA. The data architecture and the information architecture representation (along with its key considerations and guidelines for its design and usage) at each specific horizontal layer are the responsibilities of this layer.

  Industry models (for example, ACORD, IAA, JXDD) and their usage to define the information architecture, along with business protocols used to exchange business data, are addressed in this layer. It also stores the metadata required for data mining and business intelligence. Refer to the "References" section for the details of some industry models.

- **Layer 9: Governance layer**—This layer ensures the proper management of the entire lifecycle of the services. It is responsible for prioritizing which high-value services should be implemented, for each of the layers in the architecture, and for providing a rationalization based on how the service satisfies a business or IT goal of the enterprise. Enforcing both design-time and runtime policies that the services should implement and conform to is one of the key responsibilities of this layer. Essentially, this layer provides a framework that efficiently oversees the design and implementation of services so that they comply with the various business and IT regulatory policies and requirements.

  Chapter 3, "SOA Governance," discusses SOA governance and the responsibilities of a governance council in detail. Those responsibilities all feature in this layer of the reference architecture.

It is worth noting that one of the primary reasons for the SOA solution stack representation is that it helps to communicate, to the business and IT stakeholders, the evolution and realization of the enterprises SOA vision and roadmap through iterative implementation. Communicating with the stakeholders is key to ensure that the business commitment is pervasive across the various phases of an SOA initiative.

The methodology that we discuss in this chapter will help in identifying, specifying, and realizing the first-class constructs of an SOA and their placement in the various layers of the architecture stack. This logical view of the SOA reference architecture is also known as the SOA solution stack or just the solution stack. Therefore, the terms *SOA reference architecture*, *SOA solution stack*, and *solution stack* all refer to the same concept and hence can be used interchangeably.

4.2 Service Oriented Modeling and Architecture

A.4.2

Service Oriented Modeling and Architecture (SOMA) is a modeling and design technique developed by IBM that provides prescriptive steps for how to enable target business processes by defining and developing a service-based IT solution. SOMA provides the communication link between the business requirements and the IT solution. It provides guidance on how to use business model and information as inputs to derive and define a service-based IT model. SOMA, as a methodology, addresses the gap between SOA and object orientation. This methodology approach provides modeling, analysis, design techniques, and activities to define the foundations of an SOA. It helps defining the elements in each of the SOA layers (see Figure 4-2) and also to take architectural decisions at each level.

At the heart of SOMA is the identification and specification of services, components, and process flows. At a high level, SOMA is a three-phased approach to *identify, specify,* and *realize* services, components, and flows (typically, choreography of services). The first phase is that of service identification, where various techniques are used to identify an exhaustive list of candidate services. The second phase is that of service specification, in which a detailed design of services and components is completed. The realization phase focuses on making architectural decisions, justifying the most prudent approach to implement the services.

SOMA focuses directly on the services, service components, and flows. These SOA constructs reside between Layer 2 and Layer 4 of the architecture stack. However, the activities performed as a part of the end-to-end methodology influence the placement of components in the other layers of the stack. Figure 4-3 illustrates the focus of SOMA as it pertains to the solution stack.

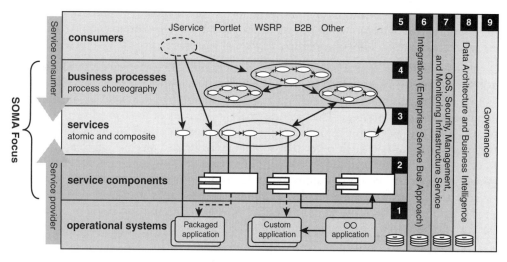

Figure 4-3 The focus of SOMA is on Layer 2 through Layer 4.

One of the main outputs of the SOMA method is a service model. It is recommended that a service model constitute of the following artifacts about services:

- **Service portfolio**—List of all the enterprise services
- **Service hierarchy**—A categorization of services into service groups
- **Service exposure**—An analysis and rationalization of which services should be exposed and which should not
- **Service dependencies**—Representing the dependencies of services on other services
- **Service composition**—How services take part in compositions to realize business process flows
- **Service NFRs**—The nonfunctional requirements that a service must comply with
- **State management**—The various types of states that a service should maintain and implement
- **Realization decisions**—Architectural decisions, for each service, around the most justified mechanism to implement the service

The techniques employed in the various phases of the method address one or more parts of the service model. Although there may be other work products that can be developed by exercising the various phases and activities of this method, we concentrate on the service model in this chapter.

4.2.1 Validation of Inputs

Before we can start identifying, specifying, and realizing service, it is imperative to validate the inputs that the method expects. SOMA takes inputs from the business.

The "to-be" business processes—their definitions and their corresponding process models that are decomposed down to second and third levels—are mandatory inputs. Services that will be summoned for implementation will be used in an orchestration to choreograph business process as a network of collaborating services at runtime.

Acknowledging the fact that SOA is primarily a business initiative where we strive to achieve flexibility, responsiveness, and agility in the business, the emphasis is on using SOA principles to solve business problems by designing and implementing an IT solution aligned with the business goals and strategy. The business goals and drivers of the company, the realization of which is the basis for commissioning an IT project, is a very important input into the method. The business goals need to be supplemented with a mechanism to measure the success of achieving the goal. Key Performance Indicator (KPI) is a metric that provides the business a measure of success of a software service against the attainment criteria for a business goal. Hence, business goals, drivers, and their associated KPIs are very important inputs to the method. These KPIs are used to measure how effective and successful an enterprise SOA initiative has been.

SOA strongly recommends the concept of reuse. Therefore, the traditional and often scary "rip and replace" approach to systems development is the last option in the philosophical premise of SOA. The idea is to reuse as much of the functionality available in currently running enterprise systems as possible. A good and solid understanding of the current IT environment represents a vital input to the method. For instance, the applications and systems, the functionalities they provide, the importance and usage of the functionalities provided, and the roadmap for enhancement or sunset of each of the systems are all key inputs that help in gaining a good understanding of the current IT portfolio.

The current organizational design and the future organization scope and requirements can also prove to be invaluable inputs. These can be used to identify which line of business will be responsible for the ownership and funding of the service lifecycle. However, this is not a mandatory input and can be categorized as "nice to have information."

We recommend the execution of a method-adoption workshop for any client engagement. Such a workshop allows the consulting team to customize the method to suit the specific requirements of the client. In an SOA-based engagement, and as a part of this method-adoption workshop, one can determine the specific inputs available for use with the SOMA method. The inputs that are available must be carefully validated for completeness. So, what happens if they are incomplete?

The first thing to do is to assess the gaps between the required and the available information, and then a gap-mitigation plan needs to be put in place. A part of the recommended approach is to perform further interview sessions with the stakeholders and subject matter experts (SME) and use that information gathered therein to incorporate the missing information. We also recommend documenting customer pain points and use them to define the customer requirements, business drivers, and priorities. These are by no means the only two ways to address gaps between available and required inputs, and the IT team might have its own gap-mitigation plan as it suits the current customer scenario.

If the mandatory inputs are not available, however, a commitment needs to be made by the business stakeholders to make them available to the degree of completeness as requested by the IT team.

4.2.2 Identification

When the validation of inputs has been completed, the focus shifts to the identification of the services that will ultimately constitute the service portfolio. The aim is to get an exhaustive list of services that are potential candidates for exposure and then categorize the services into some logical grouping. Experience suggests that the general approaches taken to identify services are sometimes too restrictive; typically we do not exploit all possible sources to identify enterprise-level services. To come up with such an exhaustive list of "candidate" services, it is recommended to use a combination of three complementary techniques: domain decomposition, existing asset analysis, and goal service modeling. After we have compiled the list of candidate services, we use a technique that extracts, from the list of candidate services, only those services relevant for exposure. Figure 4-4 illustrates the three techniques for service identification.

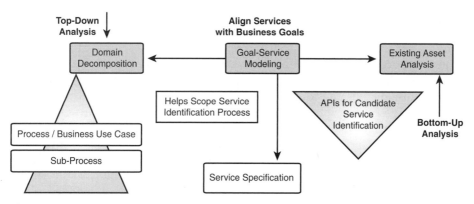

Figure 4-4   The three different techniques for service identification

Let's explore further the various techniques for service identification.

4.2.1.1 Domain Decomposition

This is a top-down technique that involves the decomposition of the business domain into its functional areas and subsystems, including the decomposition of its business processes into subprocesses and high-level business use cases. These use cases are often good candidates for business services exposed at the edge of the enterprise, or for those used within the boundaries of the enterprise across lines of business. Apart from identifying candidate services, this technique helps to identify functional areas that identify boundaries for subsystems.

This technique includes one step called functional area analysis (FAA). In FAA, we decompose the business domains into logical cohesive functional units and name each unit as a functional area. The resultant set of functional areas provides a modular view of the business and forms the basis of IT subsystem identification, nomenclature, and design. It is not necessary for FAA to be done as a part of SOMA because it can leverage similar work that could have been done as a part of any other project initiative in the same enterprise. The identification of functional areas assists in their usage in service categorization, wherein the identified candidate services can be categorized using the functional areas. The "Service Hierarchy" section of the service model work product is a formalization of the categorization of services.

FAA usually falls under the expertise realm of business analysts and domain experts. One can start with a base set of functional areas, but if and when services are identified and start to be grouped using the functional areas, one can refactor the existing functional areas so that they make sense from a service grouping standpoint. The key point we are trying to make here is that functional areas can be refactored to suit the proper grouping to services.

The next step in this technique is called process decomposition. In process decomposition, we decompose business processes into its constituent subprocesses and further into more atomic activities or tasks. The resultant process model depicts both the business-level and IT-level flow of events that realize a business process. It also forms the basis of candidate service identification. A process is a group of logically related activities that use the resources of the organization to provide defined results in support of the organization's objectives. Process models describe the work that an organization is involved in and the behavior of systems the organization uses. Each business process in the scope of the business or IT transformation is decomposed into subprocesses and further into leaf-level subprocesses. Each activity in the resultant process model or process breakdown tree is considered a candidate for service exposure. Hence, each is added to a list called the service portfolio. At this point, the service portfolio consists of all the subprocesses, activities, and tasks from the process model definitions for every single process. The "Service Portfolio" section of the service model work product is the recipient of the list of candidate services that are identified in this step.

Decomposition of processes into its activities and tasks also assists in identifying commonalities and variations between multiple business processes. The common activities or subprocesses provide good candidates for services while the points of variability enable the design of the system in a way that it fosters design resiliency and makes the system more adaptive to incorporate future changes. Variations in a system are usually identified across three aspects: structures, processes, and rules. Externalizing these variability points enables configurable injection of flexibility into system design. Variations may also suggest new services based on types, processes, and rules.

4.2.1.2 Existing Asset Analysis

Existing asset analysis is a bottom-up approach in which we examine assets such as existing custom applications, packaged applications and industry models to determine what can be leveraged to realize service functionality. This analysis is also designed to uncover any services that may have been missed through process decomposition. While you are analyzing existing legacy and custom applications, we recommend performing a coarse-grained mapping in which you map business functionality in the portfolio of existing applications to the business processes and determine which step (as identified through domain decomposition in Section 4.2.1.1) in the process can be potentially realized by some functionality in existing applications. We do not recommend performing a fine-grained mapping to specific transactions and batch processes within legacy application at this stage.

During the coarse-grained mapping activity, a detailed understanding of the application's state and quality is obtained that will allow the assessment of technical risks associated with the services that are going to be realized by the existing system functionality. For the applications that have such technical risks associated with their usage for service implementation, we recommend scoping some technical prototypes to test things like basic connectivity, protocol issues, data structures and formats, and so on. This prototyping will help mitigate the project risks that might otherwise crop up during the later stages, for example, during implementation.

So, with this technique, we can not only start thinking about service realizations using existing assets but also identify new services. These new services will be added to the service portfolio. At this point, the service portfolio consists of potential services derived from both a top-down and a bottom-up approach.

4.2.1.3 Goal Service Modeling

Goal service modeling (GSM) is the third of the three techniques and is used to validate and unearth other services not captured by either top-down or bottom-up service identification approaches. It ensures that key services have not been missed. GSM provides the key link between the business goals and IT through the traceability of services directly to a business goal. The attainment of the goal, through the supporting service, is measured through the KPIs and its metrics that were documented as a part of the inputs from the business. GSM also ensures that stakeholder involvement and accountability is maintained through their consent on the business goals that needs to be achieved. Services directly linked to the business goals would then have a higher probability of being prioritized and funded for subsequent design and implementation. It is worthwhile to point out that GSM may be used as a scoping mechanism that assists in defining the scope of a project by focusing deeper into the problem domain. A problem domain is often too large to be tackled in one iteration and hence narrowing down and identifying an area that provides the highest impact (by realizing one or more business goals) to the business in a reasonable and acceptable timeframe is a recommended way of scoping a project initiative. Once the scope is defined around a business goal, not only can services be identified through the GSM technique but also the top-down (domain decomposition) and bottom-up (existing asset analysis) techniques may be performed on the given scope of the project.

Identifying business goals is a nontrivial task. It is not uncommon for clients to be grappling for ways to articulate their real business goals. SOA architects are not the ideal consultants who can be of much help to the business people. The business analysts and SMEs are the ones who come to the rescue, helping the clients to clearly articulate their business goals.

The business goals are usually stated in a way that are too lofty and at a very high level. It is difficult and often impossible to try to identify and associate a service to these lofty goals. The recommended approach is to work closely with the business and domain SMEs to decompose the goals into subgoals, and keep decomposing until the point that a subgoal is actionable. *Actionable* here means the attainment of what I call as the "Aha!" factor—that I can identify an IT function that I can use to realize this subgoal. Hence, each business goal is usually decomposed into subgoals, and then services are identified that can realize them. This approach differs radically from the top-down and bottom-up techniques, and therefore you have a high potential of discovering new services. These new services are added back to the service portfolio. Some of the discovered services can be found to be already present in the existing service portfolio. This is a good thing, a validation step that ascertains that more than one technique for service identification has identified the same service!

So, what do we achieve in the service identification phase?

- We have taken a three-pronged approach to identify candidate services.
- Each identified candidate service is added to the service portfolio.
- FAA is performed or leveraged to provide a mechanism to group services—the service hierarchy.
- The service grouping may be iteratively refactored to provide the best categorization of services.
- For functionality in existing applications identified for use to realize service implementations, a technical assessment is performed to assess the viability of reusing the existing application for service implementation.

From a service model standpoint, what have we addressed?

- We are able to provide a service portfolio of candidate services.
- We categorized the services into a service hierarchy or grouping.

With this, we move on to the second phase in the method: specification of services.

4.2.3 Specification

The specification phase helps design the details of the three first-class constructs of SOA: services, service components, and flows. It uses a combination of three high-level activities to determine which services to expose, provides a detailed specification for the exposed services, and specifies the flows (processes) and service components. The three activities are called service specification, subsystem analysis, and component specification. From a service model work product standpoint, this phase provides the most content: The service exposure, service dependencies, service composition, service NFRs, service messages, and state management are all addressed in this phase. The rest of this section focuses on the three activities.

4.2.3.1 Service Specification

Service specification defines the dependencies, composition, exposure decisions, messages, QoS constraints, and decisions regarding the management of state within a service.

The first task concerns service exposure. The service portfolio had an exhaustive list of services obtained through the three techniques that we used for service identification. It is easy to comprehend that this list may contain too many candidate services; not all of them are at the right level of granularity to be exposed as services. Some of the service candidates may be too coarse grained and might actually be more like business processes or subprocesses rather than individual services (for example, some of the process elements derived from the first level of process decomposition), whereas some others may be too fine-grained IT functions (for example, the process elements in the lowest level of process decomposition and some of the existing system functionality). Deciding to expose the entire list of candidate services is a perfect recipe for following a perfect antipattern in SOA—the service proliferation syndrome (a phenomenon we want to avoid). Some economic and practical considerations limit the exposure of all candidate services. A cost is associated with every service chosen for exposure. The funding of the entire service lifecycle, the governance factor around service lifecycle management, and the added underlying infrastructure requirements to support security, scalability, performance, and other nonfunctional requirements make it impractical to follow the rules of economies of scale when it comes to exposing all candidate services.

Based on these premises, we recommend a service litmus test. The test consists of specific criteria applied to the candidate services. Only those services that meet the criteria are chosen for service exposure. The method provides an initial set of test criteria in the following form:

1. **Business alignment**—A service must be business aligned. If a service is not, in some shape or form, traceable back to a business goal, it may not be an ideal candidate to be chosen for exposure.

2. **Composability**—Tests the ability of a service to be used in a context entirely different from the one from which the service was originally identified. A service should be able to participate in multiple business processes without compromising the NFR compliance requirements for the process.

3. **Feasibility of implementation**—Tests the technical feasibility of implementing the service in a cost- and time-effective manner. Practical considerations limit overly complex services to be commissioned for implementation.

4. **Redundancy elimination**—Tests whether the service can be used within all processes and applications where its function is required.

This method by no means enforces these four litmus tests and recommends defining litmus test criteria taking the client environment, goals, and other relevant and pertinent client-specific factors into account. The most important point here is that some form of an elimination criterion needs to be defined that will allow the prioritization of services for exposure consideration. It is also recommended to provide a justification for the services that failed the litmus test for exposure. This justification, when documented, provides crucial information which becomes vital when the failed services might be revisited later in the scope of another SOA initiative in the same enterprise. It is quite possible that the business goals, client prerogatives, and other factors as applicable during subsequent projects might expose a service that might not have passed the exposure tests during the current scope!

Now that a filtered list of services has been determined, the services chosen for exposure constitute the refined service portfolio. Each service in this portfolio now needs to be provided with detailed specification. The first specification activity is to identify service dependencies.

Services are ideally dependent on other exposed services. Although in an ideal world of SOA everything is a service, in reality we find that services are more frequently dependent on underlying IT components. This dependency happens typically in situations where QoS requirements such as performance and availability tend to push SOA architects to design a service to be hardwired to one more technology-specific component. A service-to-service dependency is called a processing dependency because a service is dependent on one or more services only in the context of a given business process. Sometimes however, strict nonfunctional requirements mandate that services are more tightly coupled in their dependency on finer grained IT components. This type of dependency is often categorized as a functional dependency. Categorizing service dependencies into processing and functional groupings provides key architectural and design considerations for service implementation. Figure 4-5 provides an example of the two types of dependencies.

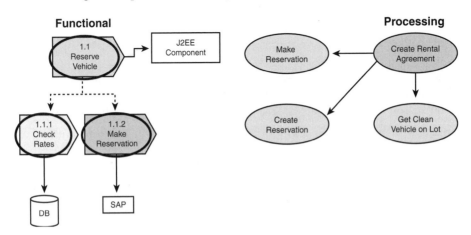

Figure 4-5   The two general types of service dependencies

With service dependencies depicted, the next natural activity is to identify service composition and flows. Services that take part in a composition are a collection of related services to solve a specific high-level business function. A business process can be either represented as a single composite service or may be realized as an orchestration of one or more composites or individual services. Each business process that is in the scope of the transformation initiative is modeled as such an orchestration. These orchestrated services and their specifications and design will influence how they may be implemented as Business Process Execution Language (BPEL) flows at runtime. See the "References" section for more information on BPEL.

The next activity is identification of the NFRs that a service must implement. Each service must, in addition to the business logic that it implements, comply with a set of NFRs. The security mandates for service access, for example, authentication requirements for external consumers or no security for internal consumers; the availability of the service, whether 99.999 or 99.9; the maximum allowable latency for service-invocation turnaround, whether 1 millisecond or 1 minute are examples of NFRs that typically must be implemented by a given service. The method prescribes the documentation of all the required and optional NFRs for each service. This information will influence downstream microdesign and implementation. Note that keeping the complexity of business logic equal, the complexity of the NFRs of a service directly affects the time, cost, and resource requirements for its implementation.

Service message and its specification is one of the most critical and significant activities in this phase. A service message—the input message, the output message, and the exception and faults—typically constitutes the syntactic specification of the service. Service messages are usually defined in XML format for the obvious reasons of portability and interoperability. This method provides some prescriptive guidance for designing service messages.

One of the main tenets of SOA is to provide business flexibility and agility to an enterprise through an IT infrastructure that facilitates the enterprise to participate in a collaborative ecosystem. Collaboration brings in the key requirement for flexible and seamless integration with other collaborating entities. One of the first things you want to do is to standardize on the message format used to define services. Following a standard message format can facilitate a better integration with other partners outside the enterprise perimeter. A growing number of industry-specific consortiums provide standard definitions for business entities and information applicable to a given industry. For example, the insurance industry and the retail industry might define a *customer business entity* differently. The attributes and even some base and common operations on the entities are being standardized per industry. These standard specifications are called industry models. There exist quite a few stable industry models, such as ACORD for insurance, enhanced Telecommunications Operations Map (eTOM) for electronics, Justice XML Data Dictionary (JXDD) for the Department of Justice, Open Travel Alliance (OTA) for travel and transportation, and so on. Refer to the "References" section for more information on eTOM and OTA.

This method recommends using the industry model, if available for the given industry, as a starting point for message specification. Acknowledging that these specifications are often all encompassing, the first level of analysis that needs to be done is to define a subset of the industry model artifacts that is applicable to the client wherein the SOA project is being undertaken. This subset of the industry model can be the base specifications. In more cases than not, there will be a need to add some specific extensions to the base specifications that incorporates client-specific requirements. The base specifications together with the extensions constitute what we call the Enterprise Message Format (EMF). Defining the EMF is the first step toward service interoperability. Sometimes, a version or a flavor of an EMF may already be present with the client. If so, it needs to be analyzed, validated, and enhanced to support the new and upcoming requirements. The input and output message elements must be compliant with the EMF. The EMF is also a perfect starting point to define the Enterprise Information Model (EIM) and it also influences the Logical Data Model (LDM), both of which, although are not necessarily a part of SOA, are mandatory architectural constructs in any enterprise application development.

> **NOTE**
>
> Note that the domain of information architecture plays a very important role in SOA. The data translation requirements together with information architecture that models the data and information flow from the consumer, through all the layers of the architecture stack right down to the operational systems layer falls under the domain of the Integration and Data architecture layers in the SOA reference architecture.

The amount of work that goes into the definition of the EMF and subsequently into service message specifications is often underestimated and becomes the widest chasm to bridge. Keep in mind that service message specification is closely, if not tightly, linked with the design of the information model and the data models and therefore not a trivial work effort.

Get your EMF well designed and documented; it will have a positive impact on downstream design and specification activities.

The last major activity focuses on analysis of the state management requirements for a service and its operations. As a general design rule, the business logic implemented by a service should not include state-specific logic.

However, requirements often mandate that some services address some state requirements. The most commonly occurring types of state are transactional state, functional state, and security state. Transaction state is required to support transactions spanning multiple messages. If an atomic transaction must include the results of multiple business actions preformed as a result of multiple messages from a service requestor to a service provider, the state of the transaction must be maintained until all the messages involved in the transaction are completed and the transaction is committed or rolled back.

Security state addresses how the identity of a consumer may be verified. In a stateless scenario, the client is authenticated each time a message is received. In a stateful scenario, a token is typically passed in the message sent by the consumer.

Functional state refers to state that must be maintained between messages while a business action is accomplished.

We must account for how the specific state requirements must be managed. Sometimes, IT technology components influence how state can be managed. For example, a security state can be managed by a product such as IBM Tivoli Access Manager (see the "References" section of Chapter 6 for more information), and the transactional state requirements between multiple service invocations in a business process may be managed by a BPEL engine. Hence, the documentation of the specific state requirements for each service is imperative. Keep in mind that during service realization, we can come up with the right architectural decisions justifying the best mechanism to implement the state management requirements. So, document them here!

This is just the first major activity during the specification phase; we have two more areas to address. Before we move on, however, we want to mention that all six recommended activities that we discussed as a part of this technique are iterative in nature and we will, depending on the scope and complexity of the project, need to run through this technique multiple times until we get a refined and robust specification of services at this level.

4.2.3.2 Subsystem Analysis

Just like functional areas provide a logical grouping of a business domain, an IT subsystem is a semantically meaningful grouping of logically cohesive IT artifacts, which are in the form of components and classes. When a functional area is too large to grasp, it is broken down into these logical units called subsystems. Although this decomposition can be done top down or bottom up, the method recommends a top-down approach.

A subsystem consists of three types of components: service components, functional components, and technical components. It is the job of the SOA architect to identify a logical grouping of services that can be implemented together by a team that has specific domain knowledge in the area. Subsystem analysis and identification is nothing special to SOA, and it has been practiced from the days of OO; therefore, I call it "architecture as usual" (AAU) work. Let's focus now on the constituents of a subsystem and how to identify them.

A functional component is an IT component that encapsulates and supplies a single type of business functionality. For example, any customer-related business logic and IT APIs can be encapsulated in a single functional component called, for example, CustomerManager.

A technical component is an IT component that provides generic functionality such as authentication, error handling, and auditing. Their implementation is usually more closely tied with the technology platform that is used.

A service component is an IT component built as a coarse-grained façade on top of more focused and finer-grained functional and technical components. Think of it as a central component in a mediator pattern. A service is usually aligned to a high-level business function. For this business function to be implemented, it might need to call finer-grained IT APIs on some functional and technical components. Let's consider an example in context. Suppose a service is to provide "details of the last reserved vehicle for a customer." This requirement will typically necessitate a call to a CustomerManager component to "retrieve the customer profile" information, use some business logic to pick the relevant customer details from the returned result, and then invoke a VehicleManager component to "retrieve the current reserved vehicle" for the given customer. In the process, it may invoke a technical component called AuditManager to log the service request. Neither the CustomerManager nor the VehicleManager nor the AuditManager has the business logic to control this microflow of steps. This control of the microflow, which component to invoke and in which sequence to realize the service request, is the responsibility of the service component. The service component can be designed to conform to the specifications of service component architecture (SCA). See Chapter 6, "Realization of Services," for detailed treatment of SCA.

For illustrative purposes only, Figure 4-6 depicts how subsystems are related to service, functional, and technical components.

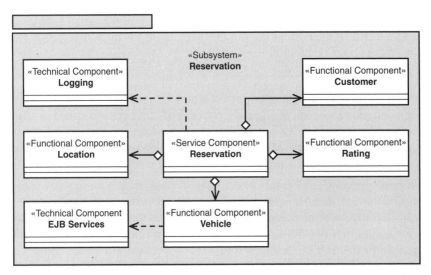

Figure 4-6   The relationship between a subsystem and its constituent service, functional, and technical components

Identifying the various subsystems followed by the derivation of the service components and its constituent functional and technical components that together define a subsystem is the crux of this major step of subsystem analysis.

4.2.3.3 Component Specification

From here on, it is AAU work! There is nothing very special about SOA that we would do. Providing the detailed microlevel design is the focus of this step (that is, the software model in terms of class diagrams, sequence diagrams, and so on). Each service component identified and designed at a high level in the preceding step is further elaborated into a much more detailed treatment. Some typical microdesign steps that apply to a service component are the following:

1. Identify component characteristics, including component attribute and operations together with the policies and rules that they implement.

2. Identify events and messages that the components must sense and respond as a triggering mechanism. Incoming and outgoing component messages are also specified.

3. Identify internal component flow (representing the internal flow of control within the service component and which can be represented as a sequence or collaboration diagram).

4. Create component class diagrams, which are class models that show the static relationships between the functional and technical components.

Similar types of microdesign activities must be performed for each of the functional and technical components so that they are designed and specified to an adequate and unambiguous level of detail to be comfortably handed over to the implementation team for converting into working code. Because these are AAU activities, they are not covered in any further detail in this chapter.

Phew! That was a long section, but we did cover a lot of ground.

Okay, so what did we achieve in the service specification phase?

We were able to filter out only those services that are perfect candidates for exposure, and we did that by applying the service litmus test.

For each of the services tagged for exposure, we provided prescriptive guidance on how to design (at a macro level) a full specification for them, including the following:

- How services are dependent on each other (service dependencies)
- How services are orchestrated together to form composites that enable business processes (flows) (service compositions)
- Identifying and documenting the nonfunctional requirements that each service must implement and comply with (service NFRs)
- Detailed specification of the service messages (service message specification)
- Identifying and documenting the state requirements for each service (service state management)

While developing service message specifications, we acknowledged how these specifications tie in with and influence the information architecture, the integration architecture, and the data architecture of the system. Services are not the only SOA construct that we designed in this phase of SOMA. The processes were further elaborated and their flows were represented as an orchestration of services and IT components. The service component was also designed using their constituent functional and technical components.

From a service model standpoint, what have we achieved?

- Provided a service exposure rationale
- Addressed service dependencies
- Addressed service compositions and how they help in realizing process flows

- Emphasized the need to document service NFRs
- Addressed the recommended approach to define service messages
- Explained why it's necessary to document state management

Having achieved this, we move on to the third and last phase in this method: realization decisions for services.

4.2.3.4 Realization for Services

The method in its first two phases not only demonstrated how to use a three-pronged approach for service identification but they also offered guidance about how to provide detailed specification for the services, service components, and process flows. The main focus of the method in this phase is to provide guidance about how to take architectural decisions that facilitate service realization. It is important to note that SOMA does not, at this point in time, address the actual implementation of services; instead, it provides enough information and detail so that an SOA implementation phase can just concentrate on the development and implementation of the services. Implementation is the phase wherein a specific technology, programming language and platform is chosen and used to transform the design specifications and the realization recipes and patterns into executable code.

This phase has three major activities: component allocation to layers, technical feasibility analysis, and realization decisions. The rest of this section focuses on these three major activities.

4.2.3.5 Component Allocation to Layers

So far, this method has identified services, process flows, service components, functional components, and technical components. It also argued that technical components belong to a genre of components that do not directly provide business functionality but instead focus on delivering infrastructure functionalities that might be used by multiple functional and technical components. Keeping the solution stack in mind, we want to provide architectural recipes to allocate the SOA artifacts that we have identified, to the pertinent layers in the solution stack.

The service components and the functional components are all allocated to Layer 2 in the stack. The services, both atomic and composite, are allocated to Layer 3 in the stack. The process flows orchestrated using services from Layer 3 and functional and technical components from Layer 2, are allocated to Layer 4 of the stack. Technical components are of different types. There can be technical components that encapsulate a persistence framework or a data access layer. This type of technical component is usually allocated to Layer 8 (the data architecture layer). Some technical components encapsulate event management functionality, whereas others might provide queue management functionality, and some may encapsulate transaction management features. These types of components are allocated to Layer 6 (the integration layer). There can be other types of technical components, such as cache management, permissions management, audit management, and so forth. These types of components, which usually assist in complying with QoS requirements, are usually allocated to Layer 7 (the QoS layer). As you can see, based on the characteristics of each layer in the reference architecture, the method assists us to map the various types of software artifacts to the layers.

Without paying specific attention to the names of the components, specifically between Layers 1 and 4, Figure 4-7 depicts how different types of software building blocks, which the method assists us in identifying, are allocated to each layer in the solution stack.

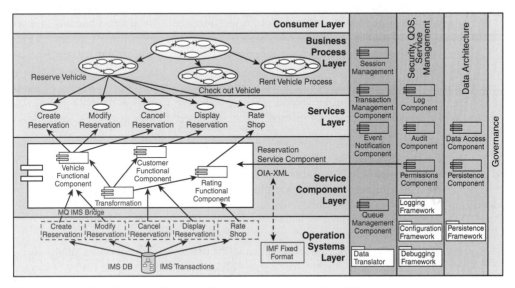

Figure 4-7   Allocation of software artifacts on the layers of the SOA reference architecture

4.2.3.6 Component Allocation to Layers—Technical Feasibility Analysis

Technical feasibility takes input primarily from existing asset analysis and takes into account the services portfolio defined during service specification. The main focus of this activity is to perform a detailed analysis of existing systems to evaluate how much of the existing technology-specific implementation can be leveraged to realize the services. This activity, as is the SOMA method itself, is primarily iterative in nature, and it can be started as early as during the EAA technique during service identification. The functionality, along with the transactions identified during the early stages of service identification, needs to be validated for feasibility for componentization. This type of feasibility analysis results in architectural decisions for either the functional or operational architecture of the system. This is the step in the method where the deep-dive technical analysis of leveraging existing system functionality is actually formalized. You can do as much service specification as you want, but if you do not provide deep insight into the implementation of the service, ably supported by its justification, there still remains that proverbial gap between where architects hand off the design and where developers start with the exact knowledge on what to implement!

Let's consider an example of assessing the feasibility of using legacy system functionality. We must consider many technology aspects of legacy systems when looking to reuse such an existing asset for service realization. Some notable examples include the following:

- Exception handling in legacy systems is typically in the form of program termination. This might not be acceptable in a real-time SOA-based system.
- Authentication and authorization are often built in to the legacy application code using proprietary technologies and protocols. If legacy functionalities protected via security credentials are considered for reuse, there needs to be a mechanism to integrate the embedded security credentials in a federated environment. Externalizing the legacy security credentials might raise technological issues that will have to be addressed.
- The typical nightly batch processes for data synchronization or request submission may just be too infrequent to be used in real-time scenarios. In such cases, the legacy processing system might need to be amended; in extreme cases, the process might prove unusable.

These examples provide a snippet of the challenges that must be addressed when considering the reuse of existing systems and their functionality. Technical feasibility analysis addresses these types of issues by taking architectural decisions and justifying them for consideration.

4.2.3.7 Realization Decisions

The technical feasibility analysis has a significant influence on how services ought to be realized in the best possible manner. Although technical feasibility analysis is initiated very early in the identification phase of the method and is performed throughout the various phases, considering all the various design and implementation alternatives, this step formalizes the final realization decision for each service and provides justification for the choice. This justification is a key step in the process and helps in maintenance and enhancement of the system in the years to come. The same realization alternatives could well be re-analyzed during enhancement of the system a few years down the road; and while doing so, the then-available technology might justify a different alternative as better suited. Thus, the snapshot in time of the architectural justification often proves invaluable.

In general, this method recommends considering six different high-level realization alternatives, as follows:

1. **Integrate**—Wrap existing legacy applications with SOA technologies and provide a service façade using open standards and protocols, for seamless integration into an SOA. Adapter technology is typically suited for this purpose.

2. **Transform**—Transform parts of legacy applications and expose them. This might involve the extraction of business rules or policies and rewriting the code in a modern SOA-aware programming language. This often falls under the discipline of legacy modernization.

3. **Buy**—Purchase products from independent service vendors (ISV) who provide out-of-the-box functionality that are exposed as services. Note that this option often results in a classic SOA antipattern in which the features of the ISV product often dictate the requirements of an enterprise. So do not fall into this trap and only evaluate the ISV functionality in the context of the project requirements.

4. **Build**—Build applications following the principles and best practices of SOA. This is often called the domain of custom application development.

5. **Subscribe**—Subscribe to external vendors who provide services that meet or exceed specific business functional requirements. Various SOA vendors are trying to find a niche in the market where they can specialize in a specific type of offering. Credit card authorization service is a classic example. Rarely would we see any enterprise developing this functionality indigenously. Instead, they subscribe to the best service provider that suits their needs.

6. **Outsource**—Outsource an entire part of the organization's functions to a third party. This is not yet considered mainstream because SOA is still undergoing some critical phases in its maturity and adoption. However, there are companies that specialize in, say, HR operations, and we have started seeing big corporations outsourcing an entire department. These third parties will provide services that need to be seamlessly integrated with the enterprise business processes.

This is what realization decisions help us achieve: a justification of the implementation mechanism for the services in the services portfolio.

So, what did we achieve in the realization phase?

- Understood how to allocate the various software building blocks onto the layers of the solution stack.
- Appreciated the justification to perform a detailed technical feasibility analysis before using existing legacy functionality for service realization.
- Identified the various options available for service realization.

And from a service model standpoint, what have we addressed?

- We were able to provide realization decisions for services.

This marks the completion of the three phases of the SOMA method. By now, I hope you can appreciate why a service-oriented analysis and design method, like SOMA, is required in any SOA-based initiative. The treatment provided here has hopefully demonstrated how SOMA is built on top of OOAD, while adding modeling and design techniques specific to SOA.

4.2.4 Using SOMA

The language of SOMA is crisp, clear, and very much focused on, providing a methodology to solve the challenges the IT community faces regarding service-oriented design. However, it is important to keep in mind that tools are integral to processes or methods, and a well-articulated method drives the development of tools in support of them. Rational Unified Process (RUP) has extended its process technique to incorporate service-oriented design, and it has used the SOMA method as the basis for its extension. This method extension is available as a plug-in in a product from Rational Software called the Rational Method Composer (see the "References" section).

SOMA method artifacts can also be expressed as a platform-independent model. Think of SOMA as providing a meta-language that helps in defining a service model. This model representation, defining not only the SOA constructs but also the relationships and constraints between them, is called the meta-model for SOMA. Any design tool that can implement the SOMA meta-model will be able to provide a tooling environment for service-oriented modeling and design based on the SOMA method. Although we do not provide the entire meta-model here, we do offer hints about how to develop one.

Hint: A *business domain* can be decomposed into one or more *functional areas*. A *functional area* can be decomposed into one or more *subsystems*. A *subsystem* contains one or more *service components*. A *service component* uses one or more *functional components* and *technical components*. If you try to enlist all the various constructs of SOMA and then model relationships between them, together with constraints on the relationships, you will be able to create the SOMA meta-model. It is then just a matter of implementing the meta-model in a software modeling tool! IBM has already developed a tool for SOMA and has been using it productively and successfully in multiple client engagements.

4.3 Conclusion

This chapter provided a detailed overview of a service-oriented design methodology, and we used the IBM-developed SOMA methodology as guidance on how to effectively develop an SOA-based system design.

The chapter also covered the SOA reference architecture, also called an SOA solution stack. It described each layer and identified the kind of software building blocks that constitute each layer. It then focused on how the SOMA method assists in the development of the first-class constructs of SOA: service, service components, and flows through the three phases of identification, specification, and realization.

As you finish this chapter, we hope that you now appreciate the need for a service-oriented design methodology and have learned how to execute the same via the SOMA methodology.

4.4 Links to developerWorks Articles

A.4.1 Arsanjani, A. et al. Design an SOA Solution Using a Reference Architecture, IBM developerWorks, March 2007. www-128.ibm.com/developerworks/library/ar-archtemp/.

A.4.2 Arsanjani, A. *Service Oriented Modeling and Architecture*, IBM developerWorks, November 2004. www-128.ibm.com/developerworks/webservices/library/ws-soa-design1/. www-128.ibm.com/developerworks/architecture/library/ar-archtemp/.

4.5 References

Gamma, E. et al. Design Patterns: Elements of Reusable Object-Oriented Software, Addison-Wesley, 1994.

Grossman, B. and J. Naumann. ACORD & XBRL US-XML Standards and the Insurance Value Chain. Acord.org, May 2004. www.arord.org/news/pdf/ACORD_XBRL.pdf.

Deblaere M. et al. IBM Insurance Application Architecture (IAA), White Paper, April 2002. www.baoxian119.com/xiazai/updownload/iaa2002whitepaper.pdf.

The complete and latest release of Justice XML Data Dictionary (JXDD). http://it.ojp.gov/jxdd/prerelease/3.0.0.3/index.html.

The official BPEL specifications are maintained by OASIS. www.oasis-open.org/committees/tc_home.php?wg_abbrev=wsbpel.

The official site that maintains the enhanced Telecom Operations Map (eTOM). www.tmforum.org/browse.aspx?catID=1647

Download the latest Open Travel Alliance (OTA) specifications from the opentravel site. www.opentravel.org/.

Download a trial version of Rational Method Composer. http://www14.software.ibm.com/webapp/download/product.jsp?id=TMMS-6GAMST&s=z&cat=&S_TACT=%26amp%3BS_CMP%3D&S_CMP=

Download the RUP plug-in for SOA. http://www.ibm.com/developerworks/rational/library/05/510_soaplug/

Chapter 5

Leveraging Reusable Assets

One of the key characteristics of a service-oriented architecture is reusing assets. Of course, this means service reuse, but service reuse is just one aspect of the potential for reusing assets and bringing the benefits of decreased costs and faster time to market for your enterprise. Many opportunities for reuse should be considered and exploited. This chapter shows you the elements of SOA reuse that you should consider.

5.1 What Is an Asset?

An asset is something that adds value and provides a solution to a problem. The asset should be reusable in similar contexts and may be customized. Three dimensions describe reusable assets: granularity, variability, and articulation:

- Granularity describes the size and purpose of the solution. Assets may range from fine-grained, meaning they are small in size and purpose, to coarse-grained, meaning it has a larger size and purpose and often contains or refers to fine-grained assets.
- Variability refers to the asset's degree of customization. Variability points allow for the specification of "spots" in the asset that are subject to change. *Low variability* means that the asset is fixed, with no variability points. *High variability* means that the asset is quite visible and changeable, with many variability points.
- Articulation is the level of completeness of artifacts in an asset that provides a solution. *Low articulation* means that the asset has very few artifacts that aid the consumer. *High articulation* provides artifacts at a great level of detail (for example, requirements, analysis, design, and testing).

5.2 Service Reuse

As described in the "Service-Oriented Modeling and Architecture" section of Chapter 4, "A Methodology for Service Modeling and Design," reusable services principally derive from three modes of thinking. The first uses "domain decomposition," a top-down breakdown of the business domain into its functional areas and subsystems, including its flow or process decomposition into processes, subprocesses, and high-level business use cases. These use cases often identify good candidates for business services. Reusable pattern techniques to be used include model-driven architecture (MDA), model-driven design (MDD), and usage of industry models in the decomposition. In doing so, architects will create new business services and leverage existing business services, reuse proven models and patterns instead of building new ones, and leverage reusable industry best practices instead of inventing their own.

The second approach is "existing asset analysis." The asset analysis is a bottom-up approach in which you examine assets, such as existing legacy applications, to determine what can be leveraged to realize service functionality. It is a mistake to ignore the business and technical value available to us as SOA practitioners from the existing enterprise legacy systems. In particular, there are four areas of legacy systems to consider reusing and transforming when you transition to SOA: the functional logic itself, the legacy business rules in the functional logic, the workflow of the function, and the interface data. Migrating legacy assets into a reusable services environment leverages the immense amount of time, effort, and cost that has already been invested by the enterprise in these assets and refactors them into something that is reusable now and into the future.

Goal service modeling (GSM) is the third of the three techniques used to validate and unearth other reusable services not captured by either top-down or bottom-up service-identification approaches. It ensures that key services have not been missed. GSM provides the key link between the business goals and IT through the traceability of services directly to a business goal.

The concept of reuse has been around for a long time in the computer industry and has been supported by such concepts as modular programming, subroutines, remote procedure calls (RPCs), remote method invocation (RMI), and object-oriented programming (OOP). The desire for reuse is equally old. However, reuse has largely failed to be exploited in the industry. Reuse does not occur in an enterprise unless the organizational and governance adjustments are made to support reuse. This is discussed in Chapter 3, "SOA Governance."

5.3 What Makes an SOA Service Reusable?

With some training, anyone can create a service. Write some application code and put a WSDL (Web Services Description Language) or JMS (Java Message Services) specification wrapper around it, and you have created yet another service!

However, there is more to a real service than technical qualifications. Is the service something that would have value beyond the project it was originally created for? Is it at a granularity that makes sense and is beneficial to the business? Has it been generalized and written in such a manner that it supports multiple service consumers and not just one? For example, see Figure 5-1. A program has been written to schedule consumer billing during off hours, and the governance policy has determined that it should start at 2 a.m. to minimize the impact on the rest of the business. As the business has grown, however, billing cycles for other markets such as business and international now need to be run. Production cycles are also needed for other applications such as payroll and general ledger. The "Run Consumer Billing at 2 a.m." program is not reusable for these purposes, but the "Schedule Production Transaction" is.

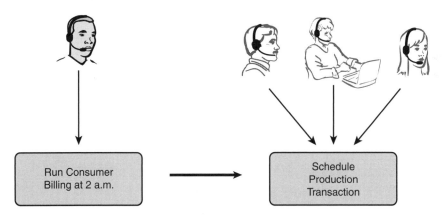

Figure 5-1   Simple example of creating reuse

SOA is an architectural style that, as a means to an end, seeks to create software building blocks that can be reused by multiple applications. If a service has no potential for reuse, it's not really an SOA service and should not be attributed as one. Specifically, the service must have the following attributes:

- The service is *self-contained* and performs a distinct business or technical function.
- The service is *loosely coupled,* meaning that it has an explicit contract (interface) independent of the technology of the invoking service consumer.
- The service is *transparent,* meaning that the specific location of the service is immaterial to the service consumer, with binding taking place at deployment or runtime.
- The service is *interoperable,* meaning that service interaction can be supported over a wide variety of platforms due to usage of compatible, industry standard communication protocols.
- The service is *composable,* meaning that it can be aggregated as part of a service at a higher level of granularity.

For example, a coarse-grained service should be generic enough to be reused by many higher-level business services and yet continue to be reused when the nature of that service changes and new functionality needs to be added. At the same time, services at a higher level of granularity that have aggregated that service should not need to change if they don't need the new functionality. Consider the example shown in Figure 5-2.

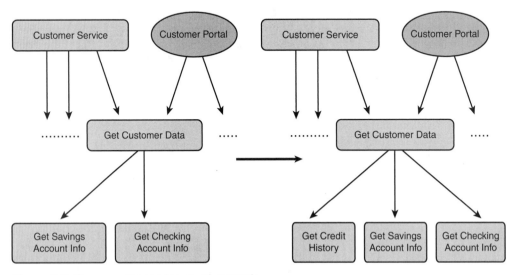

Figure 5-2 Coarse-grain service reuse example

A Customer Service business function and a Customer Portal are both business services that are composed of multiple services, including Get Customer Data. Get Customer Data is a less-granular business service responsible for retrieving any customer data needed by a business function of higher granularity. It is reused by many coarse-grain business services across many different projects and has become one of the most reused services at this sample enterprise.

The business leaders at Customer Service have determined that it needs to decrease bad debts by 10 percent and has requested IT to provide a customer's credit history upon an inbound call to the call center when the customer requests additional services. The SOA architect determines that this functionality can be provided within one week because of the inherently flexible nature of the business services design. A Get Credit History service will be added to Get Customer Data, and the Customer Service is enhanced to provide the customer credit history to the customer service representative via a pop-up screen. The Customer Portal remains unchanged and will not provide credit history, because this information is of a sensitive nature and is company confidential. No changes are necessary to the Customer Portal, because of the changes to Get Customer Data. At the same time, there will perhaps be future business services that do need customer credit history, and a reusable service has been created in a composable manner.

Note that service reuse is not limited to coarse-grain services. For example, a Credit Card Payment service is a fine-grained service that would be used by any business service that accepts credit cards for payment of retail store services or catalog store services.

5.4 Reusable Patterns

"Don't reinvent the wheel" is a tried-and-true maxim that we've all heard and used many times. The phrase itself is an example of a reusable pattern that may be applied to many different situations. It neatly summarizes a patterned response to a potentially complex discussion, while doing so in just a few words. The difficult becomes easy, and we move on to do something more productive.

The software development industry has increasingly realized the value of higher levels of abstraction, as shown in Figure 5-3.

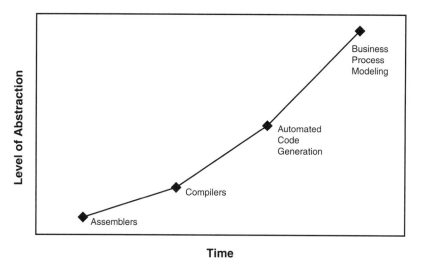

Figure 5-3 The increasing levels of abstraction for software practitioners

Aiding in this drive toward higher levels of abstraction and reuse are the concepts of industry models and MDA. An industry model summarizes a "standard practice" business model for a particular industry. Although no particular company in that industry will hew exactly to the industry model, still, the model provides a starting point to understand the business services, contract interfaces to the services, and creates UML (Unified Modeling Language) modeling of the business behavior and functionality.

A.5.1

MDA is an industry standard technique for employing reusable patterns and business-based industry functional models and application maps to assist SOA practitioners in reusing intellectual property suitable to their needs. This reuse helps to create speed and flexibility in the creation of services or software at any level.

A.5.2

5.4.1 Industry Models

Industry models, when they exist for the industry that one is working in, provide a standard taxonomy of how a typical enterprise within that industry could work. Process models then detail the end-to-end processes required to support an organization's business. Next, service-analysis and service-design models act as patterns for SOA projects.

A good industry model consists of reusable artifacts, including functional models (the business functions typical within the industry), process models (how does the business process flow), business object models (use cases for the business service), interface design models (interface designs for the business service), and a data model (standard data fields and hierarchies for this business). No industry model will be an exact fit for any existing business and will not be specific to a depth that takes you from business services all the way down to IT services and applications. But, it's a great place to start and get your IT personnel to start thinking like business people!

Examples of industry models include the TeleManagement Forum (TM Forum) Next Generation Operations Support System (NGOSS), IBM's Information Framework (IFW) for the banking industry, and IBM's Insurance Application Architecture (IAA) for the insurance industry.

A.5.3

Using an industry model enables you to start with a framework that can be adapted to your specific requirements. The steps in that process are as follows:

1. Identify business areas of opportunity (that is, identify the pain points) using the functional map as a starting point.

2. Within these business functions, identify the highly reused business tasks that may be further explored as service candidates.

A.5.4

3. Download the system use cases modeled via UML and update them to fit your organization. Doing so will provide you a complete understanding of the context of each service and a solid exploration of likely reuse.

4. Information on the data requirements for the service candidates is then used to create the contract definitions in WSDL.

5.4.2 MDA

Model-driven architecture (MDA) is an industry standard software design methodology proposed and sponsored by the Object Management Group (OMG). MDA defines an architecture that provides a set of guidelines for structuring specifications expressed as models. The MDA relates multiple standards, including Unified Modeling Language (UML), the Meta-Object Facility (MOF), the XML Metadata Interchange (XMI), and the Common Warehouse Metamodel (CWM). Further detailed information on MDA may be obtained from the OMG's MDA website at www.omg.org/mda.

The basic approach of an MDA methodology is as follows:

1. The business model should come from the business or an industry model, and the business should "sign off" that the model is correct, thereby increasing customer satisfaction and decreasing the overall development lifecycle duration. MDA titles this model the Computation Independent Model (CIM) because it is platform independent. The business model can be generated from an industry model such as the TM Forum, NGOSS, or a Component Business Model (CBM) developed in-house or by a Systems Integrator (SI) such as IBM. The requirements should be tracked and traced throughout the development process, including the resultant reuse and architecture decisions. IBM's Rational Requisite Pro (Reqpro) and Rational Software Architect (RSA) are a pair of ideal tools for this process.

2. Design should be platform independent and should be specified in a way that is independent of the underlying technology, which is likely to change over time. This type of design creates cross-platform interoperability and portability. MDA denotes this step as a translation of the CIM via a mapping to the PIM (Platform Independent Mapping). If such mappings already exist, they will be reused; otherwise, an architect will create them. IBM's WebSphere® Business Modeler enables the analyst to model the processes and specify the services in this manner.

3. The PIM is translated to usually one specific technology implementation, but additional technology-specific implementation can be created if needed. Each implementation is called a Program Specific Model (PSM) via a pattern. IBM's WebSphere Integration Developer (WID) and the Rational Unified Process (RUP) are used to integrate processes and services and then model and implement service logic.

4. Personnel with detailed implementation skills in the chosen platform and technologies should then be used to code the PSM.

5.4.3 Getting Assistance with Reusable Patterns

Because the concept of reusable patterns has been around for a while, help is available in the public domain, which you can take advantage of. One excellent site for this purpose is IBM's "Patterns for e-business" (www.ibm.com/developerworks/patterns).

A.5.5

In this case, you can leverage the experience of various IBM e-business architects when creating your e-business solution. IBM architects noticed, when creating such solutions, common problems that had common solutions. It made sense to have the senior architect create a generic template at a standard point in the system development life cycle to give a best practice solution for the problem. See Figure 5-4 for a mapping of the solution patterns to an e-business problem.

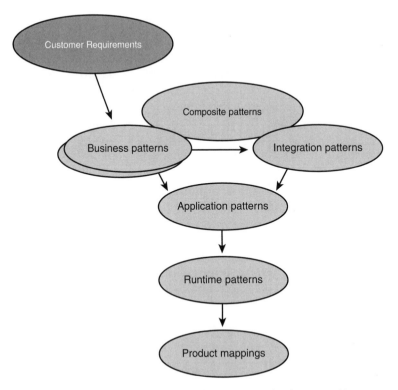

Figure 5-4   Mapping of solution patterns to an e-business problem

The patterns in the e-business approach are structured in a manner that each level of detail builds on the last. E-business is used in this section because of the availability of the public IBM e-business patterns site, but the same approach applies to any set of patterns. Note the similarity of the approach articulated for e-business and the MDA standard discussed earlier in this chapter. The approach is as follows (refer back to Figure 5-4 when needed):

1. **Customer requirements**—First, the architect must work with the business analyst and users to create the customer requirements per their current development methodology. The architect creates use cases and identify the criteria needed to create a successful solution.

2. **Business patterns**—Based on the use cases, the architect consults the business patterns and performs a gap/overlap analysis to determine whether any of the given patterns are a "good enough" fit to the customer requirements. If so, the corresponding business pattern is selected. This pattern identifies the interaction between the users, businesses, and data.

3. **Integration pattern**—In more complicated business cases, it might be necessary to use multiple business patterns. In such a case, an integration pattern can be selected to tie the multiple business patterns together.

4. **Composite pattern**—The IBM e-business architects noted a number of commonly occurring combinations of business patterns and integration patterns. As a result, they created composite patterns. These composite patterns create a common solution for the common problem of the corresponding business pattern and integration pattern.

5. **Application pattern**—The next step in the SOA development process is to create the solution architecture approach and lay out at a high level the service(s) and service component specification. The application pattern will provide a solution architecture for the e-business problem being addressed.

A.5.6

6. **Runtime patterns**—The next step in the development process is to create a more specific and detailed design. In the case of e-business, runtime patterns show the major nodes, their roles, and the interfaces between the nodes.

7. **Product mappings**—Sometimes a specific operational implementation is available that is proven and tested for a runtime pattern. In such a case, the product software implementation is specified and reused.

5.5 Making Legacy Reusable: Harvesting Reusable Components from a Legacy Monolithic Application

IT legacy applications are a mixed bag. Some are well written, using structured and modular programming that is well documented and easy to understand. Others are like multiple strands of spaghetti, with little or no documentation, that even the original developers (if they're still around) cannot understand. In either case, these monolithic applications contain valuable business logic, rules, information, workflow, and sometimes a user interface that the users have grown accustomed to and probably like.

The SOA architect can make three choices when evaluating a legacy application for applicability to an SOA approach. Each of these is described in Tables 5-1, 5-2, and 5-3.

Table 5.1 Legacy with No Value

Legacy Situation	The legacy application is a "black box" that's impossible to understand. It supports a function that's not changing or that is not supporting a high-priority business area or will not add flexibility with a services approach.
Action to Take	Leave this application as is. It's not worth considering.

Table 5-2   Legacy That Cannot Be Changed but Has Value

Legacy Situation	The legacy application is more or less understandable, with one or more operations that contain value for the business. It supports a business function that needs flexibility and a services approach.
Action to Take	Identify the operations that this application contains. Don't attempt to change the application other than to make it "accessible as a service" for these operations. Put a web services "wrapper" around the application with a schema that supports the operations and the messaging interface. At some future point in time, consider converting those legacy operations into services and retiring this legacy application. See the remainder of this section for more information about this process.

Table 5-3   Legacy That Is Componentizable

Legacy Situation	The legacy application is well written and understood. It contains valuable operations that can be migrated to a services approach.
Action to Take	Convert this application from a "monolith" to services. See the remainder of this section for more information about this process.

The term *monolith* implies that the legacy application is a single block that is impervious to all attempts at conversion. In fact, conversion of a monolithic legacy application to reusable components can be performed with an analysis that takes into account the existing user interface, system interface, workflow, system processes, functional logic, and application data. The idea is to break up the monolith and harvest reusable components. These components can be reorganized into service layers by leveraging portals, process automation, and shared enterprise data store infrastructures. System interfaces will be replaced with service interfaces (see Figure 5-5).

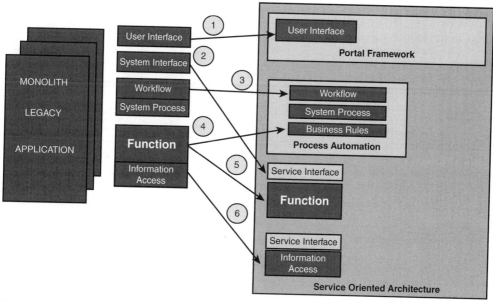

Figure 5-5   Analysis model for conversion of legacy application into reusable components

We focus now on the six conversation areas noted in Figure 5-5:

1. Creation of a user interface component that obtains information via a portal and integrates with a coarse-grained service or middleware providing the workflow for the new service.

2. Conversion of the system interface that existed on the monolith into one or more service interfaces for the functions to be harvested.

3. Creation of a workflow component within process automation by identifying and specifying the steps of the legacy workflow.

4. Creation of a business rule component to separate out the portions of the functional code that are subject to business change.

5. Creation of a functional service with one or more operations.

6. Creation of (probably) several information services that perform information brokering to an underlying information store.

5.5.1 User Interface

Often, the user interface in a monolith is using outmoded technology that should have been replaced a long time ago. Analysis and design will need to take place to migrate this functionality to a portal. Because the user community has likely grown fond of the "old" way of doing things, some diplomacy will need to be employed to understand and re-create or better the current design. In so doing, a story board should be created showing the flow of the user interface. Figure 5-6 shows a sample page from a story board.

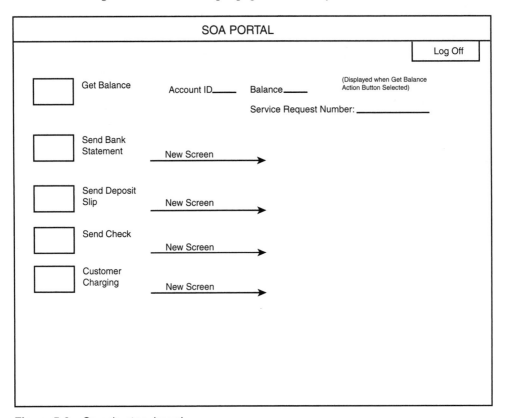

Figure 5-6   Sample story board

5.5.2 Service Interfaces

The "Service Specification" section of Chapter 4 discusses the design considerations for a service interface.

How can reuse be created when services must interface with other services that have different schemas? Middleware can assist in eliminating the creation of point-to-point interfaces. This is best done through the use of common representations (schemas) for those business entities. In other words, service- or application-specific data is mapped into a common format for use by the process-integration middleware. In turn, any data that needs to be processed by a service or application is mapped from the common format into the specific form needed by the application.

The separation of the monolithic application into reusable components requires the creation of service interfaces for each functional component created. The service interface is a formal interface contract for the invocation of the service. When one service interfaces to another service, an information brokering must take place that applies transformations to translate the schema of the calling service to the schema of the called service.

Key, in an SOA approach, to simplifying the interface of different services is the concept of a common object model, also known as a generic business object (GBO). The common object model provides a superset representation that normalizes the data associated with integration of applications and business processes. This reduces the number of transformations to two, one from the source application/process to the common object model and another from common object model to target application/process (see Figure 5-7).

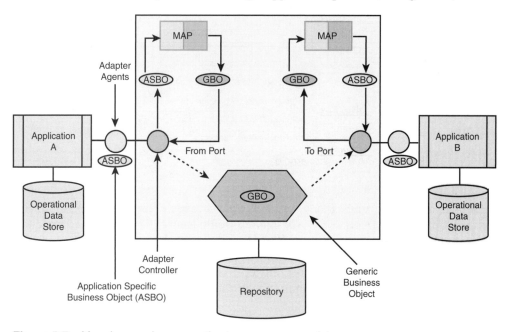

Figure 5-7   Mapping service semantics to a common model

Such an information-brokering approach provides real isolation from participating applications, thus enabling process logic integration and application independence. In addition, the integration does not require advance knowledge of all participating applications. Enterprise data is distributed in several systems, not often in the same format. Having a common view of data that is most valuable to the business (such as representation of customer) can provide enormous business value. Adoption of such a common object model is often a way for enterprises to develop an enterprise data model. XML has become the de facto standard for data representation and data exchange in SOA-led organizations.

A.5.7

The hierarchical nature of XML allows you to adopt a component-reuse approach to XML design. Think of an XML document as a set of nested containers. The outermost container is the root element. All of its children appear as containers inside it, and so on, until sub-containers contain only actual text values. For example, you might have the structures shown in Figure 5-8, each of which contains a customer address

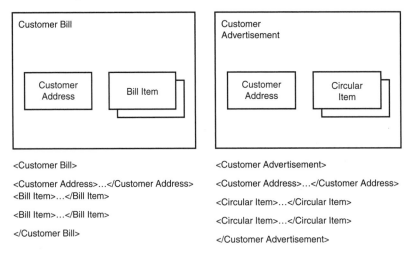

<Customer Bill>

<Customer Address>...</Customer Address>
<Bill Item>...</Bill Item>

<Bill Item>...</Bill Item>

</Customer Bill>

<Customer Advertisement>

<Customer Address>...</Customer Address>

<Circular Item>...</Circular Item>

<Circular Item>...</Circular Item>

</Customer Advertisement>

Figure 5-8   XML customer address example

For example, monolithic applications may well create different customer address formats. Setting up XML Schema Definition (XSD) libraries would enable the developer to reuse the customer address element in both of the XML documents. To do so, however, the two customer address elements used in Customer Bill and Customer Advertisement have to be syntactically and semantically identical. Not only do they have to have the same content, but the content must also have the same meaning each time it appears.

5.5.3 Workflow

Workflow is implemented in SOA using choreography, which is accomplished by defining the overall process logic steps from start to finish and then capturing this process choreography outside the service functional logic. Process logic is the decision logic that controls the execution of other functions. Figure 5-9 shows the workflow that has been initiated by a customer request from a portal to initiate service activation. The workflow to complete service activation is controlled by the Process Automation with interaction via the Enterprise Service Bus to the business services that, in turn, implements each step in the service activation process.

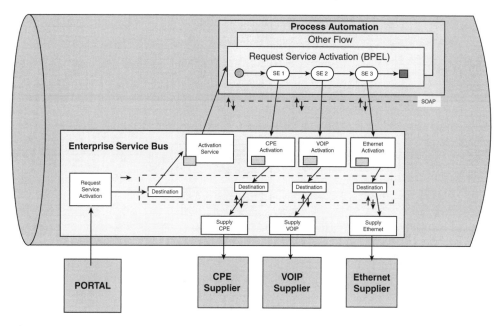

Figure 5-9 Workflow in an SOA approach

The Business Process Execution Language for Web Services (BPEL4WS) is a language to define business process models that combine inbound and outbound web service operations, describing the relationship of the operations and order of execution, fault processing, and compensation (backout). Service choreography engines can then execute the service choreography described in a BPEL model, expose such choreography as a service within SOA, and choreograph the invocation of services that provide the activity implementations.

5.5.4 Business Rules

The business rules are part of the monolithic application that is intertwined in the application code. Each time the business changes, analysts and programmers must figure out what application code needs to change, where it needs to change, and how to make the coding changes. Then they must perform unit, system, and integration testing. It is not unusual for this process to take a year or more. Wouldn't it be easier to separate out this logic that the business is likely to change? The business logic can be exposed as rules and modified by the business user via a business rules engine. The rules in the business rules engine are then accessed at runtime by the application, creating maximum flexibility.

Figure 5-10 shows the flow of the application and the rules engine. Many times, the changes needed for a new business capability merely require changes to the business policy. By separating this policy from the application code, the business can now change this policy without bothering IT. What takes months or years to change only takes the time needed for the business to change the rule and verify the change.

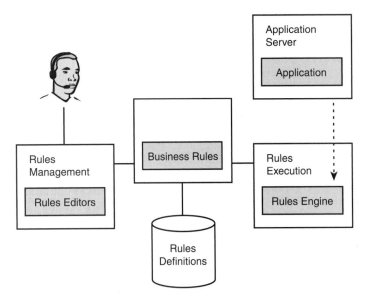

Figure 5-10   Business rules flow

The rules for expressing the business rules and their flow are easy to change. The rules are typically expressed as a set of if-then rules or decision tables. Most business users are comfortable with decision tables, and many are comfortable with if-then rules (see Figure 5-11).

Business Policy & Rule Name	Business Policy & Rule Description
Customer_Segmentation_ Policy	If customer is existing platinum or has total puchases > $100,000, send transaction to platinum line
	If customer is existing gold or has total puchases > $50,000, send transaction to gold line
	Else send transaction to silver line
Security_Level_Policy	If transaction amount > $10,000 or transaction country is not equal to home country, then set Fraud Checking = Yes
Total_Income_Rule	If marital_status is divorced, then family income = salary - alimony
	If marital_status is married, then family income = husband salary + wife salary
	Else family income = salary

Figure 5-11   Business tables

IBM WebSphere® Process Server and IBM WebSphere Integration Developer support if-then rules and decision tables, thus bringing these benefits to their customers in the context of creating business agility.

5.5.5 Service Functions

The monolith may have a function or set of functions that is of interest to us in our analysis of legacy applications. No doubt, the functional code is intertwined with accessing user data, business rules, workflow to perform various subfunctions, and interworking with various databases. The legacy code typically consists of a set of function points that can be useful. Identify what those function points are and create the interface that can be used to access the legacy functions. The original systems interface is probably a good starting point, but this is also the right time to consider and possibly modify the new interface schema to take advantage of information component reuse as described in Section 5.5.2 "Service Interfaces."

5.5.6. Information Service

It is good software design practice to never have a native database call in application code. Violation of this design practice results in a service tightly coupled to a specific physical schema and data implementation. It becomes impossible to realize information agility without time-consuming and expensive changes to the applications and services when the underlying database definition is changed. Creation of a virtualized data source and the advisability and methodology for separating data providers and data consumers is discussed in detail in Chapter 7, "Information Services."

If the monolith you are dealing with has been designed correctly, it uses either a subroutine or RPC as its data provider. In the case where the monolith is both a data consumer and data provider, it is necessary to remove these from the functional service and create a data provider service that the functional service uses.

5.6 Conclusion

An SOA is undertaken for many reasons, but certainly one of the chief ones is to accrue the benefits of reusable assets. This is a significant component in a positive return on investment (ROI) for SOA. Maximizing your ROI requires a proactive governance approach and reuse strategy, the elements of which were described in this chapter.

5.7 Links to developerWorks Articles

A5.1 Brown and Conallen. *An Introduction to Model Driven Architecture*, IBM developerWorks. www.ibm.com/developerworks/rational/library/may05/brown/.

A5.2 Kontio. *Architectural manifesto: MDA for the enterprise*, IBM developerWorks. www.ibm.com/developerworks/wireless/library/wi-arch16/.

A5.3 Gardner and Yusuf. *Combine patterns and modeling to implement architecture-driven development*, IBM developerWorks. www.ibm.com/developerworks/library/ar-mdd2/.

A5.4 Lane and Gee. *Building SOA applications with reusable assets, Part 2: SOA recipe reference example*, IBM developerWorks. www.ibm.com/developerworks/webservices/library/ws-soa-reuse2/.

A5.5 Lord. *Patterns for e-business*, IBM developerWorks. www.ibm.com/developerworks/web/library/wa-lessons/.

A5.6 Gancl et al. *Patterns: SOA Foundation Service Creation Scenario.* w3.itso.ibm.com/abstracts/sg247240.html?Open.

A5.7 Williams. *XML for Data: Reuse it or lose it*, IBM developerWorks. www.ibm.com/developerworks/xml/library/x-xdreuse/.

A5.8 Medicke. Chen, and Mago. *Create an intelligent and flexible solutions with BPM, Business Rules, Business Intelligence: Proactive Use of Business Rules*, IBM developerWorks. www.ibm.com/developerworks/db2/library/techarticle/0310mago/ 0310mago.html.

A5.9 Linehan. *SOA programming model for implementing web services, Part 9, integrating rules with SOA*, IBM developerWorks. www.ibm.com/developerworks/webservices/ library/ws-soa-progmodel9/.

5.8 References

www.ibm.com/developerworks/patterns/.

Brown and Conallen. *An Introduction to Model Driven Architecture*, IBM developerWorks. www.ibm.com/developerworks/rational/library/may05/brown/.

Kontio. *Architectural manifesto: MDA for the enterprise*, IBM developerWorks. www.ibm.com/developerworks/wireless/library/wi-arch16/.

Gardner and Yusuf. *Combine patterns and modeling to implement architecture-driven development*, IBM developerWorks. www.ibm.com/developerworks/library/ar-mdd2/.

Lord. *Patterns for e-business*, IBM developerWorks. www.ibm.com/developerworks/web/library/wa-lessons/.

Lane and Gee. *Building SOA applications with reusable assets, Part 2: SOA recipe reference example*, IBM developerWorks. www.ibm.com/developerworks/webservices/library/ws-soa-reuse2/.

Medicke, Chen, and Mago. *Create an intelligent and flexible solutions with BPM, Business Rules, Business Intelligence: Proactive Use of Business Rules*, IBM developerWorks. www.ibm.com/developerworks/db2/library/techarticle/0310mago/0310mago.html.

Linehan. *SOA programming model for implementing web services, Part 9, integrating rules with SOA*, IBM developerWorks. www.ibm.com/developerworks/webservices/library/ws-soa-progmodel9/.

Gancl et al. *Patterns: SOA Foundation Service Creation Scenario.* w3.itso.ibm.com/abstracts/sg247240.html?Open.

Williams. *XML for Data: Reuse it or lose it*, IBM developerWorks. www.ibm.com/developer-works/xml/library/x-xdreuse/.

Larsen. "Model-driven development: Assets and reuse," *IBM Systems Journal*, 45:3, November 2006. www.research.ibm.com/journal/sj45-3.html.

Chapter 6

Realization of
Services

In Chapter 4, "A Methodology for Service Modeling and Design," we covered a thorough treatment of a methodology for service identification, specification, and realization. IBM has standardized on SOMA (Service Oriented Modeling and Architecture) as the de facto standard to execute on SOA projects. The method has enjoyed so much widespread acceptance that the Rational Unified Process (RUP) has based its method extension for SOA on SOMA. The new version of RUP, version 7.1, incorporates additional information on building SOA-based solutions and is formally called *IBM RUP for SOMA V2.4 (henceforth referred to as RUP-SOMA for brevity).*

A.6.1

Although a methodological approach to service design is imperative, the challenges arise when it is time to execute the various phases, activities, and tasks laid out as a part of the method. The ability to execute on the various phases in an SOA lifecycle, in a typical design and implementation project, depends on the products and tools, along with their supported features that are used. The challenge is to choose the right tools to provide a seamless forward-engineering mechanism while moving from one phase to the next in the SOA lifecycle.

This chapter focuses on the realization of services in an SOA implementation, with an emphasis on the execution of the activities and tasks of specific tool and products. Although we have chosen a particular set of products, to demonstrate the realization of services, the choice of the product is not as important as the features that are used to execute on the activities. Other products/tools that provide similar capabilities can be easily substituted and used for the realization of services. An important rule to note here is that regardless of the set of tools and products that are used, consistency, compatibility, and usability of artifacts (across phases) generated in each phase of the SOA lifecycle is fundamental and imperative in the choice of the tool and product set. The chosen suite in this chapter follows the rule that we stated here.

6.1 Realizing the SOA Lifecycle

After being introduced to it in Chapter 4, you are now ready to delve more deeply into the SOA lifecycle. The lifecycle revolves around the *MADM* (Model, Assemble, Deploy, Manage) phases and assumes that output artifacts of a given phase should be used as software inputs for the subsequent phase in the lifecycle. This seamless incorporation and transition of artifacts between the phases is one of the key features that the tools and products ought to provide. The tools chosen for use in the *assemble* phase, for example, should be capable of importing the artifacts generated by the tools used in the *model* phase. The requirements of the tools not only need to produce artifacts consumable by the subsequent phase, but also need the capability to consume the produced artifacts from the preceding phase in the SOA lifecycle.

The SOA lifecycle is defined by the *MADM* phases, but it is critical to understand that identifying and capturing requirements is a key part of any IT project—and an SOA is no exception! In fact, additional, specific requirements need to be gathered in an SOA-based IT project. Therefore, this section examines some elements that, although do not necessarily fall under the MADM phases, are essential for the successful execution of an SOA engagement. We group them together and call them *premodeling activities*.

6.2 Premodeling Activities in an SOA

The first of the premodeling activities is to formalize on the software development process that may require tailoring for the organization or project in scope. Although the base method used for our illustration is *RUP-SOMA*, you might need to customize the chosen method. For example, you might need to exclude a few activities that are not relevant or add a few activities or tasks that incorporate some specific nuances of the organization's development process—essentially you are performing a *method adoption*.

The second premodeling activity important to the realization of services is requirements gathering.

> **Note**
>
> Some schools of thought consider requirements gathering a part of the model phase in the SOA lifecycle. There is no harm in that as long as the right requirements are adequately captured in the proper sequence of lifecycle steps. For purposes of this discussion, however, we consider requirements gathering as an activity performed *before* the model phase.

Documentation and management of requirements are critical steps in the development of an SOA-based solution. Requirement management is defined by RUP as follows:

"Requirements management is a systematic approach to finding, documenting, organizing, and tracking the changing requirements of a system."

We introduce the tools/products used in the premodeling phase, and then discuss the execution mechanism for the activities that typically are performed during this phase. In the rest of this chapter, for each phase that we discuss, we introduce the tools/products before discussing how you can use them to execute the activities in the phase.

6.2.1 Tools for Premodeling Activities

Any tool used to develop and maintain a method should provide a flexible and robust feature that supports the customization of the method and publishing a read-only version of it that is in human-readable form and made available to method users. The tool that we recommend in IBM for method development is called *IBM Rational Method Composer*.

For gathering requirements, the tool used to capture, document, and maintain them should also be capable of categorizing them into individual projects and of maintaining an intuitive folder structure while providing the key linkage between the requirements to the modeling and design tools used in the subsequent phases of a typical software development lifecycle. The traceability of requirements to their realization through architecture, design, and implementation is imperative and should be used as a determining factor when choosing any requirements management tool/product. For requirements gathering, we recommend *IBM Rational RequisitePro*.

6.2.1.1 IBM Rational Method Composer

IBM Rational Method Composer (RMC) is an Eclipse-based framework for process and method authoring targeted primarily at method customization and publishing. RUP considers RMC as its replacements for all the previous RUP authoring products. The RUP-SOMA method is available as a plug-in in RMC. RMC implements the Unified Method Architecture (UMA), which is a standard for method creation and is presently being submitted to the Object Management Group (OMG) for acceptance and standardization under the name Software Process Engineering (SPEM) version 2.0.

A.6.2

RMC enables the development of new methods and the customization of existing methods. It also enables the publication of methods in an HTML format that can be displayed in a standard browser outside of RMC, which helps separate the roles of method users versus method exponents. The method users use the published version of the method and do not need to work with RMC, whereas their method exponent counterparts use RMC to develop/customize method content. Using RMC, we can formalize the development and provisioning of the method.

6.2.1.2 IBM Rational RequisitePro

IBM Rational RequisitePro provides an in-depth traceability and coverage analysis that along with its seamless integration with the design and development tools such as IBM Rational Software Architect (RSA), IBM Rational Data Architect (RDA), and IBM Rational Application Developer (RAD) provides the linkage between the requirements and the artifacts developed in the subsequent phases of the software development lifecycle. RequisitePro also provides web-based access to its content, which assists in the seamless sharing of requirements among distributed development teams.

It is recommended that you create two different projects in RequisitePro (see Figure 6-1), one for the enterprise-level requirement and another for the project-level requirement. The minimum set of requirements for each project, which are discussed in the next section, are gathered and maintained in this tool.

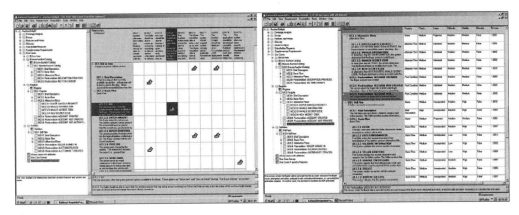

Figure 6-1 Two different views illustrating two features of RequisitePro

Refer to the "References" section for more information on RequisitePro features. The key thing to keep in mind is that whichever product or tool is chosen to capture requirements, it must be feature rich to capture all the requirements that typically constitute an SOA project and should also have the capability to seamlessly integrate with the downstream modeling and design tools that will be chosen for the project.

6.2.2 The Execution

The development and the customization of the method is usually performed by a method exponent, also called a process engineer. After the process undergoes the necessary customizations, it should be published to the architects, designers, developers, and testers in the project. An instance of a method is made available through RMC's own internal browsing mechanism. In reality, however, the content is published as a set of HTML files that can be shared in a team environment. The content can also be exported into a simple Microsoft Excel spreadsheet format or as a Microsoft Project Plan format. These various forms in which the method can be made available to project team members make the method ready for execution. (Note that the customization of a method is typically not a part of a software development lifecycle (SDLC) that follows a MADM phase approach, and in most cases the HTML, Excel, or Microsoft Project Plan version of the method is all that is required. However, in some cases, based on the scope and context of the project, method customization can be incorporated into what typically constitute the *solution inception* and *outline* level activities.)

Project requirements may be categorized into three domains:

- **Business domain**—Pertains to business use cases, business glossary, key performance indicators (KPIs), metrics, business processes, and so on.
- **Services domain**—Pertains to functional and nonfunctional requirements of a service, service policies, and so on.
- **System domain**—Pertains to system functions, system context diagrams, system use cases, and so on.

Requirements from each of the domains need to be captured and documented in RequisitePro. The various work products that need to be created as a part of the project deliverable and the relationship and dependencies between them must be defined and carefully monitored. The management and control of requirements should be captured in a requirements management plan.

Requirements can also be broken down into two broad categories: enterprise level and project level. Enterprise-level requirements are defined and controlled at the corporate level. Business use cases, business processes, business policies, system policies, and regulatory requirements are typical examples of enterprise-level requirements. Project-level requirements are more focused on a given initiative and what is expected to be achieved by looking through the project lens. System use cases, KPIs, metrics, and functional and nonfunctional requirements are some examples of project-level requirements. Maintaining these two categories separately, while preserving the relationships and dependencies between artifacts from the two categories, helps better manage the requirements and is considered as a best practice in the usage of RequisitePro.

To successfully realize services in an SOA, a minimum set of requirements must be captured. At the enterprise level, you need the following requirements:

- Business use cases
- Business policies
- Regulatory and compliance requirements
- System policies
- Business processes that are in the initial scope of the transformation initiative

At the project level, you need a minimum of the following requirements:

- Functional requirements
- Nonfunctional requirements
- Business vision
- Business goals
- KPIs and metrics supporting each business goal
- System use cases that support the scope of the project's deliverables

Each different type of requirement is captured in RequisitePro. Note that although it is prescribed to capture all these requirements, the project is usually the final dictator (based on time, resources, and cost constraints) of what requirements need to be captured.

6.3 Modeling Services in an SOA

Modeling is the first phase in the MADM-based SOA lifecycle. The focus of this phase is on service identification and service specification. We discuss both topics as part of the model phase, and we precede the discussion with a list of the products/tools that we propose be used for each of these activities. The main work product that we focus on in this section is the *service model*.

6.3.1 Tools for Modeling

In a top-down approach, the business processes in the scope of the transformation need to be modeled. The tool we recommend for business modeling is the IBM WebSphere Business Modeler. For the bottom-up approach, to identify services, we will leverage a product called the IBM WebSphere Studio Asset Analyzer, which assists in identifying function modules in legacy systems that have the potential to be used to implement a service. Some of these existing functions can also be exposed as service themselves. Finally, the identified services need to be modeled and their detailed design performed before they can be handed over to the implementation team. Most of the artifacts during service identification and service specification steps in SOMA are developed in IBM Rational Software Architect (to be discussed in Section 6.3.1.2).

6.3.1.1 IBM WebSphere Business Modeler

Business Process Modeling (BPM) is an important topic as it relates to SOA, and a lot of tools and products in the market provide the basic capabilities of BPM. The product that we use for process modeling is called IBM WebSphere Business Modeler (WBM). WBM provides a user-friendly mechanism to model the processes, add roles for each process node (that is, to subprocesses and activities), and also represent inputs and outputs in terms of *business items*. The business items collectively can be exported out as an XSD (XML Schema Definition) file and can be used as a valuable input to define the information model and the logical data model. Figure 6-2 shows how a typical business process is modeled in WBM. Refer to the "References" section for more information about WBM.

When you are modeling, the tool enables you to add cost, duration, and resources to each task in the process model and then enable running simulations of the modeled processes based on user-configurable data points. Simulations provide invaluable information about the performance of processes on various input loads, thereby providing the business with predictability in the performance of their "to-be" processes.

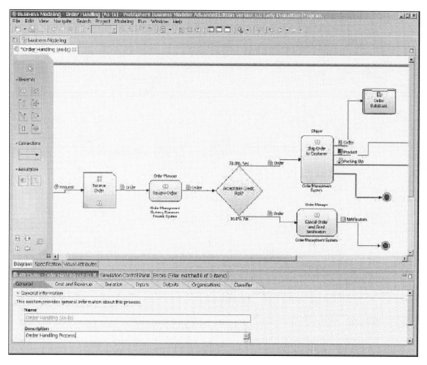

Figure 6-2 A typical business process model in WBM

6.3.1.2 IBM Rational Software Architect

IBM Rational Software Architect (RSA) is an Eclipse-based development tool for modeling
your application software components. RSA operates on standard Unified Modeling
Language (UML) notation and semantics for use case analysis, class designs, sequence and
state diagrams, deployment models, and so on. As of this writing, the latest version of RSA,
version 7.0, provides a built-in plug-in that assists in the development of a specific type of
project for service design by providing a preconfigured package structure that can be used
to develop all aspects of a service design model. It is particularly useful for using and transforming the models developed in WBM into detailed service specifications and component
models that you can then hand over to software developers for implementation. RSA has
support for plugging in design patterns that help automate development and promote reuse.
It comes already populated with some of the most commonly occuring classic patterns
described in the book *Design Patterns: Elements of Reusable Object-Oriented Software,* by Erich
Gamma et al. (often referred to as the Gang of Four, or GoF). You can obtain other predefined patterns or create pattern templates for specific design practices used commonly
throughout the software analysis and design process. Figure 6-3 provides a snippet of a UML
diagram in RSA. For more information about RSA, refer to the "References" section.

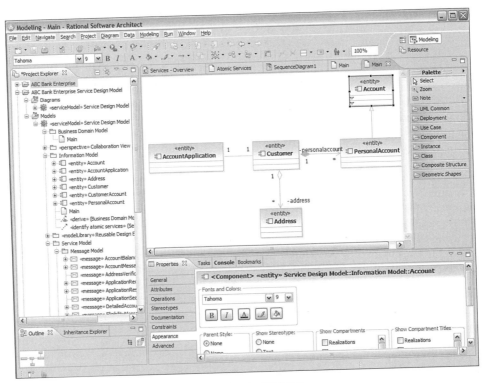

Figure 6-3 The UML Modeling perspective in RSA 7.0

6.3.1.3 IBM WebSphere Studio Asset Analyzer

IBM WebSphere Studio Asset Analyzer (WSAA) is a tool for maintaining and extending exist-ing assets through impact analysis, connector builder assistance, and graphical application understanding. This tool is designed to help enterprise customers understand their existing assets by providing knowledge about both their static environment (finding and reusing application code) and the components that connect to that code. It also helps them under-stand their dynamic environment (what code is executing in the runtime environments). Refer to the "References" section for more details about WSAA.

> **Note**
>
> Several other products in the market assist in analyzing legacy sys-tems and in mining knowledge that can be used to implement one or more services in an SOA.

6.3.2 The Execution

The execution focuses on service identification and service specification phases of *RUP-SOMA* and how to use the tools and products to model and specify services and produce artifacts for the service model work product.

6.3.2.1 Service Identification

We have already covered the RUP-SOMA method in detail in Chapter 4, and therefore the theory behind it is not covered here. We focus on how, aided by tools, we can perform the three main activities of domain decomposition, goal service modeling, and existing asset analysis and use them to identify services.

6.3.2.2 Identify Services from Domain and Process Models

The two main activities you need to perform are functional area analysis and process decomposition. For functional area analysis, you depend on the business architecture definition of the system. As a part of the business architecture analysis, you usually try to come up with a componentized view of the business, whereby you break down the enterprise capabilities into a modular set of well-defined business components. Some of those business components are identified as to be in the scope of the transformation. This subset of the business components is the starting point for identifying functional areas. Functional areas are used to categorize and group the services that will be identified. The grouping of services derived from the functional areas results in service partitions that are represented in separate packages in the service design model. At the end of the service identification phase, after all the services have been identified, the service partitions are formalized, with each containing a group of services.

For process decomposition, the main emphasis is on business process modeling. During the requirements-gathering activities, business use cases are identified. According to RUP, a business use case is a "sequence of actions that a business performs that yields an observable result of value to a particular business actor, or that shows how the business responds to a business event, to yield a business benefit."

A business use case forms a top-level view of the business as perceived by the outside world. Any business use case requires a business use case realization.

As Figure 6-4 illustrates, a business use case realization can be, for all practical purposes, considered akin to the realization of a business use case.

Each of the business use cases defined and captured in the requirements-gathering tool, RequisitePro in this case, need to be further elaborated. Business process modeling is a good starting point to refining the business use cases.

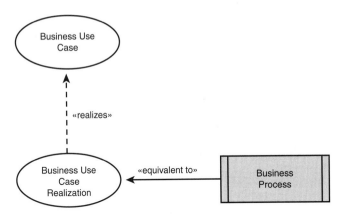

Figure 6-4   Relationship between a business use case and a business process

A business process model contains the details of the business process. Each business process is decomposed into subprocesses, which are further broken down into activities. Process models cannot be captured in a tool such as RequisitePro, and therefore a visual modeling tool is required. The tool should have a minimum set of capabilities. It should

- Visually represent a business process.
- Decompose a process into activities or tasks.
- Associate input and output information between the process nodes.
- Represent the modeling artifacts using a standard language.
- Export the process model in a format such that the resultant exported artifacts can be used seamlessly in tools used for service design and specification.
- Simulate the *to-be* process models to determine areas of bottlenecks and provide predictable results based on different data points.

> **Tip**
>
> In a decomposed process model, each lower-level (typically the leaf-level, that is, the lowest level of decomposition) subprocess is a strong candidate to be exposed as a service.

Figure 6-5 demonstrates how we took a typical business process for "opening a bank account" and decomposed it into its constituent subprocesses.

Each of these subprocesses, as shown in Figure 6-5, is a candidate service. Recall that candidate services are passed through a filtering gate to identify only those services that should be exposed. This part of the service realization is not covered in this chapter mainly because there is no tooling support yet that we have found to be able to perform this activity. For documentation purposes, we draw a simple table to capture the reasons why the service-exposure decisions passed or failed.

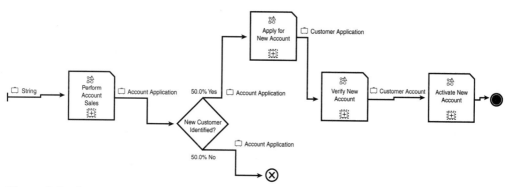

Figure 6-5 A process model for a typical Open Bank Account business process

For illustration purposes, we take the subprocess called, Verify New Account, and decompose it into a set of tasks. Figure 6-6 depicts the tasks for the subprocess.

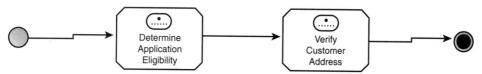

Figure 6-6 The tasks related to the *Verify New Account* subprocess

Each business process and subprocess is modeled in WBM in the manner illustrated in Figure 6-6. The processes or subprocesses in the main business process are broken down into their constituent tasks, as in Figure 6-6. In this simple example, we identify *Verify New Account* as a service, and *Determine Application Eligibility* and *Verify Customer Address* as two operations on the identified service. The business items that flow through the process nodes, as depicted in Figure 6-5 are mapped to business entities in the service model. However, service modeling is not in the purview of WBM and hence we need to turn our focus to RSA, where we perform the service modeling and design.

Figure 6-7 depicts some key conceptual artifacts of a service model that are modeled in RSA. The *VerifyNewAccount* class that is stereotyped as *serviceSpecification* depicts a service. This service makes its way into the Service Model work product document. The service is traced back to the 'Verify New Account' business process that was identified and modeled in WBM. The service uses an entity that is identified as *CustomerAccount* that has its derivation from the Customer Account business entity, from the process models in WBM. The *OpenNewBankAccount* is a service consumer derived from the main business process called Open New Bank Account that was modeled in WBM. Note that because we are focusing on performing service identification, we cannot provide the service syntax and semantics just yet. This is done during service specification.

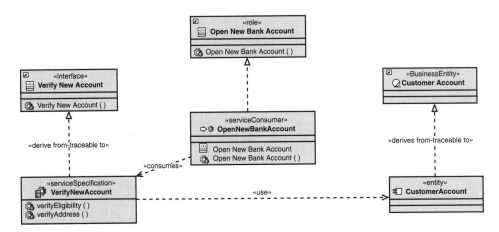

Figure 6-7   Example of services identified from business process analysis

From a tooling standpoint, a seamless integration exists between WBM and RSA. In fact, the business model project in WBM when imported into RSA creates an RSA version of a modeling project. This RSA model is a representation of the process models as defined in WBM. The recommendation is to use the imported (from WBM) process model only for reference business information and for traceability between the service design model artifacts and the activity models that are developed in RSA as a part of the design and specification of the services. The service design model is represented as a UML model in RSA. Key linkages between the activity model artifacts in RSA and the process model in WBM can also be determined and documented. If you look closely at the top three classes in Figure 6-7, you will notice a small icon to the upper left of each class, which indicates that it has been referenced from a different project; this linkage between different projects in the same workspace is a feature of RSA that is exploited.

WBM seamlessly integrates with RequisitePro too. You can open a RequisitePro client inside WBM as a different perspective and link the business use case definitions in RequisitePro with the business process models in the WBM perspective view. This way we establish the traceability between the business use case and its realization through the business processes. It is important to understand that this traceability is the cornerstone of a well-managed and controlled software development process based on SOA. This seamless traceability is possible between WBM and RequisitePro because both the tools are based on the Eclipse framework.

6.3.3 Tools for Domain Decomposition

Although functional area analysis can be performed in many ways, and is almost always a factor of the business domain expertise and skills available in the project, we recommend looking closely at IBM's Component Business Modeling (CBM); refer to the "References" section. CBM is a technique that provides a modular view of the enterprise by deconstructing the business into a set of business components. Each business component has a well-defined set of responsibilities and a set of expected capabilities that it requires to perform. A business component may also rely on the capabilities offered by other business components. The component capabilities together with the intercomponent relationships may be mapped to a model of collaborating business components. The CBM technique provides such a CBM map of business components for most of the industry sectors. Leveraging an existing industry CBM map helps accelerate the process of creating a business architecture for an enterprise. The business components identified to be the ones in the scope of the transformation are then used as the first iteration in identifying the functional areas—a business component is initially mapped to a functional area with the same name.

6.3.4 Identify Services from Business Goals

The business goals are assumed to be well captured in RequisitePro during the premodeling activities. As discussed in Chapter 4, it is common to find the business goals to be at such a high level that it is practically impossible to identify services from them. Hence, goals need to be decomposed into subgoals. RequisitePro provides the capability to not only break down the goals into subgoals and then depict the parent-child relationship between goals and subgoals but also to document them in a very intuitive and user-friendly manner. This capability allows designers to determine the traceability of subgoals to the parent business goal.

KPIs and metrics are also captured in RequisitePro. A metric is a unit of measurement for a KPI. Each KPI must be associated with a metric.

It is important to connect goals to subgoals and connect both of them to their corresponding KPI and metrics. The traceability feature in RequisitePro can be leveraged to establish this relationship. Every element captured in the tool can be "traced to" and "traced from" other elements. You can also use the traceability matrix feature in the tool to relate more than two types of information. For example, you can first relate the business goals to the KPIs, thereby forming a 2x2 matrix. For each of the cells in the matrix, you can then use the "trace to" feature to link the data in that cell to a third metric.

6.3.5 Identify Services from Existing Assets

Although installation and configuration of products is beyond the scope of this book, it suffices to say that our suggested tool, in this case WSAA, can be configured to mine most mainframe systems and databases, from CICS to IMS databases and to MVS systems and so on. Without getting into the details of the way the tool functions, existing applications can be analyzed not only at a high level to discover the main business functions that a specific application or module provides, but also at the level of transactions, data structures, batch components, and files. Employing the rules of the method as described in Chapter 4 (in the section "Existing Asset Analysis") and aided by the capabilities of the tool, you can discover some business functions or data structures that have a high potential for realizing one or more business requirements that may be identified from the domain decomposition or from goal service modeling activities.

Some enterprises that are more mature than their counterparts or competition in their SOA journey, may have their existing services provisioned in a service registry. These services are also existing assets and can be used to realize some of the service functionality identified through domain decomposition and goal service modeling. In our example, while analyzing the Create New Account business process, we discovered that the existing SAP CRM system had BAPI (business API) code that is used to store any new customer applications. Therefore, as Figure 6-8 depicts, we have a service identified as AccountApplicationService that uses an SAP CRM component called Account Application to realize some of or all of its service operations.

Figure 6-8   A depiction of how service functionality is realized by an existing asset

Tools and techniques exist for inspecting the registry during design time. The services identified from the registry are already designed, implemented, and specified through their externalized definitions. These services are added to the service model, but need not undergo the specification and realization phases.

6.3.5.1 Service Specification

During service specification, all the architecturally significant constructs of an SOA solution have detailed design and specification. At the end of service identification activities we can produce a *service portfolio* containing services that are grouped into *service partitions*. Here, we focus on three aspects:

- Deriving atomic services from the information model
- Specifying the details of the service messages in the *message model* package
- Illustrating how services collaborate with each other in the *service collaboration* package

6.3.5.2 Deriving Atomic Services from the Information Model

The business domain model defines the business entities that represent a subset of a common glossary of business terms that are standardized for an enterprise or a part thereof. Often, a business domain model is derived from an industry standard model. An enterprise information model constitutes a subset of the business domain model, that which is in scope of the transformation, and may contain both types of data: persistent and transient. The information model is typically not that well analyzed during service identification, but the analysis performed during this step often helps in the identification of certain information types that have either a high business or a high technical value and can be used in composition with other services to realize a business function. Atomic services are created out of such information types. Figure 6-9 shows a sample of atomic services that are identified.

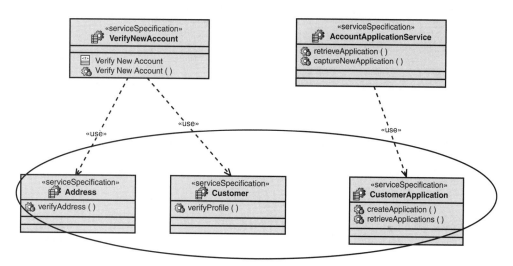

Figure 6-9   List of atomic services that are identified and specified

The figures enclosed in the ellipse are the newly identified services.

Some information types that have a close affinity, from a usage standpoint, to other services can be combined together using an atomic service.

6.3.5.3 Specifying Service Messages
Service messages define the input, output, and fault definitions for service operations. Messages define how the service consumers interact with the service provider and how some warnings and exceptions are relayed back for a better experience for the service consumer. Messages derive from the information model but do not necessarily have a one-to-one mapping between a message definition and a specific information type. Some information types may be combined to construct an input or an output of a service operation. Figure 6-10 shows how messages are derived from the information model elements.

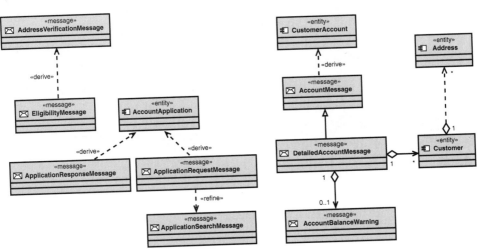

Figure 6-10 How messages are derived from business entities from the information model

Service operations are elaborated by specifying the input and output parameters in the form of messages. Figure 6-11 shows how the CustomerApplication atomic service has its operations specified using the message definitions.

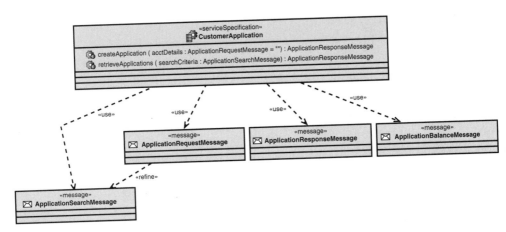

Figure 6-11 An example of a service specified with messages as parameters

This process is performed for every single service in the service portfolio. Defining the message model and using messages to define service operations are critical to service specification.

6.3.5.4 Defining Service Collaborations

Service collaborations define how one or more services interact with each other to realize an end-to-end business process or a part of that end-to-end process. To depict service collaborations, we can either use sequence diagrams or collaboration diagrams in UML. Collaborations should depict the service consumer and the list of services whose operations are invoked in sequence to realize the request from the service consumer. Figure 6-12 depicts a service collaboration represented using UML sequence diagrams.

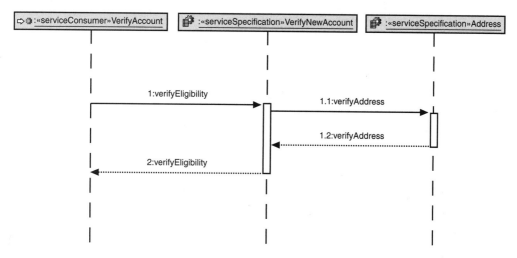

Figure 6-12   Collaboration between services to realize the Verify Account process

For each of the processes and their subprocesses, such service collaboration diagrams should be modeled. Collaborations help in modeling the dynamic view of service dependencies and are key constituents of service specification.

For the service design model, the package structure with its contents (that is, the information model, message model, and the service collaboration packages) expanded is depicted in Figure 6-13.

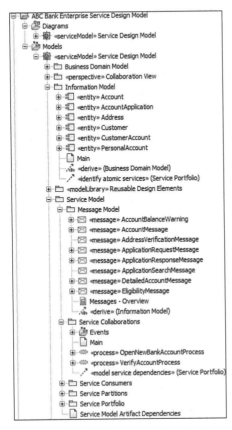

Figure 6-13 Package structure for the service design model after the information model, message model, and service collaborations are specified

Before implementation, the specifications of a service undergo detailed design. The contracts of a service that are exposed to the service consumer are essentially defined through the service's operations. A service component is a special type of an IT component that encapsulates the realization of the contracts for one or more services. The detailed design of the service components is further elaborated through low-level classes that collaborate together to fulfill the functionality. It is a standard practice to produce low-level detailed object models for each service component. It is recommended you use the well-established design patterns (for example, façade, factory, abstract factory, strategy, template, and so on) to detail the low-level design constructs of each service component.

As you can see in this section, many features available in RSA are exploited during the service modeling phase.

6.4 Assembling Services in an SOA

The two main activities of the assemble phase are the implementation of the services and assembling them together to realize business processes. Services are implemented either from scratch or from existing assets by using specific technologies, such as technology adapters. After the specified services are implemented, they are orchestrated to implement a business process. Therefore, the two main focus areas in this phase are on implementation and assembly of services.

6.4.1 Tools for Assembly

Some services are implemented as standard J2EE components that are then exposed as Web Services typically conforming to the of Web Service Description Language (WSDL) specification that is used to declare the service contract. Implementation of some other services requires access to back-end systems through integration technology (for example, adapters). The development environment chosen should be able to support both types of service implementation. On the other hand, for service assembly, a tool that provides a design-time environment to implement orchestration of services into an executable business process should be used.

6.4.1.1 IBM Rational Application Developer

IBM Rational Application Developer (RAD) is an integrated development environment for J2EE programming. RAD, like the rest of the IBM Rational tool suite, is based on the Eclipse framework and therefore can be integrated with any other Eclipse tools to provide a seamless transition from modeling, to architecture, to software development, to debugging, and so on. RAD covers the spectrum ranging from basic Java programming, to Enterprise Java programming conforming to J2EE, to the Portal Server programming model. It has a fully integrated debugging tool and a predefined unit test environment for IBM WebSphere Application Server (WAS) for creating Enterprise JavaBeans (EJB)-based business services. The developed artifacts can be deployed on popular application servers such as WebLogic, Tomcat, and WAS. J2EE components (for example, EJBs) used to implement the business logic for service operations can be exposed using WSDL, which can be published for consumption. Refer to the "References" section for more information about developing J2EE applications with RAD.

6.4.1.2 IBM WebSphere Integration Developer

IBM WebSphere Integration Developer (WID) is also an Eclipse-based tool designed to help create business process flows, state machines, and business rules. WID has full support for BPEL (Business Process Execution Language). It provides extensions to BPEL for human tasks, thereby adding the ability to capture human-to-process, process-to-human, and even human-to-human interactions. WID also has support for the Service Component Architecture (SCA), which is discussed later in this chapter. SCA includes a wiring editor for assembling service components, for importing service interface definitions, and for setting binding policies.

6.4.1.3 The Execution

The services are specified at this point, and the design model is detailed enough for realizing the services. The important point to note here is that, so far, we have concentrated heavily on modeling the service definitions and subsequently providing detailed design for each service component that realizes a service. All the work performed so far is at a model level. Model-driven development (MDD) is a discipline where we start by modeling the system and then use automated transformations to generated downstream development artifacts, which can be refined models or skeleton code that provides a jump start to the development of applications. RSA provides, among other things, two types of automated transformations: *UML2WSDL* and *UML2Java* that are available out of the box.

RSA provides a UML-to-WSDL transformation plug-in that enables the generation of WSDL documents from a UML model that represents service definitions. RSA also provides a UML-to-Java transformation plug-in that enables the generation of a Java project from a UML model. This has the advantage of leveraging MDD techniques to automate the creation of the source code artifacts from a model. Of course, the business logic needs to be implemented by the developer, as does the required integration logic to connect to information systems (for example, databases, packaged applications), but the use of proper MDD techniques enhances developer productivity and isolates any changes to the requirements right into the design model without changing the code. The changes in the model can then be used as inputs to the automated transformations and code can be subsequently generated. Refer to the "References" section for a detailed treatment of how MDD techniques can be applied in SOA using RSA features.

The J2EE project that contains all the Java programming artifacts constitutes the application to be developed. The business logic implementation for the application components is developed in RAD, or any other J2EE-compliant development environment. All the J2EE programming constructs and options can be exploited. Which technology option to use is a matter of an architecture decision, which should be made by the application architect in the team. You can develop the business logic as POJOs (Plain Old Java Objects) or as EJBs. You can also use technologies such as JDBC, entity EJBs, or an Object Relational Mapping framework such as Hibernate to connect to database systems. RAD has built-in features to convert POJOs/session EJBs into web services and their corresponding WSDL definitions. You can use either a top-down approach or a bottom-up approach to service implementation. In the top-down approach, you start with a WSDL definition by using the UML2WSDL transformation and then implementing the business logic. In the bottom-up approach, you can develop the Java code and then use the RAD features to expose the chosen ones as Web Services. The approach to use is also a matter of an architecture decision taken for the specific system's development initiative. At this point, we have the implementation of the atomic services, and they are now ready to be assembled into a service composition and orchestrated together to realize the business processes.

As mentioned previously, the tool that we recommend using for the assembly of services to implement business processes is WID. Artifacts in WID follow the SCA for assembling services together. SCA is a realization of SOA, and WID is a workbench that contains the tools to not only visually assemble the blocks into a complete solution but also to build the inner workings of each block. A *module* is a container for services in WID and also a unit of deployment on any SCA-compliant application server. A module provides services that can be used by other modules and that can be accessed by external clients used by your partners or customers. A specific SOA application being built to realize one or more business processes can be implemented as one or more modules in WID. A *component* is the part of a module that is the actual service, and each service is implemented using one of the implementation types supported by WID. Although components can be implemented inside of WID, sometimes you need to access services that are outside of a given module or even running as a service in a different system. In these cases, you can use the *Import* feature to access external services. The *Export* feature is used when the components of a module need to be exposed as services to be used by other modules. The components in a module are connected to each other using a *wire*.

Figure 6-14 shows an example of how to represent the Verify New Account business functionality as an SCA module.

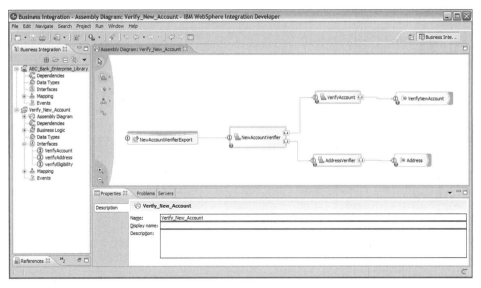

Figure 6-14   Representation of the Verify_New_Account SCA module in WebSphere Integration Developer

Because the services were developed in RAD, they are assumed to be external services in the context of the Verify_New_Account SCA module. These are represented by VerifyNewAccount and Address in Figure 6-14 as SCA imports. The VerifyAccount and AddressVerifier are just SCA components with no implementations, but are connected to their respective imports to realize the necessary business function. The NewAccountVerifier interface has the two operations that are each implemented by the two components,

A.6.4

whereas NewAccountVerifierExport is an export definition of the services exposed by the NewAccountVerifier interface.

As you have seen in this section, services can be exposed from session EJBs or POJOs that are developed in RAD. WID is used to assemble atomic services together into composite services and into deployable units called modules that can run on SCA-compliant application servers.

6.5 Deploying Services in an SOA

The assembly process not only implements the services, but also assembles them into executable business processes. These executable entities need to be deployed on a runtime infrastructure that supports SOA. The services have an implementation and a service definition. The service implementations are deployed on an application server, whereas the service definitions are provisioned into a service registry that may also provision the definitions of the executable business processes.

6.5.1 Products for Deployment

IBM WebSphere Application Server (WAS) is one of the most commonly recommended and popular platforms for deploying SOA-enabled J2EE applications. The services that are custom developed are packaged and deployed on WAS. Executable business processes implemented by orchestrating atomic and composite services and conforming to the BPEL specifications need a BPEL runtime. The IBM WebSphere Process Server (WPS) provides a robust and scalable BPEL runtime environment that is built on top of WAS, which is where the SCA libraries and modules are deployed. The individual services are provisioned in a registry and are exposed for both external and internal consumption. IBM WebSphere Service Registry and Repository (WSRR) provides a design-time and runtime platform for service provisioning and governance.

6.5.1.1 IBM WebSphere Process Server

A.6.5

WPS version 6 is a comprehensive SOA integration platform, which is based on WAS version 6. WPS provides a business process execution runtime on which business processes, that are implemented as service orchestration and composition and which are SCA and BPEL compliant, can be deployed. The SCA modules assembled in WID are seamlessly deployed on WPS. Because WPS leverages WAS capabilities, it provides a scalable and reliable business integration environment that can be used for transaction, security, clustering, and workload management. It provides full atomicity, consistency, isolation, and durability, that is, the ACID transaction support, for the business processes by providing a flexible compensation mechanism. It also provides an efficient recovery mechanism through its Recovery Manager feature. WPS also provides an efficient message-oriented integration with existing systems through its support for seamless integration with IBM WebSphere Message Broker. Through its native support for Web Services interoperability and its integration with the IBM WebSphere Adapters framework, the integration with enterprise information systems such as Siebel, SAP, PeopleSoft, and so on is made easy.

6.5.1.2 IBM WebSphere Registry and Repository

IBM WebSphere Service Registry and Repository (WSRR) acts as a single integration point for service meta-data and establishes a central point for finding and managing service meta-data acquired from a number of sources, including service application deployments and other service meta-data and endpoint registries and repositories, such as Universal Description, Discovery, and Integration (UDDI). It is where service meta-data scattered across an enterprise is brought together to provide a single, comprehensive description of a service.

It assists an enterprise IT to harness better business value from an enterprise SOA by enabling better management and governance of the services in the enterprise service portfolio. Through its robust registry and repository capabilities and its tight integration with IBM SOA Foundation, WSRR is used as an essential foundation component of an SOA implementation. Services provisioned in WSRR can be invoked from development environments such as RAD and WID, which enable a seamless method of integrating existing services into an SOA development and runtime landscape.

A.6.6

6.5.2 The Execution

The execution starts with deploying the packaged J2EE applications to an instance of WAS. The J2EE applications contain the business logic that realizes the implementation of the service definitions. Applications that are installed on WAS need to be carefully configured and administered. Configuration and administration of WAS server instances is beyond the scope of this book. The service definitions, along with their meta-data (policies, business rules, access roles, and so on), are provisioned in WSRR. The business processes developed and choreographed in WID are packaged and deployed into WPS. During runtime, the executable business processes access the service definitions in WSRR and the service implementations that run on native WAS. To take this one step further, the user interaction components that constitute the consumer layer of an application can be developed as portlets following the portal programming model, which can be deployed onto the IBM WebSphere Portal Server. Portlets running on the Portal Server have a seamless integration with the WPS and WAS. Portlets can be used to trigger business processes and interact with them. Note that portal server products from any vendor can be used to trigger business processes running on WAS and WPS so long as the portlets comply to the standard portlet programming model. Refer to the "References" section for a full list of features of WebSphere Portal Server. Figure 6-15 illustrates a high-level overview of the four WebSphere deployment platforms.

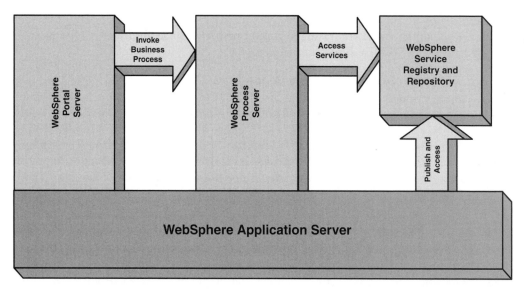

Figure 6-15   The WebSphere Deployment platform for SOA deployment

Note that the WebSphere platform is not restricted to these four products only. IBM WebSphere Adapter for technology integration with heterogeneous enterprise systems; IBM WebSphere Message Broker for message-oriented integration and mediation; IBM WebSphere DataPower Appliances for secure service invocation from outside the enterprise perimeter; and wire-speed XML processing are examples of products that can find their place in the complete deployment platform. However, a detailed treatment of the entire IT infrastructure is beyond the scope of this book.

6.6 Managing Services in an SOA

Service management is the crucial last phase in the SOA lifecycle. *SOA governance and best practices* is an overarching phase that influences the other four phases of the MADM cycle with a special emphasis on the management and monitoring of services and its associated data. SOA governance is discussed in detail in Chapter 3, "SOA Governance," and so is not covered again in this chapter.

Services need to be treated as managed resources. For any software component, certain standard characteristics need to be addressed, including the following:

- Service level or quality of service
- Ability to be deployed and configured
- Ability to be versioned and deprecated
- Ability to be monitored and optimized
- Ability to be secured and audited

All of these characteristics apply to the services in a service portfolio. SOA, however, introduces a new set of requirements to the management challenge. A service is conceptually at a higher level of abstraction than traditional IT components. Therefore, there is an added need to adequately describe the definition and contract for the service so that service consumers can discover and invoke them. Service usage also introduces additional management overhead in an SOA that is over and above the traditional requirements common in a typical IT management scenario. Examples of such usage requirements are billing, metering, SLA compliance, and tracking the relationships between the business processes, the services, and their associated IT infrastructure. The SOA runtime infrastructure is operational at this point with services, business processes, and servers all being deployed. Figure 6-16 depicts how the management and monitoring of the IT infrastructure needs to be aligned to the business services and what kind of actions need to be taken to mitigate the risks of failure.

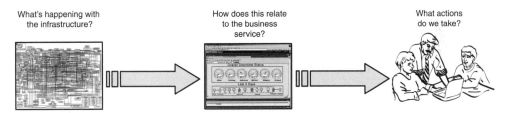

Figure 6-16   What service management and monitoring caters to

Service management also assists in transforming the typical "spaghetti" and unmanaged IT infrastructure into a set of modular components, applications, or suites. Service management then uses management and monitoring tools to provide definitive IT information from these modular components and enables the key linkage of the IT information to the business by providing targeted and role-based information views and channels to the business stakeholders, as shown in Figure 6-17.

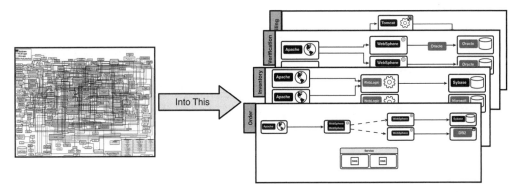

Figure 6-17   The objective is to transform the unmanaged IT infrastructure into a set of managed components and suites.

Service management and monitoring are applicable to most of the layers of the SOA architecture stack. Figure 6-18 depicts a simple example of an Account Opening business process, along with the various services, at each layer, that come into play to realize the business function. Figure 6-19 provides a sample illustration about what kind of service monitoring and management requirements are applicable across the various architectural stacks.

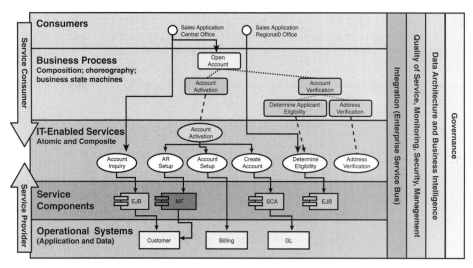

Figure 6-18   An example of services in an Account Opening process

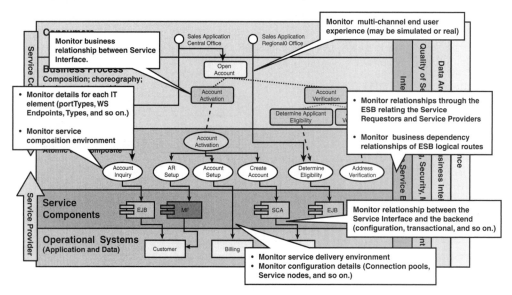

Figure 6-19   An example of service management and monitoring requirements in an Account Opening process

Figure 6-20 summarizes the commonly occuring multilayer service management requirements for a typical composite application.

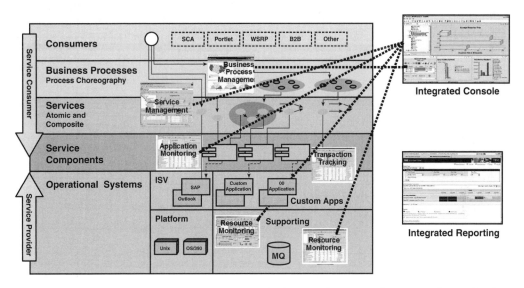

Figure 6-20   The typical management and monitoring requirements of a composite application

6.6.1 Products for Service Management

The monitoring and management of the executable business processes that run on an IBM
SOA platform are usually addressed by IBM WebSphere Business Monitor. The IBM Tivoli
line of products is specifically geared toward the management and monitoring of services
and its associated infrastructure and provides a complete diagnostic view into the SOA-based
composite applications. Figure 6-21 illustrates the most commonly used Tivoli products that
address the bulk of the requirements for management and monitoring.

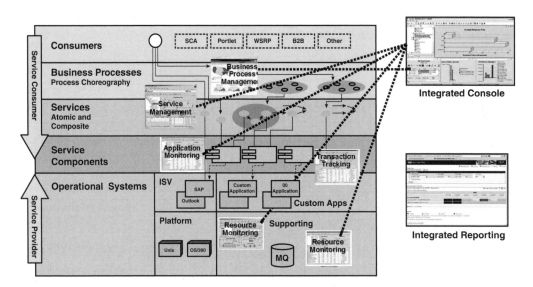

Figure 6-21   Recommended Tivoli suite of products along with WebSphere Business Monitor
are recommended for service management and monitoring on the IBM platform

IBM Tivoli exploits the brokering runtimes and the mediation frameworks provided by the
WebSphere runtime platform. Its management framework can display aggregated data, to
send event notifications to interested subscribers and to raise alerts for IT operations. Its
monitoring capabilities include not only IBM technologies but also a wide set of non-IBM
technologies. It is important to note that there are other infrastructure solutions that constitute an overall end-to-end service management and monitoring discipline. For example,
service security can be externalized from its business logic implementation and addressed at
the infrastructure level using products such as IBM Tivoli Access Manager (ITAM) and IBM
Tivoli Identify Manager (ITIM), while virtualization of service channels can be addressed by
IBM WebSphere Partner Gateway and so on. It is beyond the scope of this book to cover
every single aspect of service management and monitoring, and therefore this section discusses only WebSphere Business Monitor and the IBM Tivoli Composite Application
Management (ITCAM) product suite. A list of useful links is provided in the "References"
section for products that have not been addressed in this chapter. There you will find more
detailed information about ITAM, ITIM, IBM WebSphere DataPower Appliances, and IBM
WebSphere Partner Gateway.

6.6.1.1 IBM WebSphere Business Monitor

IBM WebSphere Business Monitor focuses on the management of the executable business
processes by measuring the defined business-level KPIs and the *actual* performance of every
instance of a monitored business process. It thus provides the executive and technical
people, who responsible for the operation of specific processes, with accurate information
about how the process is executing. IBM WebSphere Business Monitor enables users to view

dashboards to analyze how their processes are working, to track individual items, and to identify bottlenecks. It can also measure, in real time, the business metrics and measures that are defined during the design time in the IBM WebSphere Business Modeler.

A key capability of IBM WebSphere Business Monitor is the capability to take real-time data and load it back into the Business Modeler (WBM) for a more accurate representation of the existing process, thereby permitting better simulation and analysis and resulting in refined processes that usually have a high degree of confidence to meet their projected performance goals. For further information, refer to the "References" section.

6.6.1.2 ITCAM for SOA

IBM Tivoli Composite Application Manager (ITCAM) for SOA supports Web Services deployed across the most commonly used SOA and Web Services platforms starting with, but not restricted to, WAS, BEA WebLogic, and Microsoft .NET. ITCAM for SOA also provides monitoring and management for enterprise service buses (ESBs), including WebSphere ESB, WebSphere DataPower SOA Appliances, and WebSphere Message Broker. It allows architects, developers, and testers (early lifecycle users) to view service relationships, patterns for incoming requests, and detailed request data. It has built-in and extensible automation workflows and alerts to actively manage service requests by selectively rejecting some incoming requests or provisioning additional servers during periods of heavy load. ITCAM for SOA has a seamless bidirectional integration with WSRR (for example, furthering information to WSRR based on performance metrics of services). For further information, refer to the "References" section.

6.6.1.3 ITCAM for WebSphere, J2EE, and Web Resources

Monitoring of the application servers, which are the containers for the deployed SOA-based applications, is a crucial aspect of SOA management. ITCAM for Web Resources helps in maintaining the availability and performance of WebSphere applications. It provides the operational monitoring for the application server and the applications that are running. ITCAM for WebSphere and J2EE provide drill-down diagnostics of J2EE performance problems and include sophisticated composite transaction tracing that includes WebSphere MQ-based middleware infrastructure and backend mainframe systems such as CICS applications and IMS databases. Memory-leak detection and customizable performance analysis and reporting are some of the other basic features of ITCAM for WebSphere and J2EE. For further information, refer to the "References" section.

6.6.1.4 ITCAM for Response Time Tracking

ITCAM for Response Time Tracking (RTT) proactively recognizes and isolates transaction performance problems using robotic and real-time techniques and visualizes the transaction's path through the application systems, including response time contributions of each step. It supports SLA management by directly sending response time data to other infrastructure components that collate the information and make it available for representation on targeted information dashboards. Typically in a complex web application environment, it takes too long to identify and isolate performance bottlenecks. ITCAM for RTT enables you to quickly identify where and in which component the bottleneck or failure occurred.

It uses a graphical topology for such fast resolution and recovery. For further information, refer to the "References" section. For the end user response time portion, ITCAM for RTT provides enhanced end-user monitoring in an integrated solution with the Tivoli Enterprise Portal.

6.6.1.5 IBM Tivoli OMEGAMON XE for Messaging

IBM Tivoli OMEGAMON XE for Messaging provides the monitoring and management for the WebSphere MQ and Message Broker environments.

In an SOA infrastructure, the management of the supporting middleware might include the following:

- Understanding the health of the infrastructure that supports the services
- Correlating problems in the services to infrastructure issues such as a queue filling up or an exhausted thread pool

The IBM Tivoli Monitoring and OMEGAON XE family of products provide the base resource monitoring required for the environment, including the operating systems, databases, applications, and z/OS resources. This family of products work with the ITCAM product suite by providing integrated views in a portal environment using the IBM Tivoli Enterprise Portal.

The products work harmoniously in correctly configuring and deploying the WebSphere-based middleware stack, detecting and repairing problems as they happen, and emit alerts to imminent concerns. They also provide key IBM WebSphere MQ and Message Broker metrics for real-time and historical data analysis. This provides the base resource monitoring required for services and its associated information flowing through the various layers of the IT infrastructure. For further information, refer to the "References" section.

6.6.2 The Execution

SOA-based applications built in conformance with the SOA Solution Stack have constituent elements in most of the architectural layers. The business processes, the services, the applications that provide the service implementation, along with the entire IT infrastructure consisting of operational systems, integration middleware, security, quality of service (QoS), and the database systems require some form of management and runtime monitoring. The products and tools discussed in the preceding section all need to work together harmoniously to provide an end-to-end management of monitoring of an enterprise SOA. The products all work seamlessly together, and integration between them has been repeatedly and successfully executed in customer environments. Although the configuration and administration of the products is beyond the scope of this book, the key point to acknowledge is that these products have been developed with integration across the SOA Solution Stack as a salient feature.

A problem might arise in the business process usually either in the form of a failed process step or a scenario in which an unexpected amount of time is taken for the response. This problem is captured in the IBM WebSphere Business Monitor database, and after internal processing an alert or an event is sent. The event follows a specific format (for example, the

Common Event Infrastructure) and propagates through the enterprise service bus. A problem might also be detected by ITCAM for SOA when the performance threshold of a specific service is triggered. An alert or an event is sent out in such cases. The event is provided in the IBM Tivoli Enterprise Portal, so it can be displayed in context of the monitoring of the ITCAM and OMEGAMON monitoring products. It can also be forwarded to IBM Tivoli Enterprise Console or Netcool/OMNIbus, and root cause analysis may be performed. The collective results of the analysis can be processed for SLAs in products such as IBM Tivoli Service Level Advisor (TSLA) or can be forwarded on to IBM Tivoli Business Systems Manager for display in the business context. Whereas the alerts help in detecting a warning or a failure before it becomes a problem, the dashboards provide IT and business information that help in management by exceptions.

Figure 6-22 summarizes the integrated approach to the realization of SOA management and monitoring requirements.

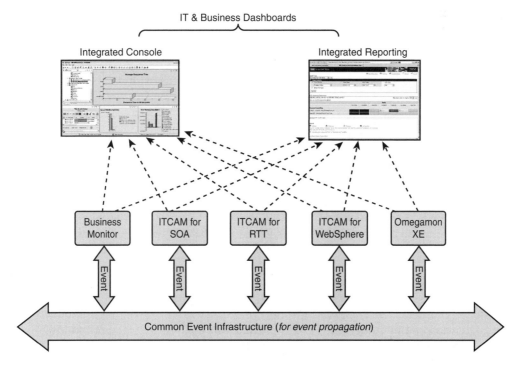

Figure 6-22   Integrated approach to realizing the SOA management and monitoring requirements

Refer to the "References" section for further information about TSLA and TEC.

6.7 The SOA Programming Model

A.6.7

The SOA programming model is an effort to mitigate the increasing difficulty of programmers and nonprogrammers to master the increasing proliferation of software technologies, best practices, tools, and platforms available today to enable business and IT transformations based on SOA principles, techniques, and best practices. The SOA programming model can be thought of as the culmination of the best practices that have been harnessed over the decades of the maturity of the software development discipline. It combines tools, techniques, and best practices into two specifications: the Service Component Architecture (SCA) and the Service Data Object (SDO).

Jointly developed by BEA, Oracle, Sun, IBM, RogueWave, Iona, SAP, and other leading companies, the emerging standards of SCA and SDO make it easy to build composite applications in a consistent manner. SCA provides developers with a single programming model for using services, and SDO provides them with a single programming model for representing and using data sources. This standardization is what makes the new SOA programming model, based on SCA and SDO, a much easier and simpler framework on which to develop SOA-based applications and ecosystems.

6.7.1 Service Component Architecture

In the early days of Web Services, Simple Object Access Protocol (SOAP) was the only protocol that was used to invoke a remote service with an XML envelope. With SOAP, although the applications were shielded from accessing the component's implementation and were invoked at runtime by the SOAP infrastructure, the applications not only knew about the component's interface at build time but also knew about the component's access method at build time (through SOAP/HTTP). SCA is a set of specifications geared toward developing even more flexible and dynamic SOA-based applications in which the SCA framework would shield the applications from both the component's internal implementation and the access method.

This section briefly introduces the SCA; a detailed treatment of the subject is beyond the scope of this book.

The SCA specification comprises four parts:

- **The assembly model**—Describes how to define composite SOA applications.
- **The client implementation specifications**—Defines how to implement SCA in different languages (for example, Java, C++, PHP).
- **Binding specifications**—Defines how to use the various access methods (for example, Web Services, JMS, RMI-IIOP, REST).
- **Policy framework**—Defines how to add security, transactions, conversations, reliable messaging, and so on in a declarative manner.

Let's now discuss the building blocks of SCA. At the lowest level, there are six SCA elements, as follows:

- **Service**—Represents an entry point into the SCA component or a composite.
- **Reference**—Represents a pointer to a service provided by something else outside the scope of the given SCA component.
- **Interface binding**—Represents two things: an interface and a binding. An interface is an external declaration of the service represented as a Java interface, a WSDL port type, a BPEL partner link, a C++ class, and so on. The binding defines the access method (SOAP/HTTP, JMS, RMI/IIOP, SCA, and so on). An interface binding may be attached to a service or a reference.
- **Property**—Represents a {type,value} pair that might be used to define some specific characteristics of a component.
- **Implementation type**—Defines the type of implementation code for a given SCA component that is used for coding the business logic. Example implementation types include state machines, human tasks, Java code, and so on.
- **Wire**—Represents the mechanism of how two components may be connected to each other. Usually a reference of one component is connected to a service exposed by another component.

An SCA component may expose one or more services, may use one or more references, may have one or more properties defining some specific characteristics, and may be connected to one or more components using SCA wiring. Figure 6-23 shows the building blocks of SCA.

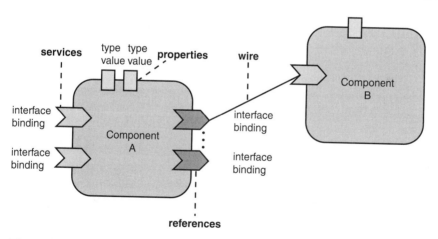

Figure 6-23 Building blocks of SCA

The building blocks of SCA can be combined and assembled together to create composite applications. A composite application can be thought of as a composition of related SCA components that collectively provide a coarse-grained business function. A composite may contain certain components that might be required only for the internal implementation of the composite and whose interfaces might not be required outside the scope of the composite in context. A composite may expose one or more composite services or composite references and may possess multiple composite properties. Figure 6-24 illustrates such an example.

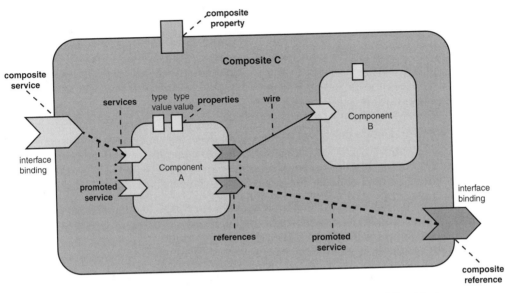

Figure 6-24   An example of a composite application built using SCA building blocks

In Figure 6-24, component B does not have any services or references exposed as a part of the composite. This illustration shows that there can be components used just for the internal implementation of the composite and thus not required to expose services and or references.

Bindings, as described previously, describe the access mechanism for a service. SCA provides a declarative and open specification for bindings. This specification means that not only can the currently supported SCA bindings (WSDL, JMS, JCA, and EJB) be represented in a declarative manner, but also that new bindings can be created.

Policies in SCA can be established in a single declarative manner. Examples of policies include *digital signing of all traffic on the wire, documenting the QoS requirements for a service component, and so on.*

SCA work is now being turned over to OASIS and is being maintained by the Open Composite Service Architecture (Open CSA) group. For the detailed specification of SCA, refer to the "References" section.

6.7.2 Service Data Objects

Service Data Objects (SDO) is a specification for a programming model that unifies data programming across data source types; provides robust support for common application patterns; and enables applications, tools, and frameworks to more easily query, view, bind, update, and introspect data. Refer to the "References" section for the entire SDO specifications. Thus, SDO assists in standardizing on a unified technique for data access to heterogeneous data sources, simplifying the mechanism of decoupling the application code from the data access logic. The unified data access relieves the developer from having to learn access mechanisms to multiple data sources and hence reduces the complexity of SOA programming. This simplification, in turn, has a positive effect in that it decreases the development time of applications that have a federated data dependency.

A.6.8

In typical web-based applications, it is a common requirement to retrieve some data in a transaction and then in a new transaction submit the updated data for persistence. SDO implements the disconnected data-usage pattern wherein it uses the optimistic concurrency semantics data-access pattern to provide an efficient concurrency mechanism to interact with the data, thereby simulating closely the typical business-level semantics of web application usage.

Instead of leaving the development of tools and frameworks for data access and manipulation in the hands of implementers, the specification provides inherent support for tools and frameworks for uniform access of data across heterogeneous sources. In particular, it provides a meta-data API framework that allows introspection of data, including data types, relationships, and constraints. This framework enables the development of generic tools around meta-data.

The rest of the section discusses the architectural premise behind SDO.

6.7.2.1 The SDO Architecture

Discussing SDO architecture in detail enables a better understanding of the "magic" behind realizing the promise of SDO—providing a unified data access technique to access all data sources in a standardized manner. Figure 6-25 presents a simple schematic of the SDO architecture.

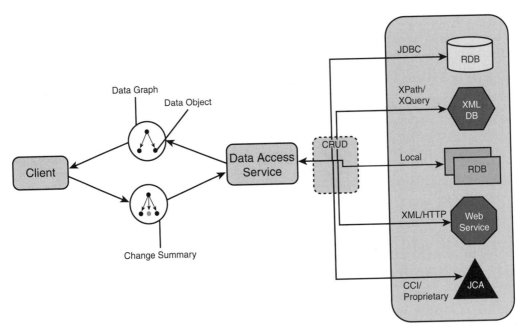

Figure 6-25 A simplistic representation of the SDO architecture

Three essential components of the SDO architecture are data objects, data graphs, and data access service, which together with the meta-data API complete the SDO circle:

- **Data object**—An object-oriented representation of the actual data. It encapsulates the data attributes represented by primitive values, references to other data objects, and a reference to its own meta-data.
- **Data graph**—A conceptual representation of a unit of data that may be transferred between the various tiers in an application. An example is an *Order* data object that contains a list of *OrderLineItem* data objects. A data graph can contain the Order, the list of OrderLineItem, along with their relationships. It also contains a Change Summary that records all changes to data, including all new, changed, or updated data objects.
- **Data access service**—The only mechanism for clients to interact with the different types of data sources. It implements the data access object (DAO) design pattern, and it produces data graphs to be handed over to the invoking client. It also uses the "Change Summary" information in the data graphs that are sent by the client and applies those changes back to the data source. Refer to the "References" section for further details about the DAO pattern.
- **Meta-data**—Represents the data about the data objects (that is, its data types, relationships with other data objects, and its constraints). The meta-data framework provides a lightweight API that enables the development of generic tools and frameworks for data introspection.

6.8 Architecture and Design Considerations

SOA, as perceived by a software architect, is an architectural style that supports the design and implementation of flexible, reusable, and dynamic applications. Any industry-proven architecture is almost always backed by a set of best practices, a subset of which is usually wrapped into architecture and design patterns. Their genesis lies in the lessons learned from successful and failed approaches and guidelines followed in projects. (The repeated and proven successful solutions to recurring problems are published as patterns, whereas the ones that have been experienced to be recipes for failures are published as antipatterns.)

With SOA projects becoming more and more pervasive as the de facto architectural style and approach to designing and implementing mid-range to complex applications and systems, new patterns and antipatterns are being continuously discovered and the existing ones refined. Because SOA is built on top of object-orientation (OO) and component-based development techniques, the prevalent patterns and antipatterns in SOA, if analyzed a little carefully, will reveal to be a composition of multiple OO design patterns and antipatterns, respectively.

The rest of this section briefly summarizes some of the SOA patterns and antipatterns worthy of consideration while embarking on a serious SOA.

6.8.1 SOA Patterns

As stated earlier, SOA patterns are higher-end patterns that are usually developed by an optimal composition of existing OO design patterns in such a way that is increases the probability of using the resultant composite pattern to solve recurring problem domains in SOA.

An overview of some of the well-established patterns is provided in this section.

6.8.1.1 Remote Service Strategy Pattern

A service definition describes the syntax and semantics of a service. The service definition can be implemented by multiple service providers, which although are contracted to provide the same business functionality might provide different QoS for the services or may vary in their billing and metering contracts. For the service consumer, there needs to be a mechanism for changing the service provider with minimal consequence to IT implementation or business functionality. This pattern introduces a service broker that will have the intelligence to introspect the consumer requirements, from the service request, and route the request to the best-fit service provider. The service consumer knows only about the existence of the service broker and is unaware of which service provider provides the service at runtime. This pattern is built on the premise of the *Strategy* design pattern; see the "References" section for further detail about the Strategy pattern. Figure 6-26 summarizes how this service is used.

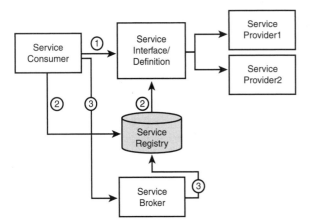

Figure 6-26   The building blocks for the Remote Service Strategy pattern

This pattern provides dynamic reconfiguration rather than hard-coding between the consumer and provider.

6.8.1.2 Service Adapter Pattern

Also known as the service wrapper, the Service Adapter pattern allows high-value business functionality present in traditional and legacy systems to participate in an SOA. Typically, we find that legacy systems comprised of interfaces, data attributes, and invocation protocols that are either proprietary or nonconformant to open standards. A service is usually business aligned, and when defined using a top-down business-driven approach does not usually take into account how they are implemented. A service definition is based on open standards and uses standard protocols for communication. When we need to address the implementation of a service, the existing legacy applications must be assessed to determine whether any existing functionality may be leveraged to implement the business logic for the service. The service adapter is used to hide the implementation details of transforming the standards-based service semantics into the data and function calls for the legacy application. Figure 6-27 summarizes the pattern's building blocks.

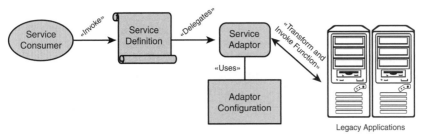

Figure 6-27   The building blocks for the Service Adapter pattern

Also note that although we mention introspecting legacy systems to identify existing functionality that may be leveraged for service implementation, the same is equally applicable to packaged application implementations such as Siebel, SAP modules, and so on, that may be present in the enterprise IT portfolio and capable of being leveraged to take part in an SOA.

6.8.1.3 Virtual Service Provider Pattern

The Virtual Service Provider pattern might be used in situations in which you do not implement services on your own but instead rely on services provided by other service providers (and these services from external service providers might not yet be available for consumption). In such cases, a virtual provider may be created by specifying the service needed and assuming that it is provided by some service provider. The crux of this pattern is summarized in the following steps:

1. Create the provider by using a proxy to communicate with the legacy system while using an adapter to transform the protocol used to one that has been specified in the service description.

2. Encapsulate the proxy and adapter in a façade. This façade addresses the issue that arises from a random increase in the number of adapters to accommodate new systems that use different protocols and hence may need to be transformed in the future.

3. Use Rule Objects for routing and policies, and use a special type of façade to encapsulate the policy-based routing and mediation.

Figure 6-28 summarizes this pattern's building blocks.

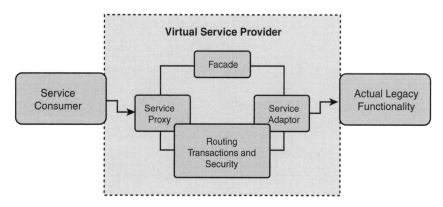

Figure 6-28   Building blocks for the Virtual Service Provider pattern

6.8.1.4 Enterprise Service Bus Pattern

The Enterprise Service Bus (ESB) pattern assists in the provisioning of a common infrastructure that provide the capabilities of transformation, routing, and mediation between disparate channels, service consumers, and service providers. The common infrastructure created also acts as a single point of control to apply service management, security, monitoring, and instrumentation to the constituents of the SOA. The ESB pattern is a confluence of multiple patterns, such as the Virtual Service Provider, Remote Strategy, Service Adaptor, and so on, and how they can work together to create a middleware infrastructure layer that enables robust and efficient service interactions.

Figure 6-29 summarizes the high-level schematic of the ESB pattern.

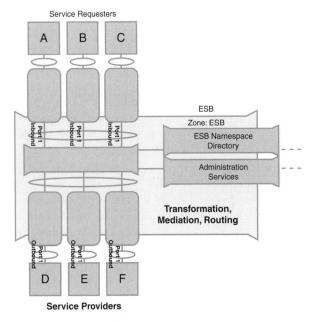

Figure 6-29   Logical view of the simplest ESB model

For a detailed treatment of the ESB pattern, refer to the "References" section.

This section discussed the Remote Strategy, Service Adapter, Virtual Service Provider, and the ESB patterns.

A.6.9

6.8.2 SOA Antipatterns

Just as patterns are obvious choices to obtain repeated success, antipatterns identify a specific type of usage of architectural and design guidelines and practices that when practiced become clear recipes for failure. As developers and architects seek to fully understand SOA

A.6.10

best practices, it is just as important to be aware of the common pitfalls of SOA adoption. This section lists the most common SOA antipatterns and pitfalls to avoid and warns of a few caveats for your SOA adoption:

- Beware of vendor-proprietary service offerings. Do not get locked into SOA vendor offerings that are proprietary in nature; you could lose the interoperability and flexibility benefits of a true SOA.
- Seek stability when using open standards. The latest open standard specification in the industry is not always the most stable; therefore, it might not be mature enough for adoption.
- Carefully assess your legacy modernization approach. Take a holistic view of the enterprise when choosing particular legacy systems for modernization. Silo approaches for SOA transition might create redundancy.
- Avoid "waterfall" development and lack of service versioning. An SOA transition should be iterative in nature. A service lifecycle management should possess the capability to maintain multiple versions of a service.
- Know the technical constraints of your legacy system. Consider all the technology limitations of a legacy system before jumping ahead into a legacy-modernization effort.
- Don't equate SOA with Web Services. Acknowledge the difference between SOA, which is an architectural style, and Web Services, which is a set of standards for SOA implementation.
- Avoid the silo approach to service creation and ownership. Understand the paradigm shift between traditional application development and an SOA-based development. Service lifecycle management, along with service ownership, should factor in organization structure and stakeholder commitments.
- Steer away from the use of fine-grained services. A service is a higher-level abstraction than are fine-grained APIs. Services should be coarse-grained and at the right level of granularity to be business aligned.
- Avoid point-to-point invocation. Make an SOA-based ecosystem manageable and loosely coupled. Bring in a mediation layer that not only handles service discovery and invocation but also neutralizes the underlying technical heterogeneity between different SOA implementations.
- Avoid lack of adherence to standards. Adopt stable and proven industry-specific standards. This approach will bring in interoperability benefits to your SOA.
- Use redundant data stores. Concentrate on a data-consolidation strategy. Mask the data redundancy by creating a virtualized data service.
- Stay away from using a "Big Bang" approach. For complex SOA transformation efforts, forget a Big Bang approach to the finish line. Acknowledge and respect that a smooth SOA transformation with minimal risks is best achieved by adopting an iterative approach.
- Allocate service ownership. Do not orphan a service, and ensure that there is a business owner to fund the service's lifecycle. This ownership enables someone to be responsible for maintaining the nonfunctional characteristics of your services.

- Institute SOA governance. Empower a governance body to manage the entire service lifecycle.

The list of common pitfalls to avoid in SOA (a.k.a. antipatterns) will get more refined and updated as enterprises embark on their incremental adoption of SOA.

6.9 Conclusion

Up until now, we have discussed SOA governance, the SOA lifecycle, a logical view of an SOA reference architecture, and the methodological approach to SOA. This chapter discussed how a team of SOA architects, designers, and developers, aided with the right tools and products, can design and implement an entire SOA-based application. This chapter also introduced the IBM SOA products and tools commonly used during each phase of the MADM cycle, and it illustrated how they work together toward a complete SOA design and implementation. This chapter also introduced an SOA programming model based on SCA and SDO, and concluded with a discussion about some of the common patterns and antipatterns related to SOA.

6.10 Links to developerWorks Articles

A.6.1 Download the IBM RUP for Service Modeling and Architecture V2.4 plug-in for IBM Rational Method Composer. www.ibm.com/developerworks/rational/downloads/06/rmc_soma/

A.6.2 Haumer, P. *IBM Rational Method Composer: Part 1: Key Concepts.* IBM developerWorks, December 2005. www.ibm.com/developerworks/rational/library/dec05/haumer/.

A.6.3 Portier, B., Ackerman, L. *Design SOA services with Rational Software Architect, Part 1: Getting started with requirements, process, and modeling* (a four-part series). IBM developerWorks, September 2006. www.ibm.com/developerworks/rational/education/dw-r-soaservices1/index.html?S_TACT=105AGX15&S_CMP=EDU.

A.6.4 Adams, G. et al. *A guided tour of WebSphere Integration Developer—Part 1.* IBM developerWorks, February 2006. www.ibm.com/developerworks/websphere/techjournal/0602_gregory/0602_gregory.html.

A.6.5 Kulhanek, W., Serna, C. *WebSphere Process Server: IBM's new foundation for SOA.* IBM developerWorks, September 2005. www.ibm.com/developerworks/websphere/library/techarticles/0509_kulhanek/0509_kulhanek.html.

A.6.6 McKee, B. et al. *Introducing IBM WebSphere Service Registry and Repository, Part 1.* IBM developerWorks, September 2006. www.ibm.com/developerworks/websphere/library/techarticles/0609_mckee/0609_mckee.html.

A.6.7 Ferguson, D., Stockton, M. *SOA programming model for implementing Web services, Part 1: Introduction to the IBM SOA programming model.* IBM developerWorks, June 2005. www.ibm.com/developerworks/webservices/library/ws-soa-progmodel/.

A.6.8 Portier, B., Budinsky, F. *Introduction to Service Data Objects.* IBM developerWorks, September 2004. www.ibm.com/developerworks/java/library/j-sdo/.

A.6.9 Arsanjani, A. *Toward a pattern language for Service-Oriented Architecture and Integration, Part 1: Build a service eco-system.* IBM developerWorks, July 2005. www.ibm.com/developer-works/webservices/library/ws-soa-soi/.

A.6.10 Mitra, T. *Avoiding common pitfalls in SOA adoption.* IBM developerWorks, June 2006. www-128.ibm.com/developerworks/library/ar-soapit/.

6.11 References

The complete set of features of IBM Rational RequisitePro can be obtained at ftp://ftp.software.ibm.com/software/rational/web/datasheets/version6/reqpro.pdf.

Download a trial version of IBM WebSphere Business Modeler from www.ibm.com/developerworks/downloads/ws/wbimod/?S_TACT=105AGX28&S_CMP=TRIALS&st=3&sp=20.

A dedicated space in IBM developerWorks for a consolidated source of information on IBM Rational Software Architect: www.ibm.com/developerworks/rational/products/rsa/.

Kahm, L. et al. IBM redbook *Using WebSphere Studio Asset Analyzer.* www.redbooks.ibm.com/abstracts/SG246065.html?Open.

Official site in IBM to obtain more information about CBM: www-935.ibm.com/services/us/igs/cbm/html/bizmodel.html.

Parkin, S. IBM white paper on *Rapid Java and J2EE Development with IBM Rational Developer.* ftp://ftp.software.ibm.com/software/rational/web/whitepapers/wp-radrwd-medres.pdf.

Wahli, U. et al. IBM redbook on *Building SOA Solutions Using the Rational SDP,* April 2007. www.redbooks.ibm.com/abstracts/sg247356.html?Open.

The complete set of features of IBM WebSphere Portal Server can be obtained from www-306.ibm.com/software/genservers/portal/features/.

Single consolidated site to browse all the Tivoli Products by category: www-306.ibm.com/software/sw-bycategory/subcategory/SWK10.html.

Find out more details about IBM Tivoli Identity Manager at www-306.ibm.com/software/tivoli/products/identity-mgr-express/.

A good starting point to browser information regarding IBM Tivoli Access Manager for Business Integration: www-306.ibm.com/software/tivoli/products/access-mgr-bus-integration/.

Get all information about IBM WebSphere DataPower SOA Appliances:
www-306.ibm.com/software/integration/datapower/index.html?S_TACT=102A9W01&S_CMP=campaign.

Information about IBM WebSphere Partner Gateway is available at
www-306.ibm.com/software/integration/wspartnergateway/.

Visit the IBM site for further information about IBM WebSphere Business Monitor:
www-306.ibm.com/software/integration/wbimonitor/index.html?S_TACT=102A9W01&S_CMP=campaign.

Detailed information about IBM Tivoli Composite Application Manager for SOA is available at www-306.ibm.com/software/tivoli/products/composite-application-mgr-soa/.

Detailed information about IBM Tivoli Composite Application Manager for WebSphere is available at www-306.ibm.com/software/tivoli/products/composite-application-mgr-basic-websphere/.

Detailed information about IBM Tivoli Composite Application Manager for Response Time Tracking (RTT) is available at www-306.ibm.com/software/tivoli/products/composite-application-mgr-response-time/features.html?S_CMP=rnav.

Detailed information about IBM Tivoli Monitoring for Business Integration is available at www-306.ibm.com/software/tivoli/products/monitor-integration/.

Learn about IBM Tivoli Service Level Advisor (TSLA) at www-306.ibm.com/software/tivoli/products/service-level-advisor/.

Learn about IBM Tivoli Enterprise Console at www-306.ibm.com/software/tivoli/products/enterprise-console/.

The Service Component Architecture (SCA) specification is available at www.osoa.org/display/Main/Service+Component+Architecture+Specifications.

The Service Data Object (SDO) specification is available at www.osoa.org/display/Main/Service+Data+Objects+Specifications.

The Data Access Object (DAO) design pattern is available at http://java.sun.com/blueprints/corej2eepatterns/Patterns/DataAccessObject.html.

Gamma, E. et al. *Design Patterns: Elements of Reusable Object-Oriented Software* (Addison-Wesley, 1994).

Adams, J. et al. An IBM redbook on *Patterns: Implementing an SOA Using an Enterprise Service Bus,* July 2004. www.redbooks.ibm.com/abstracts/SG246346.html.

Chapter 7

Information Services

In Chapter 6, "Realization of Services," we discussed the realization of services using methods and tools commonly available today and the practical steps that should be considered when building the most robust, composable, and reusable services possible. In this chapter, we move on to consider a specific class of services, those that deliver information.

So often we hear this cry for help: "We are surrounded by a sea of data but cannot get the information needed to run our business." But, how can SOA provide a best-fit solution? Many detractors have argued that SOA is too heavily focused on application function and not enough on business data or information in enterprise systems.

The volume of data that enterprise systems must handle is expanding faster than ever, and with so many disparate sources—from mainframe databases, to distributed file systems, to web pages, Really Simple Syndication (RSS) feeds, and many more—the actual quality of data available to managers and professionals is insufficient to support the adoption of SOA for many business initiatives.

What is required to bring the data dimension into SOA thinking so that both business logic and business data contribute as equal partners? This chapter begins to answer this important question.

7.1 Data or Information Services

First, we must address some issues that confuse many as they design and deploy service-oriented architectures. These issues concern the essence of the class of services we discuss. Are they data services or information services, and is it true that all services deliver data? The answers to these questions are important, as explained later in this chapter, and yet they are often lost in discussions about SOAs.

Do services deliver data or do they deliver information? This is not a trivial question, as some might presume. To academics, a clear distinction depends on the context within which data is used. Data becomes information when the context provides meaning. To marketers, the distinction depends on the value of the data delivered to the client or consumer. Often, the intention is not made clear, and the two labels are used interchangeably.

First, in realizing an SOA, we prefer to think about services that deliver data and not information. The reason for this preference is that SOA principles guide us to minimize coupling between consumers and providers and to promote reuse of services (as discussed later in this chapter). The immediate consequence is that from the service provider perspective, there must be no presumption about the *context* within which consumers may expect to use data delivered or the value of any service response to consumers. Services provide data and not information by this line of thought. The opposing argument is that consumers provide a context for service invocation and that, once received, response data is always ascribed value and becomes information. Different consumers ascribe different value to the data delivered but, from the consumer perspective, information has been received. Paradoxically, the same data can be interpreted in different ways by different consumers, but that is another topic for later consideration.

Second, it isn't true that all services deliver data, although most do. Some services accept data encapsulated in a service request but do not deliver any data in response. Such services might, for example, accept business values for entry into an audit journal or archive without acknowledgment. Most services, however, accept business values for handling in some way and then deliver derived values in response.

How and why is the category of "information services" considered to be different from business partner services, infrastructure services, or any other category of services? This is the question we address in the rest of this chapter.

7.2 Data, SOA, and Loose Coupling

In the book *SOA Compass* (Bieberstein et al.), the concept of loose coupling is introduced as it is applied in SOAs. Multiple dimensions, including time, location, protocol, format, language, and platform must be considered to provide loose coupling between service consumers and providers in an SOA (see Figure 7-1).

A.7.1

When you allow coupling between consumers and providers, you build in unwelcome dependencies and introduce complexity and fragility into an SOA. This is now the basis for a well-accepted SOA principle.

Each of these coupling dimensions applies equally well to data services and, by implication, an additional consideration is introduced. Service consumers must be isolated from timing, location, access protocol, data format, interface, platform, and language dependencies introduced by specific *data sources* in an SOA. This is extremely important and yet difficult to achieve.

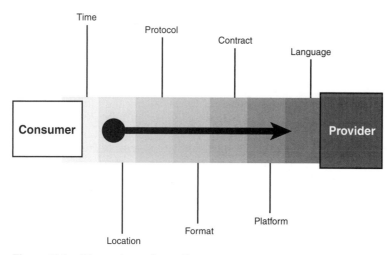

Figure 7-1   Dimensions of coupling

In the majority of enterprise SOA deployments, the number and variety of data sources that must be incorporated is large and complex. Similarly, the number of service interfaces and providers is also large, and so the critical issue is how best to provide data that can come from multiple sources in the most coherent and flexible manner. In Figure 7-2, this issue is illustrated in its generic form.

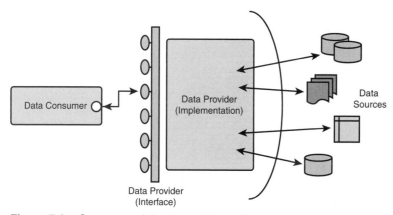

Figure 7-2   Consumer–data source decoupling

The service consumer is bound only to the contract offered by the provider in its service interface description. It is not bound to the service provider logic or to the sources of data that may or may not be accessed to provide the service response. This implies that service provider logic may be replaced at any time and that data sources may also be changed at any time without service consumers being made aware of those changes. In practice, this is difficult to achieve unless designers, implementers, and operators of the several components are physically different people acting under well-formed governance rules and management policies.

7.3 From Data Sources to Consumers

Data sources as widely varied as spreadsheets and web documents, message queues and RSS feeds, and simple files and relational databases coupled with data held in enterprise content management systems, e-mail, and other servers are available to consumers through service interfaces. It's a simple matter of programming to provide the necessary access, cleansing, consolidation, transformation, enrichment, and presentation of the data sources! In practice, this task may be overwhelmingly complex in enterprise SOA deployment projects without the appropriate knowledge, tools, and procedures.

A.7.2

With the advent of SOAs, there has been a strong focus on the identification, organization, composition, and reuse of business function; however, until recently, there has not been a corresponding focus on business data. Perhaps the same set of organizing principles applied to business functions can and should be applied to business data for a more complete and realistic picture.

What would it mean to add a layer of abstraction, a data layer, to the typical multilayered SOA illustrated in Figure 7-3? Certainly, the components that provide implementation for services in the component layer of an SOA depend on data sources that in most real enterprise systems are many and varied in nature.

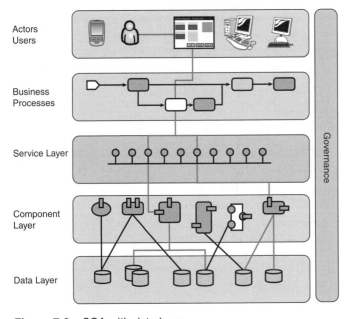

Figure 7-3   SOA with data layer

First, it implies an extension to the already healthy separation of concerns between users, business processes, services, components, and now data sources. Some of the same organizing principles apply to the data layer that apply to the other layers, and these often translate into decisions made to exploit new types of middleware infrastructure technology for business advantage.

Second, to add a data layer would imply the collaboration of a wider community of both business and technical professionals in the development of an SOA vision and deployment strategy. This more holistic involvement should result in an enterprise architecture that is better able to deliver organizational flexibility and responsiveness in the face of competition and a changing business climate.

For data to be a first-class citizen in the SOA world, a clear separation must exist between data consumers and data providers. This separation mirrors the principle that service consumers and providers must be distinct and separate in an SOA. Furthermore, this separation must be delineated by an interface, or contract, that both providers and consumers share (see Figure 7-4).

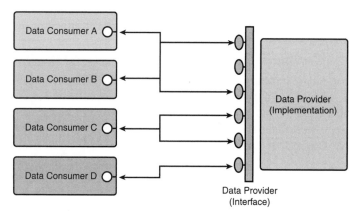

Figure 7-4   Data consumer–provider interactions

Given that this can be achieved, data consumers and providers must be loosely coupled. The benefit of loose coupling is that new data consumers can be added, and new or changed data provider implementations and sources can be introduced into an SOA without impact to existing deployments.

A data consumer may well be a business service or it may in turn be a data provider that meets the obligations of its contract. A data provider, on the other hand, must be encapsulated by its interface so that consumers are unaware of how data is being served. This implies that no matter whether data is being retrieved from persistent stores, such as relational database management systems (RDBMs), e-mail servers, RSS feeds, or enterprise messaging hubs, the obligations of the contract are being met.

The separation between the data provider interface and its many possible implementations is another critical dependency that must be met for data to be considered a first-class SOA citizen. The interfaces must also be published so that they are discoverable by potential data consumers; this separation supports reuse and flexibility in an SOA deployment. Each interface may then be considered a *virtualized data source* that can be composed with others to provide higher-value sources.

The application of the same principles to both services and data in an SOA leads to greater flexibility and reuse in the configuration of critical components (both programs and data), which in turn may lead to greater business value from existing and planned investments. That this application of principles is possible is fundamentally reassuring because it is the flow and the processing of the same business information that unites the service and data perspectives of an SOA.

Loose coupling of consumers and providers in an SOA proves to be one of the most liberating factors for consideration and one that is most often facilitated by middleware technologies. The numerous important dimensions of loose coupling shown in Figure 7-1 may be individually addressed using specific strategies. For example, data consumers and providers may be decoupled over time using asynchronous access, whereas indirection or brokering by an enterprise service bus (ESB) may be used to decouple any dependency upon location.

The use of industry-standard compliant middleware technologies can effectively decouple consumers and providers from protocol, format, platform, and language dependencies, but the remaining interface (or contract) dimension is extremely important for successful interaction in an SOA. It, too, should be standards based for maximal reuse, but it requires extremely careful design to avoid semantic anomalies and interface volatility.

7.4 Qualities of Data

The relationships between the elements of data provided by a service and the types of those elements are essential to the contract between data consumers and providers. These considerations are fundamentally the same for service and data provider interfaces because they focus on the flow of consistent sets of elements (business information) across architectural boundaries. However, there are other important considerations for data providers.

The qualities of data, such as the qualities of service, must be carefully defined to ensure success. Business professionals insist on "trusted" sources of data for inclusion in an SOA. The qualities of data implied by this trust are *provenance* (assurances about the origins and ownership of specific information), *completeness* (assurances about the presence or absence of specific information), *consistency* (assurances about information expressing real meaning within a specific business context), and *timeliness* (assurances about information being current with respect to a meaningful timeframe).

These qualities of data are by no means trivial when it comes to designing data provider implementations. In a typical enterprise scenario, there are hundreds of different data sources—some structured, some unstructured, some trusted, and others with doubtful provenance. Most are somewhat incomplete and inconsistent. Repeatable, automated procedures are required to improve the quality of this data if service-oriented business systems are to be successful.

A.7.3

Ensuring the quality of data delivered by a service is extremely important in an enterprise SOA. The qualities of data and the qualities of service—for example, availability, responsiveness, and throughput—must be considered together when assessing the overall suitability of an information service for the purpose intended.

The roadmap to successful inclusion of trusted reusable data sources and information services in an SOA starts with an understanding of existing data sources, the catalog of the data elements available, a profile of the actual data values present, and a clear definition of the rules by which the available data may be "cleansed" and extracted to become both consistent and complete.

Armed with this understanding, it is possible to design business rules and activities that may be composed into "data processes" for identifying those elements of data that are problematic and applying techniques to create data sources with higher qualities of data. The SOA data architect must have this understanding of existing data sources, an understanding of the business rules that guarantee consistency as well as an understanding of the available (middleware) technologies that may be deployed to provide needed infrastructure.

When an understanding of existing data sources has been captured and cleansing activities have been defined, it might be necessary to define merging, matching, transformation, and enrichment activities that convert source data elements into those needed to meet the obligations of a defined SOA data provider contract. Imagine these activities, and many more, on a virtual "palette" of possible activities that could be wired into data processes to deliver those obligations.

7.5 Data Processes

The processes that deliver data to meet specific information service or data provider contracts implement the virtualized data sources in an SOA context (see Figure 7-5). Such processes may be highly complex sequences of activities required to guarantee the provenance, completeness, consistency, and timeliness demanded. They may also conceivably be null when real data sources with the required qualities already exist.

Data processes may have relatively few access, matching, merging, or cleansing activities but be judged highly complex because they involve consolidating or federating data from many widely distributed data sources or involve processing of large volumes of data to produce a high-quality virtualized data source. Whether simple or highly complex, when data processes are made available as providers to SOA consumers, there is a new degree of freedom added to an SOA that integrates data as a first-class citizen.

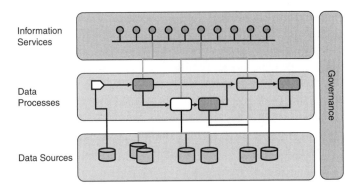

Figure 7-5   Information services and data processes

Figure 7-5 shows the lower layering in an expanded SOA. Information services are added to the service portfolio with well-formed published interfaces. The interfaces are implemented by data processes with business rules and activities that access and process data from a wide variety of different existing, industry standard, highly structured, and many other types of data sources.

Often, a significant difference exists between business information services and business logic services in real-world SOA scenarios. When the data provider implementation involves processing large volumes of data, there may be a significant time delay between service requests and the corresponding service responses. Compare this to the simplest business logic service request with its almost instantaneous response. In practice, a typical SOA has a wide spectrum of different service response time characteristics.

Many simpler information services that provide access to highly reusable data transformations and data consistency rules, for example, will often respond without significant delay. Information services of all types provide access "on demand" to high-quality trusted data for integration into a larger SOA fabric.

7.6 Data Service Provider Logic Patterns

In a typical SOA deployment, there is often a wide range of different data providers serving data to meet business needs. The implementation of those data providers will also be widely varied from simple Java programs to complex configurable middleware procedures. No matter how they are implemented, however, the value to the SOA stakeholders is that the data service provider logic has been captured in a highly reusable form and, with appropriate governance, that value is delivered every time it is reused.

A number of different logic patterns are often implemented in data service providers. These patterns cover the tasks commonly found in serving quality data to consumers, whether they be business partners, business process operational staff, business managers, or executives at their dashboards making strategic decisions.

7.6.1 Data Federation

The Data Federation pattern aims to efficiently join data from multiple heterogeneous sources, leaving the data in place, without creating data redundancy (see Sauter, Guenter et al., *Information service patterns, Part 1: Data federation pattern*). This pattern supports data operations against an integrated but transient (virtual) view where the real data is stored in multiple diverse sources. It implements the decoupling of consumers from data sources (location transparency), as illustrated in Figure 7-2.

With Data Federation, the consumer sees a single uniform interface to data required. The transparency of the data's stored location means consumers are not aware of where the real data is stored (see Figure 7-6). Decoupling consumers from the language or programming interfaces supported by specific data sources (invocation transparency) is also achieved by using this pattern as is decoupling from platform (stored format transparency) and networking dependencies (protocol transparency).

A.7.4

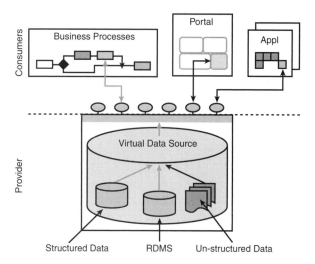

Figure 7-6 The Data Federation pattern

In this SOA context, a federation server may act as a service provider by dynamically collecting data required to satisfy a published service interface. The same federation server may also act as service consumer (not shown in Figure 7-6) by composing data from other virtual data sources to satisfy the same published service interface. The Data Federation pattern may be seen to be implementing reusable dynamic integration of data from disparate sources. This dynamic integration contributes significant value in SOA deployments.

7.6.2 Data Consolidation

Another popular pattern is commonly used to provide data integration in complex data usage scenarios. The Data Consolidation pattern is similar to Data Federation, in that it serves to collect data from multiple possibly heterogeneous data sources. In this case, however, the data collected is extracted, transformed, as required, and then loaded into a single persistent target data source (see Figure 7-7). The data service provider accesses this new data source to deliver the data according to an information service description.

When large amounts of data must be extracted to satisfy the service contract, this Data Consolidation pattern is often used in preference to the Data Federation pattern. When data must be extracted within a certain window of time to satisfy the *timeliness* quality of data, this pattern provides a valuable solution that could not necessarily be provided by other logic patterns (see Sauter, Guenter et al., *Information service patterns, Part 2: Data consolidation pattern*).

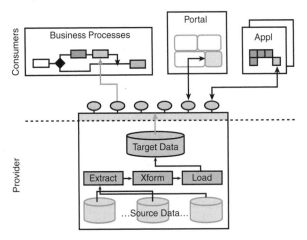

Figure 7-7   The Data Consolidation pattern

In general, this pattern allows for configurable extraction from data sources of many different kinds and processing of the data extracted in many different ways before loading in final form into the target data source. For example, data might be extracted from customer databases on different platforms to be consolidated with marketing campaign data to satisfy business development queries. The merging, matching, and filtering that must be routinely accomplished to provide such queries as a reusable service can be implemented using this pattern.

7.6.3 Data Cleansing

A variation of Data Consolidation is the Data Cleansing pattern, which focuses on meeting quality of data requirements for service consumers (see Figure 7-8). This pattern may be applied to large amounts of data or to individual records.

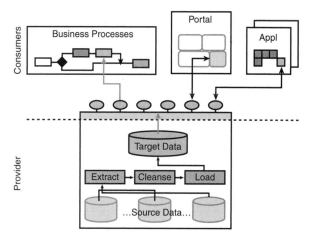

Figure 7-8   The Data Cleansing pattern

The essence of this pattern in an SOA context is the application of a set of cleansing rules to data extracted from relevant data sources to ensure *completeness* and *consistency* at the service interface. The rules may be relatively simple or extremely complex. Data must be correctly identified by type, values properly delineated and standardized, and relationships validated according to industry or enterprise standards.

A.7.6

Cleansing is often necessary when data sources are known to be incomplete or when specific inconsistencies must be detected and corrected. Sources external to an enterprise are not usually trusted, and data extracted from them must always be cleansed before use by consumers. By contrast, data originated within an enterprise would normally be cleansed upon entry into carefully controlled data sources. However, this ideal is extremely difficult to achieve and maintain in the real world.

The value of having standard cleansing procedures within an SOA available to all consumers as information services is enormous. With careful governance, this value can be realized every time those services are reused.

7.6.4 Master Data Management

Master data is the collection of enterprise-wide information describing key business entities. There are many different types of master data, such as facts and relationships among customers, employees, partners, and suppliers as well as details of hierarchies of products, items, materials, and bills of materials. Master data can also include facts and relationships of locations, entities, devices, and equipment. No matter what types of master data are important to an enterprise, the management of that data is essential.

Master data management (MDM) is a set of disciplines, strategies, technologies, and solutions used to create and maintain consistent, complete, contextual, and accurate business data for all stakeholders (users and applications) across and beyond the enterprise. A number of

A.7.7

different data logic patterns are in common use for MDM. These fall into three major categories (as in Sauter, Guenter et al., *Information service patterns, Part 4: Master Data Management Architecture pattern*):

- **Application Integration Patterns**
  - MDM Transaction Interception
  - MDM Publish / Subscribe
  - MDM Message-based Integration
- **Information Integration Patterns**
  - MDM Information Integration
  - MDM Information Synchronization
- **MDM System Deployment Patterns**
  - MDM Business Intelligence Analytical
  - MDM Data Warehouse
  - MDM Multiple System

Many of these patterns are available to consumers as information service interfaces in an SOA deployment, where they may be collaborative, operational, or analytical. Figure 7-9 shows the architectural approach for deployment of such MDM-related services.

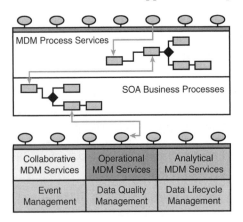

Figure 7-9   MDM patterns

Note that these data logic patterns for implementing MDM are the same whether deployed in an SOA or conventional enterprise architecture. For example, Figure 7-9 illustrates the way in which the operational style of MDM supports the consumption of master data by business processes to perform transactions. Also illustrated is the way in which master data may be leveraged by applications through MDM process services. These services provide control over master data creation, management, quality, and access. For example, as part of a process to add a new customer, a line of business (LOB) system consumes an MDM service to validate that this customer is a unique customer or one already represented in master data. The MDM service cleanses and standardizes the new customer information and performs matching logic against an MDM repository to determine whether the customer already exists within the LOB system or within the enterprise.

If it is determined that the customer is a new customer for that LOB, the LOB system could commit the new customer information to its transactional database. The MDM system would then have the new customer information in the MDM repository and in the LOB system. After the information has been successfully processed, operational MDM would support the integration and the synchronization of new master data with legacy systems, enterprise applications, and data repositories within the enterprise, and the exchange and synchronization of information with business partners.

Operational MDM is especially important in an SOA. MDM systems include libraries of common services on master data that other systems can call (for example, one centralized procedure that any application can call to query customer information, to adjust the price of a product, or to create a new supplier) to ensure information quality and consistency. MDM provides common services to support information-centric procedures across all applications.

MDM enables companies to realize internal efficiencies by reducing the cost and complexity of processes that use master data. It reduces manual translation and analysis to improve repeatability and speed to insight. In addition, MDM improves the ability to share, consolidate, and analyze business information quickly, both globally and regionally. It also makes it possible to assemble new, composite applications based on accurate master information and reusable business processes rapidly.

These are the most common data logic patterns implemented in information service providers. Note that whatever the pattern, the real value in an SOA is the accessibility and reusability of logic by consumers of all kinds through well-formed service interface contracts. This reuse avoids the cost and complexity of re-implementing the same patterns over and over again as new business challenges are met.

7.7 Composite Service Logic

As an enterprise service portfolio develops to include both business logic services and business information services, the opportunity arises for composition to realize new higher-order services, such as those required to implement a new business process. This composition realizes the value of an SOA by reusing investments that have already been made. Investments in data profiling, cleansing, federation, and consolidation are particularly valuable in this context. With appropriate governance (see Chapter 3, "SOA Governance"), the composition of services, including information services, delivers improved time to market and cost efficiency. Greater detail on how best to capitalize on this important aspect of SOA has been covered in Chapter 3, "SOA Governance."

7.8 Semantic Interoperability

A.7.8

There must be a common thread of understanding that enables integration of business logic with business information in an SOA. It might seem obvious to say that services must understand the data that they depend on, but when an SOA is assembled with a large number of moving "reusable" parts, that understanding must be captured reliably and at a high level. The emerging focus on capturing and managing meta-data attempts to achieve that higher level.

7.8.1 Common Semantics and Tools

Of course, meta-data in IT systems is not new. However, the marriage of SOA with data attempts to make explicit the identification, encoding, exploitation, and management of meta-data in middleware systems and supporting tools. Existing data sources may already contain rich meta-data (such as catalog information in relational databases), but some might need careful profiling and encoding of meta-data to fully describe the meaning of data content (transactional data, web page content, flat files, spreadsheets, e-mail, and so on).

By contrast, meta-data is also emerging in the form of semantics that result from an analysis of business domains and the common language that must be shared between business and technical communities as they collaborate to define SOA vision and deployment strategies. If services and data are to be strongly aligned with business goals, there must be a common understanding of key business entities, their relationships, constraints, and properties.

In an ideal world, the semantics of business domains would translate seamlessly into the meta-data needed:

- To define business operations as services
- To define elements of business information

In time, we may see a convergence upon this ideal, but in the meantime, new middleware products and tools are available to support meta-data in each of these areas.

For example, IBM Rational Software Development Platform tools support the capture of requirements using a common (user-defined) glossary of terms and the development of models (UML and others) based on those terms. These may then be translated into service implementations ready for deployment.

At the same time, the IBM Information Server platform includes tools for capturing meta-data in a wide variety of existing data sources. This meta-data may be used to define reusable rules and transformations as information services that are added to the service portfolio in an SOA. Many other vendors, such as Informatica, also have tools to capture such meta-data.

Such tools provide a growing momentum toward consistency in our understanding of both function and data that transcends individual services and data sources in an SOA. The impact of this momentum, given enabling governance support, is the realization of significant reuse in an SOA and the responsiveness to change required by today's business systems.

However, no matter how good tools are, they are necessary but not sufficient. A good SOA deployment also requires a sophisticated middleware infrastructure to support reusable services and data processes.

7.8.2 Common Infrastructure

The infrastructure needed must provide configuration and deployment facilities for both business logic and business information services into execution environments that support high levels of reuse and composition. Particularly important are the facilities needed to apply enterprise policies for access, authentication, authorization, standardization, communications, sharing, and workload distribution in a highly efficient manner (see Figure 7-10).

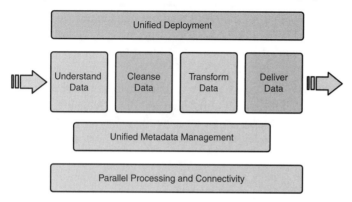

Figure 7-10   IBM Information Server architecture

When service-oriented function and data are integrated by such an infrastructure, both are subject to the same set of policies and management controls, and this consistency can deliver great value. When the infrastructure also provides industry standard support for services and their management, that business value is magnified further.

The combination of powerful IBM Information Server middleware products with IBM WebSphere SOA Foundation products already supports deployment of an SOA that includes both business function and business data services. These products can be used to deploy any number of process, application, and information servers connected by a service bus to implement composite business processes in a service-oriented infrastructure.

A.7.9

The Information Server architecture (see Figure 7-1) supports the deployment of multistage data profiling, cleansing, matching, merging, and transformation from a wide variety of data sources. It also supports wide-ranging connectivity to those data sources and large numbers of predefined data quality functions available to "wire" together as data processes. These data processing activities are based on common meta-data tools and runtime infrastructure incorporated into product packaging.

Delivery of data through industry standard service endpoints using this technology can be affected by using on-demand federation of disparate data sources or through highly parallel processing, caching, and consolidation of possibly large volumes of data using underlying job-scheduling server technology. The result is presented to data consumers as industry standard service response messages that encapsulate the data provider implementation details.

7.9 Conclusion

While functional services are a key ingredient for business agility, information services are an equally important capability for the service practitioner. Many of the business problems that the enterprise faces are actually caused by poor data quality, multiple sources of the same data, and data schema differences. Creating information services to hide and resolve legacy complexity is a simplifying concept that is a powerful source of value for the business.

This chapter demonstrates a number of information patterns that assist the reader in creating such value. This includes data federation, data consolidation, data cleansing, master data management, composite services, and semantic interoperability. Failure to use these techniques to resolve your information issues is the pain that keeps on giving, project after project. Get control of your data using information services!

7.10 Links to developerWorks Articles

A.7.1 Selvage, Mei Y. et al. *Information management in Service-Oriented Architecture, Part 1: Discover the role of information management in SOA.* www.ibm.com/developerworks/ webservices/library/ws-soa-ims/.

A.7.2 Byrne, Brian et al. *The information perspective of an SOA design, Part 2: The value of applying the business glossary pattern in SOA.* www.ibm.com/developerworks/db2/library/ techarticle/dm-0802sauter/.

A.7.3 Selvage, Mei Y. et al. *Information management in Service-Oriented Architecture, Part 2: Explore the different approaches to information management in SOA.* www.ibm.com/ developerworks/webservices/library/ws-soa-ims2/.

A.7.4 Sauter, G. et al. *Information service patterns, Part 1: Data federation pattern.* www-128.ibm.com/developerworks/webservices/library/ws-soa-infoserv1/.

A.7.5 Sauter, G. et al. *Information service patterns, Part 2: Data consolidation pattern.* www-128.ibm.com/developerworks/webservices/library/ws-soa-infoserv2/.

A.7.6 Sauter, G. et al. *Information service patterns, Part 3: Data cleansing pattern.* www-128.ibm.com/developerworks/webservices/library/ws-soa-infoserv3/.

A.7.7 Sauter G. et al. *Information service patterns, Part 4: Master Data Management architecture patterns.* www-128.ibm.com/developerworks/db2/library/techarticle/dm-0703sauter/.

A.7.8 Selvage, Mei Y. et al. *Achieve semantic interoperability in a SOA—Patterns and best practices.* www-128.ibm.com/developerworks/webservices/library/ws-soa-seminterop.html.

A.7.9 Harris, Simon et al. A *flexible data integration architecture using WebSphere DataStage and WebSphere Federation Server.* www.ibm.com/developerworks/db2/library/techarticle/dm-0703harris/.

7.11 References

Jones, Keith. "SOA and Data," *MiddlewareSpectrum*, 20:4, November 2006.

Devlin, Keith. (1999) *Infosense: Turning Information into Knowledge,* New York: W. H. Freeman and Company.

Bieberstein, Norbert et al. (2005) *Service-Oriented Architecture (SOA) Compass: Business Value, Planning, and Enterprise Roadmap,* IBM Press.

Chapter 8

Collaboration Under SOA: The Human Aspects

In the previous chapters, we concentrated on technical and organizational aspects of SOA in the enterprise. We provided practical hints and experiences for setting up the IT development. But, SOA is like other innovations, not just another technology the IT shop incorporates. Each time a new technology is introduced or innovative technologies are applied in the enterprise, humans are involved: Employees, managers, business partners, and the customers decide whether a change is successful.

This chapter discusses the development of working in a service-oriented enterprise and how the SOA-based infrastructure enables people to collaborate more effectively and receive benefits of the enterprise. An important part in this is the human interface, the way the IT systems are presented to the user. Especially in this context, we highlight the impact of new technologies that arrived with web 2.0 in the company and the organizational changes that benefit from them.

8.1 What Does SOA Mean to People?

Before discussing the technical solutions and tools, it is important to look at the impact of an SOA-based infrastructure on an organization and its people. As stated in Chapter 2 of *Service-Oriented Architecture Compass* (Bieberstein et al. 2006), business agility is a major goal of SOA-based infrastructure. This cannot be achieved with just new IT infrastructure; it also requires organizational changes. Those changes involve different ways to build IT solutions, to utilize the reuse of enterprise assets at large as we discussed earlier, and to care for appropriate governance in the enterprise.

Any change to the system results in an impact on the people working in the enterprise. In *SOA for Profit* (van den Berg et al. 2007), the authors describe the change in enterprise operation, a business transformation that is most important for getting the desired results from becoming an SOA-based company.

On one hand, the changes involve new or changed roles that reflect cooperation under the service-oriented paradigm; on the other hand, the changes involve employee and management behavioral changes. Naturally, as with any change or new idea, you will encounter resistance and overly enthusiastic acceptance. It is the task of the leadership teams, the company management, to moderate the emotions and to manage the change process.

8.1.1 The Service-Oriented-People in the Enterprise

In Chapter 3, "SOA Governance," we outlined the SOA governance structure and organization of authorities for a service-oriented operation in the company. Now, we summarize the key ideas that are important or indispensable for the service-oriented people in the enterprise—let's call them the SO-managers and SO-employees.

SO-Managers

- Primarily act as observers instead of directors (*who issue top-down orders*).
- Monitor the business (adequate tools and systems support this).
- Define rules and processes, such as building a constitution that includes the fundamental laws for the company (golden rule or constitution).
- Recognize talents and temperaments as well as know the skills of the employees to staff roles/pools (act as mentors for personal development—especially matching talents and temperaments, not just acquired skills and experiences, to the tasks).
- Allow satisfying freedom to the employees under the set rules (equivalent to the loosely coupling of services in an SOA).
- Motivate employees by addressing the individual talents and preferred tasks. (This applies especially to people managers who are responsible for dedicated teams, versus business generals who are in charge of the overall corporate directions and are not dealing with daily execution at the bottom.)

SO-Employees

- Get information and take initiatives (solving tasks autonomously by acting and cooperating with best matching peers).
- Execute the tasks that are necessary to satisfy customer demands. (Employees should be empowered to perform the company rules and processes and not have to be entitled to single actions by their managers.)
- Build ad hoc teams and organize their work within the legal framework. (Incentives and punishments can be used to enforce this.)
- Know their strengths and publish them (populating the employee repository accordingly) to become engaged (the individual employee advertises one's capabilities, preferences, and strengths to the company to get the work to the person who can do it best).

- Offer services and act (publishing experience records and service offerings within the enterprise repository).
- Maintain motivation by working on what they do best and being directly recognized for achievements. (Peer reviews, awards, and suitable incentives support this.)

Most of the items in the previous lists can be reached in a company when both sides, managers and employees, get together to define business transformation goals and a path to reach them. Certainly, education is required to gain support and understanding for why the transformation goals will help the enterprise and, even more important, who the individuals involved will be. With an SOA-based organization and a motivated team, the enterprise can become as agile as expected.

In a way, we see the roles and responsibilities of managers and employees, executives, and professionals changing toward a more service-oriented behavior, which requires the listed personal qualities. Summarizing, we can state that a manager in a service-oriented enterprise becomes more the role of a thoughtful leader, one who thinks out the services framework their company can offer under the corporate strategy as set by the business generals. More details about how to govern the enterprise in a loosely coupled manner are given in the *IBM Systems Journal* article by Bieberstein et al. (SJ44-4 of 2005).

In turn, the individual employees are getting more active to perform within the given framework. To achieve agility, each individual will advertise one's services in an enterprise repository, specifically skills, expertise, talents, and other reasonable data. In the case of a project requested by a customer, project managers or other people in charge will look in the repository to find the most suitable professionals.

8.1.2 Research on the Impact of SOA in the Enterprise

During the business transformation toward a service-oriented enterprise, there are not just technical issues to consider, but also the impact it has on a company's operation and all involved people, as well as the way the enterprise operates on the global market and deals with their customers. The observations made are being published in scientific journals (for example, see the papers in the section "Business Aspects of Service-Oriented Thinking" in the *IBM Systems Journal* issue 44-4, www.research.ibm.com/journal/sj44-4.html). Furthermore, there are researchers working on related issues, finding new ways to govern "loosely coupled" enterprises and defining guides to smoothly and surely reach the set goals. In this context, we like to refer to Peter Weill and his team at Sloan School of Management at MIT, Cambridge, Massachusetts, and other researchers who recently published books and articles on this issue (see the reference list).

The academic disciplines involved do not limit themselves to a computer sciences or business focus, but extend to psychology, political sciences, and sociology, as these get fueled by ideas through the evolving Internet and its influence on nearly every society around the globe. The scientific results from studying groups of co-workers, individual behaviors within teams, and individual temperaments support the idea that a service-oriented organization is ideal.

There are several publications based on long-term observations that can be applied to how people cooperate within a service-oriented enterprise so that the goals of agility are reached. We also found several research results that can be best applied at a company based on SOA principles, as we have described in this book.

There is Meredith Belbin's research published in *Management Teams*. Belbin's work shows that teams perform best when there is a certain mixture of dedicated team roles. In numerous experiments, he proved that so-called A-teams won't deliver the best results, because in a team made up by alpha personalities (those who always score the highest as individuals and get the A marks in school), too much time and effort is lost to ranking fights rather than concentrating on the subject. In his books and publications, Belbin shows what constellation of team player types leads to the best results. In a service-oriented enterprise, the knowledge of those types[1] can be stored as attributes in the enterprise repository. This lets a project manager staff the team not just with people who are educated in the requested areas and bring appropriate experiences with certain situations, but also helps to get the right combination of team players for a winning team.

In this context, it is worth mentioning the studies executed by Gallup over many decades. They are published in the book by Marcus Buckingham and Donald Clifton, *Now, Discover Your Strengths*. Based on millions of individual data and supported by real-life results from applying the knowledge about one's individual strengths to the personal records, the authors show that many people hide their talents instead of letting their strengths play for the team's and the company's benefit. Publishing these could also help staff teams to deliver services because each individual can get insight and knowledge about strengths and how one can best contribute to the team's success.

Personality traits are an important aspect for successful business operation as the results from research in psychology show. Philosophers, HR professionals, and especially psychologists around the globe have been interested in human stereotypes, in classifying people based on their temperaments to better understand individual drivers (what motivates you?) and reactions (why did you get so angry?). Some of the ideas are dated. In the 1980s, the psychologists David Keirsey and Marilyn Bates developed their temperament sorter and published it (1986) under the title *Please Understand Me: Character and Temperament Types*. Based on the temperament types, several tests, guidelines, and advice have been developed, all with the intention to clarify the individual personality. Better understanding other peoples' behaviors, feelings, and thinking processes can avoid friction among team members. Enlightenment can be an advantage for anybody working on teams. The knowledge about the individual temperaments is another key in staffing winning teams.

8.1.3 The Role of a Service-Oriented Architect

Team building in a service-oriented enterprise can happen in various ways. For SO-managers and SO-employees, empowered individuals ideally seek each other rather than have to be told to fill an explicit position in an organization chart. However, there are people in roles who are better at knowing the people and more capable than others at building a successful team. Those are addressed as people managers in the earlier section of this chapter.

Certainly, professional project managers, who are not just administrators, are predestined for staffing a project team. However, there is a need for translation between IT and the company business languages, a strong request for a role that spans wider than just solving IT issues for the enterprise. A person in this role has to know and cooperate with and within the executive management teams to develop the most suitable solutions.

This role takes on a certain mediator function, which we like to call the service-oriented architect, or a classical enterprise architect within a service-oriented enterprise. Best suited are persons who have been educated in IT and business administration, and probably equally important, who have the diplomatic talents to act as a mediator between both sides. This role becomes then the guarantor for the business transformation en route to the SOA-based company. It is a team play that involves change activists from almost every business unit to become successful.

This change does not end at the company gates. It goes far beyond, as individuals work from home, no longer penned up in corporate office buildings, or participate in business via the Internet from almost any place on Earth. In other words, this all is an all-embracing transition; a revolutionary movement that touches everything in everybody's daily lives, at work and certainly at leisure time, too.

8.2 Web 2.0 and SOA

In the context of the changes we expect and see ongoing to make an enterprise SOA based, it is necessary to look at what web 2.0 brings to the table. Sandy Carter (2007), in her book *The New Language of Business,* describes how the meeting of SOA and the new Internet facilities changes the way companies do their business today. She describes it as an irrevocable and impelled movement that determines a company's survival.

8.2.1 Definition of Web 2.0

When searching the Internet for "web 2.0," you easily get many millions of hits. This indicates certain hype attached to it. Let's summarize the idea behind the term.

Although the term *web 2.0* suggests a new version of the World Wide Web, it does not refer to an update to any technical specifications, but to changes in the ways software developers and end users use webs. So, it refers to a perceived second generation of web-based communities and hosted services. Those services can continuously be updated and allow various ways of social networking among the users filling the new roles as we described earlier

The term was brought up at an O'Reilly event in 2005 following a brainstorming session that Tim O'Reilly documented on the World Wide Web. The core idea is to facilitate creativity, collaboration, and sharing among users on the Internet. This applies as well to the relationship between those who create assets and those who consume them, those who provide a service and the technology behind it, and those who use it for their business or just for leisure activities.

Hence, this means a strong involvement of every user, a turn away from IT being a secret science reserved for the 2 percent in population with an IQ over 130, or for people with mathematical thinking who sit isolated in their offices and produce applications that hit the users with fixed screens, and predefined processes. Often the users merely understand the mechanism behind their screens and wonder about weird behavior of the system not suiting the immediate needs in a given business situation. With web 2.0, IT becomes everybody's thing, and most important, it becomes changeable to one's personal needs. The border between the IT providers on one side and the IT consumers on the other blurs.

The closing of the chasm between IT and lines of business is intended for best success with SOA. Besides that, the young people leaving school and starting their jobs are more used to IT than any generation before. This underpins the move of SOA and web 2.0 to become the normal way of doing business, communicating, living, and running one's daily errands.

In his web article, Tim O'Reilly provides detail about how web 1.0 (the web we currently use) is going to change toward web 2.0. Several items show a move from a predefined and company-set way of presenting and doing things toward a community-based approach. So, personal websites will be replaced by blogging (that is, a place where several people post their comments). The wiki[2] technology (that is, a place that allows a community to edit common web pages) increasingly will be used. He refers to Wikipedia as a trusted replacement for printed encyclopedias.

At the end, Tim O'Reilly (2005) summarizes the envisioned core competencies for a web 2.0 company that we are going to explore in this context. According to Tim O'Reilly, the web 2.0 core competencies of an enterprise are as follows:

- Services, not packaged software, with cost-effective scalability
- Control over unique, hard to re-create data sources that get richer as more people use them
- Trusting users as co-developers
- Harnessing collective intelligence
- Leveraging the long tail through customer self-service
- Software above the level of a single device
- Lightweight user interfaces, development models, and business models

With this in mind, we concentrate the remainder of this chapter on those items that immediately support SOA, and that are important to the enterprise architect to consider when helping the company on the journey toward a service-oriented enterprise. Before that, a few more observations are helpful to understand the whole extent of the impact from SOA and web 2.0 in our societies and economies.

8.2.2 Some Observations of Web 2.0 in Use

We concentrate here on a few, but essential observations that help to understand how web 2.0 and SOA can generate the desired results for an enterprise. There are many more trends and certainly not yet widely accepted uses and patterns of dealing with and via the Internet that we cannot include in this book. The Internet medium enables the very fast development of new ideas. Known items become obsolete, and with a generally dynamic development, any claim for comprehensiveness in a book quickly becomes outdated.

Therefore, we select a few key observations using well-known examples of today's Internet business world to exemplify how the idea of service-orientation as a platform for the agile business can be applied with today's tools, concepts, and existing services. In the following, we regard three established Internet-based business and community services: Wikipedia, Google, and YouTube. These three examples demonstrate how web 2.0 elements become the key success factors for these endeavors to start and gain importance, acting as role models for other companies, start-ups, and even for established players in a certain market. More than that, these initiatives and the innovations they bring to the market change the way we do certain things.

8.2.3 User Contribution

The example of Wikipedia.org demonstrates the factor *user contribution* and adds the aspect of starting and operating successfully a nonprofit organization on the World Wide Web. This wiki[3]-based free encyclopedia allows everybody to contribute and edit the content. Before Wikipedia (www.wikipedia.org), encyclopedias were the work of a closed circle of experts, each of them being a prominent luminary in a well-defined scientific area.

Now the wiki technologies opened it up for a large number of "experts," who all contribute their bit of knowledge and expertise to grow Wikipedia to a global matter. Wikipedia, an artificial word created from *wiki-wiki* (Hawaiian for quick) and *encyclopedia,* is a website launched in 2001 for hosting multinational, multilingual, web-based encyclopedias. The content and formatting are created by everybody who wants to contribute.

The Wikipedia community[4] meanwhile has created an immense amount of useful information, not just in English. Today, the Wikipedia site shows articles in more than 200 languages, of which English has grown to more than 2 million articles, followed by the German[5] (700,000+ articles) and the French[6] (600,000+ articles) section. Among the languages, you also find extinct ones like Latin (10,000+ articles),[7] and artificial languages like Esperanto[8] (10,000+ articles), and languages spoken by small minorities like *Pennsilfaanisch-Deitsch*[9] (1,000+ articles). Almost every language is represented, and thanks to the underlying database technology for many articles in one language, you find a direct link to the same item in one or more other languages.

Wikipedia shows impressively the public use of bidirectional information services. Concerns about incorrectness, errors, and malicious contents are countered by the control of the masses. The same model as for Linux applies, where a large community with many more eyes, specialized knowledge, and experiences monitors and contributes to a reliable instrument coming close to and with regard to agility and speed of change outperforming the classic model of the encyclopedia.

The trustworthiness became so evident that many people today seriously refer to Wikipedia as their source of wisdom. If one does not know something, the first check is Wikipedia instead of opening a printed version of Encyclopedia Britannica or its regional equivalent. This is a strong change that was triggered by IT functionalities on the Internet.

In a company, this example of user contribution can result in an encyclopedia of the company's internal terms and items not found or not allowed outside the premises (or better, outside the internal network). It might also be a repository, as described in Chapter 5, "Leveraging Reusable Assets."

8.2.4 Services for Mashups

Besides its searching functionality, which was Google's first intention when getting on the Internet, their website is a good example of providing *services for mashups.* Mashups are web applications that combine data/functionality from more than one source. Allowing any user via the web to use the services offered within applications on his or her end devices, you have the provision of services for mashups. For example, you can add geographical information to items that have been found by the Google search. As a service for mashups, Google Maps services can be used directly by end users in a very convenient fashion. Any Maps service itself can be combined with other services (for instance, Google's own Find Businesses function), generating higher value to the users. Google exposes the Maps services as remixable services so that there are now a huge number of mashups (programmed combinations of those) using these services.

 Transferred to IT and business operations at a company, you can ask your company's IT shop to provide several distinguished services that the end users, your employees, can combine with any other accepted services and applications to create suitable solutions for them. The A.8.1 services that are ready, approved, and accepted by an authority unit within your company can be kept in a pool with appropriate trust marks or certifications issued by the IT shop or a trusted provider.

The end users can then access the services in their mashups that run on their site. Enabling services for mashups and providing appropriate support by your IT shop means that every employee becomes a kind of programmer who shortcuts the traditional way of getting application solutions. For the IT shop, this means a change from a general solution provider to becoming an authority who cares for the infrastructure and the standards and who develops services and approves external services that are ready to be used within your company.

In the sense as earlier described by O'Reilly, concrete applications development becomes more an end-user task, and no longer shows version cycles and release dates. However, there has to be a sufficient number of useful and valuable services available that can be found in the repository and are made available via the enterprise service bus (ESB) infrastructure.

Going a step further, as Google offers a certain set of services from their site, it will cause more service providers to offer software that runs at some place in the network and delivers well-defined results. Over time, we can expect more providers to come to the market so that economically we see the start of a *software as a service* (SaaS) economy. This means a new software-delivery model where software vendors are developing web-native software applications (web services) that are independently hosted and operated by application providers to the users. The customers no longer pay any fees for owning the software, but for the use of it.

As soon as Internet service providers begin charging for the use of their services or services of third parties that they are hosting, there is a new market. That new market consists of software vendors who develop and offer services implemented in software and application service providers (or perhaps better, *SaaS* providers) who make those services available for end users to build their solutions on their ends.

Assuming a market for SaaS has developed, there are new alternatives for companies to choose from. The available services can be used to complement the existing IT, for example if there is a need for support of special tasks that are too expensive to develop a solution for.

This complementing job can be done by specialists at the IT department, or a company can decide to fully rely on a service provider to deliver the services according an agreement. Or depending on the policies, the trustworthiness of the application services providers, and finally the savvy of the employees, the CIO can develop a strategy of allowing (or in certain cases, encouraging) the use of mashups within the enterprise, especially when the advantages outweigh the risks. In fact, as Tim O'Reilly envisions it, this may become the norm for a web 2.0 company.

8.2.5 User Contribution and User Ratings

YouTube leverages *user contribution and user ratings*. With YouTube, we see a platform that addresses the human urge to express oneself. Digital cameras enable people to create films at a low cost, and more and more people become their own film directors, editors, and actors.

Not everybody makes it to Hollywood to become a star, but cameras at affordable price points enable every person to star in home movies and publish them via the Internet. Rating systems fuel competition, and the published number of downloads and good ratings are what motivate people to produce and upload more films and better films.

When it comes to inappropriate material, this platform supports a self-controlling system in which each user can remove those films he doesn't want to view. In this way, a democracy is in place here in which everybody can become a star if so elected by one's peers. Groups, subgroups, and discussion forums can be initiated by anyone because everyone determines what goes on the site and what changes. Users keep it dynamic, making other people want to visit the site to see what has changed, what new ideas came up, and what new discussion topics are online among one's family and friends or other social contacts. In this way, advertising is mouth to mouth as well as the traditional, electronic way. Other media takes input from the site and publishes information about these stars, reinforcing the attraction.

For companies, you can imagine innovation campaigns presented on an internal platform, discussed, and voted on. Ideas are easier spread than ever before. For any consumer/customer-oriented idea, the ratings, visitor counts, discussion content, and remarks by the target groups provide valuable input and help to determine corporate decisions.

For the IBM CEO Report 2007, the participating CEOs were asked what they considered to be the most significant source of innovative ideas for their company. The results (see Figure 8-1) clearly show that the power of innovation that comes from the direct participation of employees and customers is stronger than what the think tanks and highly paid experts in the research and development laboratories create.

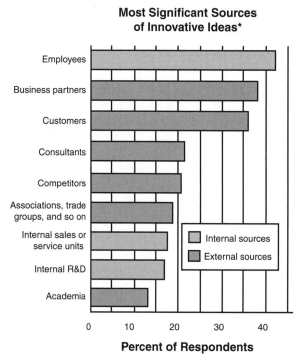

Most Significant Sources of Innovative Ideas*

Percent of Respondents

*Respondents could select up to three choices

Source: IBM CEO Report 2007

Figure 8-1   The power of innovation comes from employees and customers

Besides YouTube, there are several other examples of how quickly ideas become widely known and accepted, and finally turn into a serious business. Consider, for example, a site that offers royalty-free images and graphics by members to members. The contributors are mainly ambitious amateurs who start for recognition reasons. The site has ratings and comments, offers discussion forums, and so on. These build and foster a community of self-help members. Hints and experiences are exchanged around the globe, and thus the quality of the images improves and reaches professional levels. There are rules, processes, and distinguished roles (inspectors who monitor for quality standards and administrators responsible for any "issues" among the members).

As a business, the low prices attract buyers, especially those who would not be able to pay high prices for artistic work (perhaps available at professional sites). The quality level is kept high; contributors are motivated to deliver to high standards; software and technical equipment are available at affordable prices. The community helps to achieve all of that.

Normally, in such communities, about 1 percent or 2 percent of the members act as contributors, whereas the rest are mere consumers/customers. You can find a detailed analysis of such an organization and how it developed its business in the *iStockPhoto Case Study: How to evolve from a free community site to successful business,* by Kempton Lam and Nisan Gabbay (2006), published at Startup-Review.

8.2.6 Summary of Observations

Web 2.0 brings social and technical aspects to the table. For businesses, social aspects are more fundamental and determining than the technologies. The web 2.0 sites offer infrastructures and guidelines that enable members to participate in a community, which makes them feel connected. The members see themselves as not just employees who have been asked to deliver a requested work item; instead, they feel free to deliver what they think is their best work.

This type of open platform means that ideas often quickly become a hit and spread more quickly than an advertising campaign could. Communities of people with similar interests or complementary interests (the providers and customers of images) merge to make the audience more alert for innovation. This generates well-defined, well-known (due to voluntarily outing oneself) audiences in these interest groups that can more precisely become targets for marketing campaigns, unlike with many other media

People are attracted to these sites because of the common interests they share with the people participating in them. This implies a certain level of motivation to participate, mainly as consumers; but the small number of contributing members is highly motivated to improve their offered products. Items are often posted simply because members want to gain recognition or become famous among their peers. Some of these contributors make it to stars beyond the reach of a site and often act as advertisers for followers.

A site can grow to huge memberships, millions of daily hits, and millions or even billions of value created and traded. They reach the critical mass to become a valued business interest. Recently, Google acquired YouTube for $1.65 billion, and the established professional agent Getty Images bought the Canadian photographers platform iStockPhoto for $50 million. In each case, the new owners leave the platforms, rules, and guidelines in their core because these community-based ideas are what made them successful.

8.2.7 Technical Terms of Importance

From the technical perspective, most web 2.0 sites have APIs for use by developers of mashup applications. Typically, web 2.0 user interfaces apply the Ajax technology to achieve more responsive UIs.

8.2.7.1 What Is Ajax?

In the context of web 2.0, Ajax stands for Asynchronous JavaScript and XML. The term was introduced in 2005 by Jesse James Garrett. The purpose for this development technique is to create more dynamic and responsive web pages, as well as to build web clients in an SOA that can connect to any kind of server: J2EE, PHP, ASP.NET, Ruby on Rails, and so on.

It draws upon existing technologies and standards, including JavaScript and XML. Generally, it follows the operation pattern that a page view displayed in a web browser retrieves data or markup fragments from a service and refreshes just a part of the page. Different from some easy-to-use end-user tools for mashups, AJAX is nontrivial. It requires deep and broad skills in web development, but the benefits to be gained can be huge compared to classic web applications that are programmed in the traditional way. Ajax enables major improvements in responsiveness and performance of web applications. (For instance, it is used at Yahoo! Mail, Google Maps, live.com, and others.)

8.2.7.2 What Is REST?

REST stands for Representational State Transfer. It is the architectural model on which the World Wide Web is based. The term was introduced in the year 2000 in a Ph.D. dissertation by Roy Fielding.

Principles of REST include the following:

- Resource-centric approach.
- All relevant resources are addressable via Uniform Resource Identifiers (URIs).
- Uniform access via HTTP: GET, POST, PUT, and DELETE.
- Content type negotiation enables retrieval of alternative representations from the same URI.
- REST style services are easy to access from code running in web browsers, any other client, or servers, which is popular in the context of Ajax.
- Takes full advantage of the WWW caching infrastructure.
- Serves multiple representations of the same resource.

In short, these network architecture principles allow a seamless appearance of the websites to the users. Due to REST, the Internet is a dynamic network, not just point-to-point connections that could be based on remote procedure call (RPC) technology.

8.2.7.3 What Is RSS?

Another technical term that is important in this context is RSS. It stands for Really Simple Syndication, which describes a family of so-called web feeds, ways to put information by independent users onto common platforms and enable a close to real-time representation of the updated content to its users subscribed to such a feed. This technique allows for updating one's websites in an automated manner, instead of manually editing them. Therefore, it is often used for blog sites, news headlines, sports tickers, and podcasts.

A.8.2

The history of RSS goes back to 1995, when Ramanathan Guha and his team at Apple Computer's Advanced Technology Group developed their first approach to syndication on the web, called Meta Content Framework (MCF). Delivered by the RSS Advisory Board in 2002 under the name of RSS 2.0, it found initial acceptance as a standard. However, it still took a few more years before RSS gained broad acceptance in the IT industry. One can say RSS became the standard when finally, in 2006, all usual web browsers incorporated RSS readers.

8.2.8 Everybody Knows Everything

The idea behind web 2.0 is that *everybody knows everything*. In a way, the individual partici-pant connected to the Internet becomes more involved and more empowered than ever before when dealing with technologies, especially with IT.

Self-help groups often emerge and become serious businesses, such as when a hobbyist plat-form on the Internet run by a photographer turns into a leading stock photography provider relying on thousands of hobby or semiprofessional photographers who sell millions of images to millions of customers at lower prices than any established vendor or broker. In this case, stock photographs become affordable to a larger clientele.

8.2.9 New Models

In other words, the market has been turned over. Everybody can offer everything to every-body else; one just needs to be connected by the Internet and using a platform for commu-nication, which involves mainly advertising, searching, selling, and recommending. This means that new social models, technologies, and businesses will arise:

- **New social models** in which user-generated content can be as valuable as tradi-tional media, where social networks form and grow with tremendous speed, where truly global audiences can be reached more easily, and where rich media from pho-tos to videos become a part of everyday life online. Here community mechanisms play a role similar to the essential one they had historically under rural or small-town conditions. The difference is now the participants no longer meet in one real place in town to discuss the issues and to develop new ideas; instead, they meet "virtually" all over the network at any time.
- **New technology models** let software become a service. The Internet becomes the development platform, where online services and data are mixed and matched, and syndication of content becomes the glue across the network that is based on reli-able high-speed, ubiquitous access as the norm. Tools are developing that allow every user to arrange IT as it is needed in any current situation.
- **New business models** that are facilitated by changes in infrastructure costs, allow-ing companies to reach the "long tail" as defined by Chris Anderson (2006), which describes the large number of rather individual websites versus a small number of heavily accessed sites. Analyzing the resulting Pareto distribution,[10] it shows that the sum of all visitors to the individual sites is as high as the ones on the favorite sites; in certain cases, it outnumbers the mainstream. This makes companies turn to viral network-driven marketing, pay attention to the individuals, and gain from new advertising-based revenue opportunities. Based on these new technologies, a market for software as services and new ways to drive innovation by the customers emerges and quickly becomes the normal way to do the business.

These changes happen simultaneously for all three models. Figure 8-2 illustrates this.

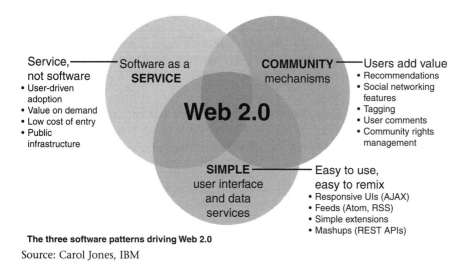

The three software patterns driving Web 2.0

Source: Carol Jones, IBM

Figure 8-2   The rise of new business, technologies, and business models

8.2.10 Web 2.0 and the Service-Oriented Enterprise

You've already read in this chapter some web 2.0 business concepts. Now take a look at the following list of principles that should be of interest to businesses, especially those enterprises that adhere to the philosophy of SOA:

- Self-establishing *communities* are collaborating around topics of common business interest.
- *User contribution* is a norm and requires treating users as coauthors and leveraging their skills.
- *Accumulation of user knowledge* is used to make applications smarter the more people use them.
- *Users are enabled to add value* by adding meta data (for example, rate, tag, bookmark, comment).
- Users *take control,* and contribute to make applications most useful to them.
- *User interface are separated from services* to make services more reusable.
- Fine-grained *access to data* that supports mashups.
- The general use of *mashups* allows combining existing services into new, useful applications and joining information from various sources.
- *Situational applications are developed by line of business users* on the spot and help to make businesses more agile.
- The general use of *Ajax* allows to enable rich, interactive, highly responsive web UIs.
- Use of *semantic tags and microformats* enables dynamic augmentation with contextual menus or information.

This list is not and will never be complete. After all, new ideas are continually being conceived and propagated, and then after having been accepted by the masses of Internet users they are finally turned into business innovations. However, from insight we have gained to the present, we can derive valuable guidelines to build the SOA collaborative environment.

8.3 Building the SOA Collaboration Environment

Characteristics of the web 2.0 enterprise build primarily on services, not packaged software, with cost-effective scalability. Due to control over unique, hard to re-create data sources that get richer as more people use them, a kind of "democratic" control mechanism is established, and users are trusted as "co-developers." Therefore, businesses have to harness the collective intelligence of all the employees in the company to reach the business goals more directly, and so that the goals are finely tuned to match customer demands at an unforeseen degree.

To reach the "long tail" as it was described before, means a different way to market, and finally a more sophisticated way to present the company services to the world. As education levels throughout the world rise, the demands become more and more specific. Those services have to match a myriad of individual needs by rather small groups of customers. This trend is irrevocable and businesses have to address those needs, because those enlightened customers know to find what they need and want anywhere in the www. This development increases the pressure by competition, and forces enterprises to adequately address the growing "long tail".

Using services via the Internet means, in a transferred sense, to extend one's personal system capabilities. As a user, you have access to application services and data sources that go far beyond traditional client/server implementations. The network itself truly becomes the computer by offering services to run, and even more, lightweight user interfaces, development models, and business models enable flexible use of services fitting the situational needs.

8.3.1 The Situational Application Ecosystem

As mentioned previously, end users of IT systems are taking on the role application programmer by building mashups or using Ajax to create applications for their immediate needs, without the often-tedious process of IT requests, requirements definitions, and following the traditional software lifecycle. The more services become available in an SOA-based IT, the more the composition of enterprise data and business logic processes becomes less a matter of the IT experts. Mash-able content helps to enable end users to do client-side composition for the browser. Those situational applications built by the user from available services for discrete business situations are the key to agile business operations.

This raises a question: Why is a situational application ecosystem important?

Surely, frameworks are only as good as the data and widgets they have access to. Less skill is required to connect components together using widgets that can interact, compose, and display mashed content in new and interesting ways. Further integration "on the glass" is easier for the average user than integration deeper within platforms or applications, and situational software is enabled by mashable data, and widgets has a proven market demand. The marketplace is clearly indicating value, as stated before.

However, there is total incompatibility and lack of interoperability between widget vendors, and most enterprise data is not available in a form easily consumed by existing frameworks. Therefore, there is a clear need for a reliable framework that enables users to assemble applications: the situational applications ecosystem.

Such a framework must include highly intuitive construction methods allowing line of business end users to create their own situational applications, mashups, services, and RSS feeds. As shown in earlier examples in this chapter, such online environments should support both personal and collaborative assembly to satisfy community and personal needs.

Certainly, collections of highly useful "starter" service components ready to easily mash up are welcome, because their availability lowers the threshold for nontechnical users to engage in building their own situational applications. Finally, to become the agile enterprise that one expects from SOA-based organizations, the enterprise must provide easy access to enterprise data sources and APIs.

To set up your company for SOA, you follow the guidelines for governance, introduce a team-based and open development process, and embed all of this in the business transition for the entire organization. When doing so, it is important to include collaborative aspects and to build the ecosystem for situational applications that enable the users to become agile in the intended sense.

8.3.2 User Conditions in the Situational Application Ecosystem

No one solution fits all situations; and in the future, we see the increasing need for more individualized applications that fit a certain business situation. No longer will packaged standard business solutions meet the quickly changing requirements, nor will they become modifiable at high speed. Therefore, the situational application ecosystem has to satisfy several conditions for the user and the technical infrastructure perspective.

For the non-IT end user, the following conditions are regarded as key:

- **User-assembled applications.**
  Intuitive construction methods for line of business (LOB) users are required and must be provided and supported by the IT shop.
  Support both personal and collaborative assembly.
  There should be high-value service components for enterprise mashups (data, feeds, collaboration, and so on) covering the most common functionalities.

- **Global contextual collaboration.**

  There are to be rich collaborations that dynamically adapt to available devices. The IT system aggressively manages dynamic collaboration contexts.

  Real-time language translation and other accessibility adaptation are provided and supported by the IT shop.

- **World Wide Widgets.**

  The IT providers in the enterprise are exploiting the emerging post-browser, cross-device interface metaphor.

  Micro-contexts and micro-templates are made available for fine-grained assembly.

8.3.3 Infrastructure Conditions for the Application Ecosystem

From the technology perspective, the following conditions have to be achieved:

- **Provide an enterprise-ready web 2.0 platform.**

  Drive the architecture of web 2.0 deep into the enterprise, including the organizational and development aspects described in Chapter 4, "A Methodology for Service Modeling and Design."

  Deliver end-to-end quality of service (QoS) that is demanded by enterprise environments (transactions, security, reliability, availability, and so on) without compromising the simplicity of the REST/web 2.0 paradigm.

- **Establish a service provisioning for REST components.**

  Create a distributed infrastructure that is capable of hosting and managing millions of transient and situational applications.

  Enable fine-grained, dynamic mediation, caching, acceleration, and discovery from inexact description. This is a challenge for the middleware, the ESB, and related infrastructure services—a semantics support in the repository.

  Enable integration of "browser-based middleware" for end-to-end management of all elements.

- **Care for security, provenance, and governance.**

  Build fine-grained distributed protection and rights management for both data and services.

  Allow "real-time" monitoring of regulatory compliance, including alerts and notifications.

  Enable provenance management in a remix-and-republish environment, matching the reuse promises of SOA.

Detailing all the listed items goes beyond the scope of this book. The items we mentioned and the collective thoughts we conveyed should help you build the ecosystem that is needed to gain the most from situational applications in the enterprise. At the time of this writing, several tools[11] that support this approach are under development or being improved.

8.4 Benefits from SOA to Enterprise Operations

To determine the benefits to the enterprise operation, a look at the stakeholders is advised. The higher-level view lets one state that the market forces are aligning the stakeholders in the following ways:

- The end users want access to their preferred data and widgets even as they change their framework of choice.
- The content providers want their content to be available to as many users as possible (that is, on as many platforms as possible), but do not want to be saddled with providing different widgets for each framework.
- The gadget and framework vendors need content and widgets for their frameworks or middleware products to be viable.

This means for *real* online services, the markets of all three types of vendors have to come together and find a common ground. There are already widely accepted standards for the technology base, namely web services.[12]

Now, need is based on this standard definitions for the contents, the processing, and the use of any item offered. Some of those definitions are developed as so-called industry models, dictionaries, or encyclopedias. They contain and define all essential elements of a certain industry. Others define a catalog of common services that can be used in various contexts across industries. Those might be used to link business partners together similar to the APIs for SWIFT (Society for Worldwide Interbank Financial Telecommunication) for international money transfers between banks and EDI (Electronic Data Interchange).

A.8.3

Having such industry standards in place results in advantages for all involved parties, because one can concentrate on the essentials rather than fight for naming something or insisting on certain attributes for an entity used by a service. As always, after awhile, vendors recognize the larger benefits for their platforms that stem from open standards (as opposed to trying to chain all involved parties to proprietary definitions).

8.4.1 Social Networking Effects for the Web 2.0 Enterprise

Another kind of benefit comes from the social networking that web 2.0 offers. Figure 8-3, the enterprise Web 2.0 spectrum, shows the broad range of the relevant aspects spanning from completely social items on one side of the scale to the rather technical definition of SOA, its underlying technology, on the other end.

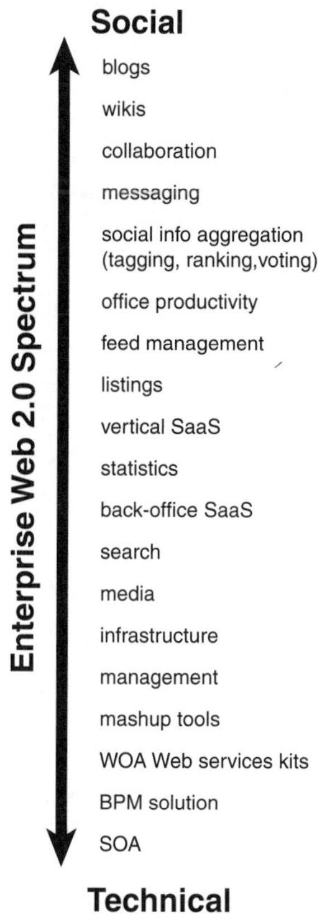

Social

blogs

wikis

collaboration

messaging

social info aggregation
(tagging, ranking,voting)

office productivity

feed management

listings

vertical SaaS

statistics

back-office SaaS

search

media

infrastructure

management

mashup tools

WOA Web services kits

BPM solution

SOA

Technical

Enterprise Web 2.0 Spectrum

Source: Thomas Schaeck, IBM

Figure 8-3   The enterprise web 2.0 spectrum

From the social end of the scale, there are several benefits that a company can realize. The predominant items, which count for larger organizations, are as follows:

- Discovery of new relationships in the company
- Access to knowledge of the organization and beyond
- Connections to information and subject matter experts far beyond one's current network
- Shared work by leveraging the connectedness of everything and everyone to work together in new ways
- Improved quality of one's work via expert peer testing, reviewing, and commenting in community forums
- Execution of better business decisions (and faster) through access to the right people, information, and new tools to manage tasks and expedite collaboration with others

The larger an organization, the more these advantages apply. The web 2.0 elements reduce the anonymity of large enterprises. In the past, an employee relied on one LOB to point to the partners within the company to cooperate; Reorganizations, then, required changes to organizational charts to reflect changed conditions. New LOBs, new managers, and new employees in the line needed to be nominated. When web 2.0 elements are in place and actively used by the workforce, each individual is more powerful. The individual employee can find the best connections, team up for better solutions, and deliver higher satisfaction to the customers.

8.4.2 Business Opportunities from Web 2.0 in a Service-Oriented Enterprise

Introducing an SOA-based organization with required IT services and implementing the described web 2.0 elements helps the company to gain business opportunities. Summarizing, we can state the introduction of SOA and web 2.0 in the enterprise:

- **Empowers the LOB.**
  Enables innovation (and thus quick reaction to business situations) at the departmental and individual levels.
  Eliminates (to a large degree), via the guided introduction of mashup and other situational applications, the often-frustrating communication and interpretations of requirements.
  Improves employee morale through empowerment and reduced bureaucracy. Important here is that the guidelines and rules be general purpose. In other words, you define and communicate the constitution of the company adjusted to service-oriented operations with web 2.0 elements.
- **Generates business fit of IT.**
  Applications are better suited to the LOB needs.
  Short-term business domain needs are satisfied because the user becomes the developer.
  Addresses the long tail of the company's customers (as explained earlier in this chapter).
  Tactical solutions become part of the IT portfolio.
- **Shortens lifecycle and results in better ROI.**
  Less time is spent on development (utilizing reuse—see the earlier chapters, especially Chapter 5).
  The development process itself becomes less expensive because the IT shop provides a platform, the rules, guidelines, the repository, and the governance instrumentation. The IT shop provides satisfying support for tools to allow end users to build situational applications to their individual needs.

Generally we can state that our experiences from projects at various organizations, including IBM, support the benefits of SOA and web 2.0 to the individual and the business goals. It fits to the changing world, which is interconnected via the Internet, operating, trading, and dealing globally with employees on every continent. It allows 24 hours operating, developing, and production of the goods demanded by the customers worldwide.

As people discover the advantages of web 2.0 in their private lives, they call for getting similar power at their fingertips at work. As shown, the advantages exist, and are ready to be exploited. However, there are also challenges to face and obstacles to overcome that derive from the introduction of SOA and web 2.0 in the enterprise.

8.4.3 Challenges of the Mergence of SOA and Web 2.0 in the Enterprise

The first and most often the most worrying aspect is about *controlling the chaos* that seems to arise when everybody starts creating his or her own applications from company and external services. With the infrastructure in place, the end users start to build and run their mashups under the radar of the teams who are responsible for the IT in the company. There are no formal budgets assigned because the users create the mashups as part of their work. This means companies have to revise IT plans and business plans to reflect what employees are doing.

A.8.4

As explained earlier, users become co-developers, making the immediate implementation of solutions the objective. The board of IT architects or an equivalent governance institution should find ways to let users learn about architecture, installing watchdogs to gain control and support quality assurance. Certain education should be set up for the mashup-savvy users to ensure the required level of security and avoid malign behaviors. The latter should be cared for by quality assurance of the offered services by the providers, be them internal IT or external.

The tools and means of web 2.0 invite spontaneous evolution, keeping every application in a perpetual beta state. Again, this is a question of automated quality assurance and inspections for severe violations. What an end user regards as "good enough" certainly will not pass traditional quality assurance, and when delivered by a professional IT shop, it may cause protests. Now the users themselves develop and implement many of their applications, and the service levels lower. Well-defined company standards or reliance on an industry canon can avoid poor quality, which would certainly counteract the expected benefits.

A.8.5

Finally, best practices do not yet exist for the enterprise- or industry-wide use of web 2.0 elements outside the web communities where those have been developed. This means the involved parties feel left alone. But, in turn, it can fuel the community aspects and the team spirit to overcome it. In this context, pioneers among the employees are the ones taking the lead, connecting within and beyond the company boundaries, and it might become the norm for application development, as it is desired for agile lines of business.

A.8.6

Setting standards, implementing a governance board, and teaching the guidelines, as well installing control mechanisms are there to avoid that integration is pushed to the edge. Over time, we have no longer standard applications control the business processes and the operation flows, but services and RSS feeds take over.

A mix of internal and external services on a global scale will bring multiple development environments and middleware platforms into the game. Preferences of individuals may determine directions rather than a reuse-oriented standard. A trusted board of IT experts, not just knowing the existing systems but well experienced with web 2.0 and recognized by the community, is needed to keep control of the framework and tools used by the users.

A.8.7

Letting happen uncontrolled developing any kind of mashups may cause severe problems to management of the situational and enterprise applications. So, the hard problems at enterprise IT gets harder (for example, the root cause analysis, error detection, data protection, and patch management). This all is, as you now know, part of SOA governance.

8.5 Conclusion

As shown, there are plenty of opportunities to gain benefits from an SOA in the enterprise. The described elements of web 2.0 are providing the end user access to services. The loosely coupled nature of the services allows the end user to combine applications to suit immediate needs. A well-organized registry and repository of services is the backbone for a governed operation and supports most efficient application development.

A well-defined and deliberately cared for repository of people lets employees get instantaneous access to each other and allows them to collaborate at solving customer demands in shortest time at highest quality. All the described elements help to create the desired business agility in the company.

However, as shown in this book, there are practical guidelines, lessons learned from first pilots and enterprises that started the journey toward SOA several years ago. All this we collected from our project teams working on real-life solutions, and it should be helpful to every enterprise architect who is responsible for his/her company transition. In the last chapter, we give an outlook on expected technology and business development based on SOA and web 2.0 as we know it today.

8.6 Links to developerWorks Articles

A.8.1 Stephen Watt. *Mashups—The evolution of the SOA, Part 2: Situational applications and the mashup ecosystem.* www.ibm.com/developerworks/webservices/library/ws-soa-mashups2/index.html.

A.8.2 IBM developerWorks, *SOA and Web Services zone.* www.ibm.com/developerworks/webservices.

A.8.3 S. E. Slack. *Social computing: Maximizing the power of Web 2.0—Learn how to maintain influence and build acceptance for your ideas.* www.ibm.com/developerworks/library/ar-soccomp/.

A.8.4 Luba Cherbakov, Andy J. F. Bravery, and Aroop Pandya (2007),   23 August 2007, SOA meets situational applications, Part 1: Changing computing in the enterprise, http://www.ibm.com/developerworks/webservices/library/ws-soa-situational1/index.html?S_TACT=105AGX04&S_CMP=ART.

A.8.5 Scott Laningham. developerWorks Interviews: *Taking Web 2.0 into the enterprise: What mashups, social collaboration, and enhanced data management mean for the workplace.* www.ibm.com/developerworks/podcast/dwi/cm-int082807txt.html.

A.8.6 Constantine Plotnikov, Artem Papkov, and Jim Smith. *Java EE meets Web 2.0—Adopting asynchronous, event-driven architectures to meet the challenges of modern Web applications.* www.ibm.com/developerworks/web/library/wa-aj-web2jee/.

A.8.7 Anirban Dutta. *The future of SOA—A service-based delivery model with Web 2.0 capabilities.* www.ibm.com/developerworks/rational/library/oct06/dutta/.

8.7 References

Bieberstein et al. *Service-Oriented Architecture (SOA) Compass: Business Value, Planning, and Enterprise Roadmap,* IBM Press, 2005.

Martin van den Berg, Norbert Bieberstein, and Erik van Ommeren. *SOA for Profit—A Manager's Guide to Success with Service-Oriented Architecture,* IBM & Sogeti, 2007.

Bieberstein et al. "Impact of service-oriented architecture on enterprise systems, organizational structures, and individuals," *IBM Systems Journal,* 44:4, 2005. www.research.ibm.com/journal/sj/444/bieberstein.html.

Peter Weill and Joanne W. Ross. *IT Governance: How Top Performers Manage IT for Superior Results,* McGraw-Hill Professional, 2004.

Koen Brand and Harry Boonen. *IT Governance Based on CobiT 4.0: A Management Guide,* Van Haren Publishing, 2007.

Sandy Carter. *The New Language of Business: SOA & Web 2.0,* IBM Press, 2007.

Bob Glushko and Erik Wilde. Service Science, Management, and Engineering Lecture Series, Course 290-16, lectures at U.C. Berkeley School of Information, Spring 2007. http://rosetta.sims.berkeley.edu:8085/sylvia/s07/view/290-16.complete.

Luba Cherbakov et al. "Impact of service orientation at the business level," *IBM Systems Journal,* 44:4, 2005. www.research.ibm.com/journal/sj/444/cherbakov.html.

Meredith Belbin. *Management Teams* (2nd Edition), Academic Press, 2003. www.belbin.com/.

Marcus Buckingham and Donald O. Clifton. *Now, Discover Your Strengths,* Free Press, 2001. www.marcusbuckingham.com/.

David Keirsey and Marilyn Bates. *Please Understand Me: Character and Temperament Types.* (3rd Edition), Prometheus Nemesis Book Company, 2001. www.keirsey.com.

David M. Keirsey, Richard Milner, and Vince Wood. *The Temperament Discovery System,* Advisor Team, Inc., 2004. www.keirsey.com.

Linda V. Berens and Dario Nardi. *The 16 Personality Types, Descriptions for Self-Discovery,* Telos Publications, 1999.

Tim O'Reilly. *What Is Web 2.0?* 2005. www.oreilly.com/pub/a/oreilly/tim/news/2005/09/30/what-is-web-20.html.

IBM, The CEO Report 2007.

Kempton Lam and Nisan Gabbay. *iStockphoto Case Study: How to evolve from a free community site to successful business*, 2006. www.startup-review.com/blog/istockphoto-case-study-how-to-evolve-from-a-free-community-site-to-successful-business.php.

Jesse James Garrett. *Ajax: A New Approach to Web Applications*, AdaptivePath Ideas, 2005. www.adaptivepath.com/ideas/essays/archives/000385.php.

Roy Thomas Fielding. *Architectural Styles and the Design of Network-based Software Architectures*, Dissertation for the degree of Doctor of Philosophy at University of California, Irvine, 2000. www.ics.uci.edu/~fielding/pubs/dissertation/top.htm.

RSS Advisory Board, RSS 2.0 Specification, 2007. www.rssboard.org/rss-specification.

Chris Anderson. *The Long Tail: Why the Future of Business is Selling Less of More,* Hyperion, 2004. www.wired.com/wired/archive/12.10/tail.html and www.thelongtail.com/.

Endnotes

[1] Belbin offers a test for the team role types on his website: www.belbin.com/onlinetest.htm.

[2] Wiki technology—a term describing a service on the web to quickly (wiki-wiki = quick) build, change, and update webpages hosted by a wiki service provider.

[3] Wikis are a way to quickly and informally allow possibly large communities to collaborate on authoring content.

[4] One can assume that mere users of such sites outnumber the contributors at large degree, probably in the range of 99:1 or close to that. Exact survey results have not been available at time of writing this book, though.

[5] http://de.wikipedia.org/wiki/Hauptseite (German Wikipedia landing page).

[6] http://fr.wikipedia.org/wiki/Accueil (French Wikipedia landing page).

[7] http://la.wikipedia.org/wiki/Pagina_prima (Latin Wikipedia landing page).

[8] http://eo.wikipedia.org/wiki/%C4%88efpa%C4%9Do (Esperanto Wikipedia landing page).

[9] http://pdc.wikipedia.org/wiki/Haaptblatt (*Pennsilfaanisch-Deitsch* = Pennsylvania German/Dutch Wikipedia landing page).

[10] That is, a mathematical term for a type of distribution curves that shows a heavy head of many users (hits in Internet speech) for a few number of sites, but a very large number of other sites with fewer users, which is called the "long tail." The sum of users in the long tail may easily outnumber the impressive number of users at the few strongly visited sites. In other words, the niches are larger in sum than the mainstream.

[11] Further, we like to point to the IBM developerWorks and IBM alphaWorks sites where the individual solutions are discussed. Research results are presented and available for early users.

[12] For web services standards definitions and ongoing activities, visit the W3C.org at www.w3.org/2002/ws/.

Chapter 9

The Future of SOA

It might sound like fortunetelling when you read in a chapter title the term *future*. Interest in the future of SOA is high, just as it would be in other technologies. Based on their own methods, analysts regularly publish what they expect to come, which innovations will hit the market and what benefits companies/consumers can get from them. Although many of those experts' predictions might not become reality, trying to predict the future fuels discovery and innovation in one's own business. Therefore, it is worth checking out such predictions. Everybody realizes that there are plenty of opportunities for enhancement, innovation, and cures for the many ailments that we encounter when applying SOA principles to an enterprise.

In this chapter, we do not take over the job from analysts who derive projections in a scientific manner. Instead, we summarize some of our ideas, discuss what is being worked on in the laboratories, and share what we have heard in IT and business expert circles and what we think is developing from the issues we cover in this book.

The order of the items discussed in this chapter does not imply any degree of probability of their reaching fruition, nor is the order a timeline in which the technologies will come to market or reach the plateau of productivity on the hype curve (Gartner 1995). When talking about SOA and when including web 2.0 elements in the considerations, we face an almost overwhelmingly large number of factors that determine future development, not just in IT and business, but also in gaining acceptability at both the individual and societal levels.

9.1 Composite Business Services and Composite Applications

SOA as a discipline is out of its infancy, and the industry is now enjoying a significant maturity. The maturity also based, among other things, on its widespread acceptance as the de facto enterprise architecture (that is, a comprehensive architecture for the enterprise based on SOA principles and philosophy). We expect the industry will see the emergence of an asset-based development approach wherein the common IT services are developed as software services.

More and more organizations have started the transformation toward an SOA-based operation and have put the appropriate infrastructure in place. Now they are looking beyond service enablement. They want to take larger process units of their business and develop end-to-end composite applications for them.

Perhaps history will repeat as it did when packaged solutions were developed to replace bespoke IT systems for common tasks such as booking and order entry. Nonetheless, companies will demand those composite business services be deployed out of the box and with the user interface, the business services, the IT services, and any other software implementation modules required to enable an entire business capability. The deciding factor for packaged applications as we know them today will become the underlying standards, not just technical definitions. Industry business models to come will define a common language and standard operations. With this in mind, we think building end-to-end composite applications will be the next big wave in the application of SOA.

9.2 Standardization of Industry Models and Industry-Wide SOA Enablement

The drive toward composite business services and applications is different from a single vendor's standards-based packaged application. SOA is built on the foundation premise of standards-based interfaces and implementation techniques and technologies. This premise leads industries as a whole to standardize on their business models. Standardized industry business models include a common definition of business processes and business entities.

These standard business processes will be mass enabled using SOA, deployed, tested, and hardened based on multiple implementations. Most of the enterprises in a given industry run at 80 percent those standard business processes (for their industry). This mass enablement through the development of composite services and applications will jumpstart IT modernization efforts. Therefore, common things won't be invented over and over again, but due to business and industry standard definitions, there will be an exchange of compositions. Those models will finally allow the business to concentrate on the uniqueness for each organization. Standard interfaces and semantics will make this possible at a higher degree of integration.

9.3 Packaged Applications Mutating to Point Solutions

The trend toward composite solutions and the increasing use of standardized industry models are likely to initiate another developing market for point solutions—that is, composites that do one thing the best without any need of an overhead that normally comes with a packaged application. Because standards evolve, the industry—companies that do not live from applications and regard IT just as a necessary instrument for doing their actual business—will push for exchangeable, loosely coupled, and proven software solutions to populate their SOA-based infrastructure. These solutions must easily integrate with IT in the company.

In this context, we see two things happening:

1. Commercial-off-the-shelf (COTS) software is being developed to expose service interfaces for certain key "external" functions. In other words, new versions of COTS packages will include not only service interfaces and adaptors but also new stand-alone service implementations; so, a kind of patchwork quilt of services is being developed that shares a common built-in SOA. Those solutions certainly have a need to be "harmonized" with in-house SOA projects. As a side effect, it will change the software services market, too.

2. The development of the software as a service (SaaS) market is more likely than before. Due to standard industry models, software vendors are going to offer units of code that can be integrated based on the SOA infrastructure. Application service providers (ASP)—deriving from companies that already deliver outsourcing services or platform vendors that know their backbone the best—are running those point solutions in any required combination for their customers. This means the ASPs act as a hub supplied by services (increasing offerings dedicated to solve a clearly defined point issue) from various software vendors on one side and their customers on the other side. The end customers will choose between ASPs and select the best offer, among other criteria based on the ability of the ASP to compile the fitting set of services for the individual needs and who can ensure a satisfying level with regard to security of data and operation. Reliability, time to change, and other service levels will become the differentiators among the ASPs.

As the known application vendors reform their packaged applications to comply with the standards and make them SOA ready, certain vendors are building composite application packages from the ground up using SOA principles. These point solutions will be either directly integrated at an enterprise or by a trusted ASP. In the latter case, the ASPs will expose their expertise and experiences and develop acceptance criteria for those composites they are going to host.

In the future, we believe these two worlds of software providers will converge, but the issue of integrating several different SOA implementations may become more and more annoying, if there are no widely accepted industry standards in place. Depending on the market forces, it might happen that ASPs set the standards or that a respective industry organization determines this world.

9.4 Hybrid Architectural Approach of SOA and EDA

In addition to the previously mentioned anticipated trends, we expect another to occur: a confluence of SOA and event-driven design (EDA) will bear a hybrid architectural style that takes advantage of the two trends we described in the previous section. You might see some parallels here, just as we encountered with the real-time extensions to Yourdon's structured design method (1979). Paul Ward and Stephen Mellor (1985) added finite state machines that are coupled with entity relationship models and structured design method to express the dynamic behavior of the system. To a certain degree, this then enabled the building of animation/simulation engines based on the formal design documents.

Technically, SOA is based on a deterministic request-response paradigm, and EDA is based on a completed decoupled pub-sub model. Again, any real-world and complex system would need such a hybrid model wherein some scenarios are best implemented using the request-response model and other scenarios are better implemented using the pub-sub model.

In the future, SOA and EDA can both live together inside a single architecture premise. Where a few steps in the business process will always need to stay together in a functional kind of dependency and within an organizational unit, SOA is the way to go; whereas in situations where processes or process steps transcend recognizable functional organizational boundaries (both internal and external), EDA is the better approach. Similarly, EDA is used across organizational boundaries, whereas SOA inside the organizational unit is a good starting recipe for hybrid architecture, which is going to become increasingly common.

9.5 SOA Methodology Evolution

To better and more efficiently act to identify, model, specify, realize, test, deploy, operate, manage, and monitor services, methodological approaches and models are being honed quickly in real-world SOA projects. The integration of this methodology and the required governance will be infused into existing systems' development life cycles (SDLC). This will become the focus for many IT departments.

A.9.1

Tension exists between those who believe in sophisticated control and traceability and those who want something called agile SOA. This tension will generate the need for optional variations in the methods as explained in the SOMA approach in Chapter 4, "A Methodology for Service Modeling and Design." We believe that in the future, industry focus will evolve to a full round-trip "continuous improvement life cycle" for service portfolios and for their provisioning on a large scale.

9.6 Business Processes and SOA Not Without People

While selling SOA to the corporate executives, we always talk about the closer relationship between IT and lines of business in the enterprise that has to be achieved for success. The merging of the architecture approaches and a flexible methodological background contribute to this goal at a certain level, but more important are the roles of people just in between the two worlds. In earlier publications (*SOA Compass* and *SOA for Profit*), we talked about the enterprise architect acting as the mediator.

They are not alone, but strongly linked with their counterparts at both sides. Business analysts won't just design enterprise operation without taking IT in the boat. Central operations staff won't create business processes to be implemented not knowing about available services at any level up to composites or without knowing whether they are ready to use by employees who will build their situational applications within a business process.

The role of the business analyst is going to be more critical because of standard industry models that are modeled and implemented as composite applications and services. Any enterprise that tries to implement them will have standard business processes with not much variability in them. Here, as always, the subtle differences are what count and make the company unique, recognized, and more effective than the competitors. This will lead to a new set of domain experts and business analysts whose job will be to identify points of variability in the standard business processes. These variable points will lead to the identification of new and enterprise-specific services that need to be injected as identified.

Besides those newly developing experts, the usual employees become more self-governed and autonomous based on the provided services, the tools, and the support to build their solutions on the spot. We can expect more young people to join the enterprises. They are the ones who grew up using computers, the Internet, mobile phones, and other electronic devices earlier and more intensively during their childhood and education time than any other generation before. As discussed in Chapter 8, "Collaboration Under SOA: The Human Aspects," collaboration under web 2.0 and SOA mashups by the end users will be the rule rather than the exception. They won't even shy away from programming in AJAX or from tools to build their software as needed based on a rich offering of services in the company and beyond.

9.7 SOA Metrics

When we are talking about business processes in context with SOA, quantifiable metrics come to mind. Any business activity (any operation executed in the company) needs to be measured for cost and revenue, resources, and time spent to achieve income. When envisioning software as services offered by third parties, or by an internal unit, one asks for return on investment, the cost for getting the service delivered.

Therefore, we see measurement systems coming to clearly prove the gain from using or embracing SOA. It is going to become common and one of the likely requirements from enterprises. We have so far been able to demonstrate qualitative gains from the adoption of SOA. Quantitative gains have only been post-usage of SOA (for instance, from the numbers obtained from successful SOA implementations). But being able to predict and measure a quantifiable advantage from the adoption of SOA is going to be key moving forward.

Following the paradigm of a closer link between lines of business and the supporting IT, we find that measuring all contributions and costs of operations (IT or human intervention, as we do it with machines in production lines) becomes indispensable. With the expected growth of the SaaS market, ASPs need to know their costs to determine prices for their service offerings. Their customers can evaluate the benefits from any use of services within given business processes and gain a sharper view of their operations. Here we certainly find the first SOA metrics in action, and from there you can calculate further returns on investment as the enterprise journeys toward becoming SOA based.

9.8 Ubiquitous SOA in the Enterprise

After we have the appropriate measurement systems in place, the scope and scale of SOA-based applications expands quickly. As explained in the preceding section, the numbers will tell. More services are built and more composite services are made from existing assets. Services are being used for more general purposes, and it becomes easier and less costly to integrate new applications in the SOA-based IT infrastructure. The more this is coming true, the more followers will ask for their software to be based on the SOA platform.

We work on SOA projects around the world, in any industry, and for any business purpose. The principles of SOA are applicable to almost any situation, and more and more advantages are documented and reported. So, we can state that adoption entry points are now well established; and transition from project to line of business, to division, to enterprise, to the virtual enterprise is coming into focus. The vision of a dynamic IT for an agile operation is about to become reality: a business with empowered employees and enlightened customers who determine the action rather than one with unnecessary boundaries and restrictions from software that determines the process.

More than being a point solution for one or the other company, now entry points and transitions are being facilitated by industry initiatives to standardize vocabularies, schemas, message formats, service operations, and interfaces. There are examples in industries such as telecommunication (NGOSS),[1] insurance (IAA),[2] banking (IFW),[3] retail, and travel and transport. In addition, standards bodies such as OASIS and OpenGroup (for example, TOGAF and COBIT)[4] support this standardization. We believe that this trend to SOA standardization will continue in the future.

Tension always exists between those who favor industry standards and those who favor proprietary standards. However, the advantages of standards, especially for the initial steps toward the SOA-based enterprise, will become obvious, and it will help to reach the desired and necessary business agility to stay competitive.

A.9.2

9.9 Global Use of SOA

SOA has the potential to be used by a large numbers of companies in a spectrum of industries around the world. Certainly not all companies want to declare their success or failure, because SOA is at the heart of a proprietary strategy to become more agile and competitive. However, the more pressure rises to stay competitive in a fast-changing global market, the more proprietary solutions for IT will become obsolete.

Company leaders will concentrate on the differentiators in their industry—finding the gaps to fill in by best fitting solutions integrated from day one—that do not require months or even years of integration projects to finally go into production (perhaps after something is no longer needed and the opportunity has gone). To adopt the industry models and standards most effectively, there needs to be a transformation of IT, as described in this book.

Most important, a trusted framework, the technical foundation, has to be in place. As crucial as this is to have, however, the organization and people must be ready for a new model. This model must address governance, reuse, end-user involvement in the discussed mashups, and self-service support in all lines of business.

To realize this model, adequate tools and solutions are certainly needed, but there is also a need to transform people's minds and expectations. Enterprise architects, or as we call them, the service-oriented architects, for whom we wrote this book, have an important role to play. They will have to answer this question: Can SOA "cross the chasm" and become the de facto style for enterprise-level architecture? We believe SOA will become the de facto style for enterprise architecture in the future.

The "SOA hype" is beginning to wane, and that's good because clarification and enumeration of SOA concepts, principles, and best practices will be more important in determining what's good about SOA and what's not. The definitions of models, meta-models, and meta-meta-models are becoming established as best practices for service-oriented design.

9.10 SOA Opens the Amateur Software Services Market

A last point is that "amateurs" are determining the market more than they did before. This will not just happen internally within a company when lines of business employees use mashups. However, applications or better software services are going to be offered online by web brokers. Today, you can find millions, probably billions, of pictures, films, music pieces, graphical designs, and other electronically available items that are traded by "amateurs" braving the worldwide competition. More and more marketing agencies take advantage of those less-expensive offerings. They use them for absolutely serious orders as cost-efficient alternatives to high-price artists.

Similarly, credible providers who deal with freelancer-developed software services are establishing themselves. Like the exchange platforms for the previously mentioned electronically available goods, the offered software will pass quality checks to gain trust with customers. Customer and peer ratings will further drive the respect and contribute to these providers' success.

Depending on the size of the enterprise, the business situation, and the underlying infrastructure, including a responsive support solution, it becomes easier for any business user to build an application ad hoc. Those can be mashups that simply combine certain web services and do some limited calculations on those that gain a meaningful result, such as a ticker service or any other Really Simple Syndications (RSS) you subscribe to.

Or you can get more expert-like solutions based on the services inside the enterprise or from the web when using higher-value languages (in this context, sophisticated development tools). Such tools are currently entering the market, and they will certainly increase in user friendliness and power over time, as the demand grows.

9.11 Conclusion

In summary, we can state that the trend toward coalescence of IT and lines of business and even the board continues. The chasm between IT and the business world in an enterprise is about to vanish. Whether this will be achieved with the people who are on board, whether external consultants will aid the transition, or whether a new generation of young and less-IT-loathing people will be the drivers depends on the individual situation of the company and the market it operates in. With the availability of services, one will eventually rather check for existing services than start with a formal definition, and then combine the results with the business application that serves the immediate business needs the best.

This scenario wholly depends on the flexibility and courage of the involved parties, but it definitely will change the way we generate software, redefining the meaning of IT as business centric and an integral part of the enterprise. This book was written based on a vast array of experience. We hope that it encourages the building of adequate SOA foundations and that our readers are now motivated to "jump on the SOA train."

We cannot address every situation that you might face in actual practice, but you can rest assured that the practical advice in this book is based on our and our colleagues' experience. And, SOA principles can provide the foundation for an agile enterprise that will be ready for change in the future. After all, the challenge facing many enterprises today is ultimate survivability, and history has shown that progress often results from changing the way one operates. The positive reception that our first book, *Service-Oriented Architecture (SOA) Compass*, received encouraged us to continue the path and further collect the practical things that make SOA real. We are happy to have shared them with you here.

9.12 Links to developerWorks Articles

A9.1 Anirban, D. *The future of SOA: A service-based delivery model with Web 2.0 capabilities.* www.ibm.com/developerworks/rational/library/oct06/dutta/.

A9.2 Laningham, S. *developerWorks Interviews: Taking Web 2.0 into the enterprise: What mashups, social collaboration, and enhanced data management mean for the workplace.* www.ibm.com/developerworks/podcast/dwi/cm-int082807txt.html.

9.13 References

R9.1 Gartner, *Understanding Hype Cycles*, 1995. www.gartner.com/pages/story.php.id.8795. s.8.jsp.

R9.2 Yourdon, E. and L. Constantine. Structured Design: Fundamentals of a Discipline of Computer Program and Systems Design, Prentice Hall, 1979.

R9.3 Mellor, S. J. and P. T. Ward. Structured Development for Real-Time Systems: Essential Modeling Techniques, Prentice Hall, 1985.

R9.4 Bieberstein et al. Service-Oriented Architecture (SOA) Compass: Business Value, Planning, and Enterprise Roadmap, IBM Press, Pearson Education, 2006.

R9.5 van den Berg, M. et al. SOA for Profit: A Manager's Guide to Success with Service Oriented Architecture, IBM & Sogeti, 2007.

R9.6 Reilly, J. P. and M. J. Creaner. NGOSS Distilled, The Lean Corporation, 2005.

R9.7 IT Governance Institute (ITGI), TOGAF and COBIT—Mapping of TOGAF 8.1 and COBIT 4.0, July 18, 2007. www.opengroup.org/architecture/wp/.

Endnotes

[1] NGOSS = New Generation Operations Systems and Software, a standard supporting SOA in the telecommunication industry. See John P. Reilly and Martin J. Creaner (2005).

[2] IAA = Insurance Application Architecture, IBM's offering of an enterprise model architecture for the insurance industry. See www-03.ibm.com/industries/financialservices/doc/content/solution/ 278918303.html for details.

[3] IFW = Information Framework, IBM's service offering based on an enterprise model for financial service organizations. See www-03.ibm.com/industries/financialservices/doc/content/solution/ 391981303.html.

[4] See details under Open Group architecture forum at www.opengroup.org/architecture/WP.

Index

X-Y-Z

This could be the best advice you get all day

The IBM® International Technical Support Organization (ITSO) develops and delivers high-quality technical materials and education for IT and business professionals.

These value-add deliverables are IBM Redbooks® publications, Redpapers™ and workshops that can help you implement and use IBM products and solutions on today's leading platforms and operating environments.

See a sample of what we have to offer

Get free downloads

See how easy it is ...

ibm.com/redbooks

- ➢ Select from hundreds of technical deliverables
- ➢ Purchase bound hardcopy Redbooks publications
- ➢ Sign up for our workshops
- ➢ Keep informed by subscribing to our weekly newsletter
- ➢ See how *you* can become a published author

We can also develop deliverables for your business. To find out how we can work together, send a note today to: redbooks@us.ibm.com